Contents

Severe physical disability

Responses to the challenge of care

John Harrison

CASSELL

Cassell Educational Limited
Artillery House
Artillery Row
London SW1P 1RT

British Library Cataloguing in Publication Data

Harrison, John, *1932–*
   Severe physical disability: responses
   to the challenge of care.
   1. Physically handicapped – Care and
   treatment – Great Britain
   I. Title
   362.4′0941   HV3024.G7

   ISBN: 0–304–31406–4

Phototypesetting by Fakenham Photosetting Limited, Fakenham, Norfolk
Printed and bound in Great Britain by Mackays of Chatham Ltd.

Last digit is print no: 9 8 7 6 5 4 3 2 1

Foreword

In 1984 the Royal College of Physicians of London decided to produce a report on 'The Young Disabled Adult'. This was an expression of a widespread feeling that services for the young disabled adult were far from satisfactory. We recognised that young disabled people had to live with their disabilities for a long time, and better co-ordination of services was needed to help them to do so.

Dr John Harrison is a physician-turned-geriatrician in Birmingham who had been conscious of the deficiencies of the services for some time and had previously prepared a report on the topic. He seemed the ideal person to undertake the study that was to form the background to our College report and he generously took a year's leave from his hospital duties to prepare it. The official College report ('The Young Disabled Adult') and this new book testify to the wisdom of our choice. Dr Harrison has approached the topic in a scholarly way, amassing as much evidence as possible, discussing it with patients and their relatives, with doctors and nurses and with all varieties of helpers – professional and non-professional. To this evidence, and its analysis, he has added a unique blend of training and experience and his own distinctive style of argument and presentation.

Dr Harrison draws attention to the change in philosophy that has led to a shift of patients from long-term institutional care back into the community. This important and proper step has sometimes taken place without adequate planning, so that facilities for community care have not always been appropriate. He also emphasises the new and wider role played by the speciality of disability medicine which takes into consideration the psychological, social and economic consequences of disability, as well as the purely physical consequences.

Although Dr Harrison's original terms of reference were to survey the residential facilities that were available to the young disabled adult, his interests have clearly ranged more fully over the whole field. This contribution sets out, for government, all health workers and the public, what the issues are and makes recommendations for improving the services. Dr Harrison feels strongly about these needs and says so firmly. A glance at the checklist of requirements in his last chapter will indicate what he feels should be done to provide the sort of service our young disabled people require. I hope his efforts will be well rewarded.

Sir Raymond Hoffenberg
President
Royal College of Physicians
July 1987

Preface

Now that there are such greatly enhanced opportunities for people with disabilities, to write in general terms about disabled living demands a fair breadth of vision and something of a balancing act as well. Severe disability in particular has so many different aspects – personal, consumer, social, political, economic, medical, to name just a few – that it can be very difficult to comprehend the whole picture. It is only too easy to understate one aspect while apparently overstating others.

This book reflects the point of view of someone who is actively engaged in medical practice. Some disabled people see the medical profession as a source of unwarranted authority over their lives, and others have come to the conclusion that doctors are too uninterested to give them the help and support that might reasonably have been expected. Many members of the profession do in fact believe that disability and rehabilitation lie outside the limits of medical responsibility, yet some of their colleagues are quite deeply involved with both. Whatever the prejudices or convictions, the fact remains that innumerable people choose or are obliged to seek medical help, or support which is dependent on the medical services, simply because they are so severely disabled. It is not a responsibility that the profession can easily escape.

The specific issue of residential care demonstrates the same conflict of opinions and reality. Widely believed to be outmoded and no longer the main priority for development, the facility offered by residential homes and hospitals for disabled people is still very much in demand. Most medical and social services indeed depend on the availability of such places when the problems of caring become severe. Almost all that has been written on the subject, however, has been from the angles of sociology, psychology, charitable enterprise, management or consumerism; medical writing about it has been minimal.

This book therefore attempts to bridge two gaps: between the medical profession and all the other active, interested groups who are working to improve the lives of people with severe disabilities, and between those who take long-term institutional care for granted and those who believe it should be dispersed as soon and as drastically as possible. But in describing the medical aspects of residential care it is essential to take a far wider view of disabled living, and here the problem of balance is only too apparent.

In the course of writing I have been particularly aware of the kind of audience whom I regularly meet at conferences and seminars about disability: professionals of every kind (except, usually, doctors) with a number of other actively concerned people including those who have disabilities, carers of all kinds, workers in voluntary organisations and (occasionally) politicians. This account relates almost entirely to the United Kingdom but many of the issues seem likely to be the same in other so-called advanced societies. A briefer version, principally directed at the medical profession, has already been issued by the Royal College of Physicians; this version includes some of the same material and is intended to be its counterpart.

The project has been wholly dependent on help I have received from far more people than it is possible to mention, although many of them are listed in Appendix 1 either by name or by the institution they were working for. It certainly would not have been undertaken at all without the active help and encouragement of the Royal College of Physicians, especially its President, Sir Raymond Hoffenberg; its now-retired secretary, Mr G. M. G. Tibbs; and the chairman of its disability committee, Dr C. B. Wynn-Parry. Equally essential has been financial support from the Development Trust for the Young Disabled, and especially the involvement of the director of the Royal Hospital and Home for Incurables, Dr J. Wedgwood, who has also now retired. Here in Birmingham I am deeply indebted to my medical colleagues, especially in the department of geriatric medicine at Selly Oak Hospital, and to the unit and district managers of Moseley Hall Hospital and Central Birmingham Health Authority, for the way in which they have allowed the practicalities of the project to be realised.

One of the most valuable experiences during a period of sabbatical leave was to talk to people with disabilities as an interested person and as a doctor, but not as *their* doctor; they were able in this way to give me insights I had not possessed before. Equally, over the eleven years in which I have been involved with severe disability, my own patients (I have to call them that) have taught me more than any medical literature. This book contains a number of short personal anecdotes based on these contacts; for obvious reasons I have chosen to make them as anonymous as possible while retaining just enough detail to show the interaction of disability with individual experiences and aspirations. The two longer accounts which open and close the book are less anonymous, and in each instance the person concerned (in the second case, including her family after her death) approved of what I was doing.

Finally, the two people most closely involved with the work have been my two secretaries: Debbie Hickey who assisted with the Royal College of Physicians' Report, and Margaret Ritchie who has helped with the later drafts and the final version of this book. It has been a pleasure to work with them both.

John Harrison
Birmingham
June 1987

1
Severe physical disability in perspective

PROLOGUE

One day when Mr R was out driving with his wife some 70 miles away from the district where they and their close relations were all living, he had a disastrous accident. Mrs R died almost at once; he was left with a broken neck which caused his legs and trunk to become permanently deprived of movement and feeling, he lost control over his bowel movements and bladder, and he could only make imperfect use of his upper limbs. There is no need to elaborate on the devastating way in which the accident affected his entire life. He was 54.

After a month in a general hospital he was moved to a spinal injuries unit which was just as far away from his home. Physically he did quite well there but he could not face the prospect of living in that helpless condition on his own. His daughters had small houses and full family commitments and his other relations lived hundreds of miles away: they were all concerned about him but having him to live with one of them was not pursued as a realistic proposition. The spinal injuries unit had to move him on and after well over a year, essentially for lack of any alternative, he was taken into an orthopaedic convalescent ward in his own local general hospital. The district had no special Health Service unit for younger disabled people although there was a Cheshire Home nearby to which he went for a short stay. For reasons he could not quite explain he did not like it there and instead he continued to live in the same ward for two and a half years. Eventually, at the age of 58, he was given a bed in the local geriatric department ten miles away.

The ward in which he now found himself, and where he still was when I met him two years later in 1985, was part of a typical late nineteenth-century pavilion-style building in the grounds of a modest-sized hospital which had once been a rural workhouse. The hospital staff had been working hard in recent years to introduce the pattern of modern geriatric care – better furnishings and fabrics, a more liberal regime, more emphasis on rehabilitation, better levels of rehabilitation staff and better liaison with the community. Mr R responded well to his new environment although he remained unable to dress himself and the clothes he had to wear belonged to the hospital and were not his own. His chin-controlled electric wheelchair was made more manageable with a new hand control and he was even encouraged to move about with the help of a swivel-walking body splint. The nurses still turned him three times every night but he had never had a pressure sore. Once a month he would go out to spend a day or two with members of his family. All but two of the other men who lived in the ward were older than he was and he passed most of his days and nights among them, either in the dormitory area or in the pleasant but rather crowded ward day room. Many had organic brain disease and at times one or two of them could be noisy and disturbed.

Mr R spoke with enthusiasm of the kindness and encouragement the geriatric depart-ment had given him in comparison with the orthopaedic ward; he accepted the situation as it was, valued the safety and security very greatly, and had made up his mind to go on living there if necessary for the rest of his life.

This brief account of one man's experience demonstrates several issues which crop up regularly in relation to severe disability. The cause of Mr R's predicament was damage to a central part of the nervous system. He was neither very old nor particularly young and he had remained a responsibility of the Health Service ever since his accident. The effect on his life, his own reactions and the actions of the many people who had tried to help him are all completely understandable, but there can hardly be any doubt that it should have been easier to find him an appropriate place in which to start a new way of living. There are value judgements to be made: the majority will probably believe that he should not have ended up in a geriatric ward, many will say that any form of continuing hospital care for him would have been inappropriate, and yet others will argue that he should have been rehabilitated to the point of living in his own household where all the necessary help should have been supplied. The more hard-headed will also want to discuss financial cost. But even assuming that Mr R himself and people like him are free to decide their own future, who should help them and how much information do they need in order to make their decisions? If having made them they then find inertia and obstruction which cause further improvement to seem impossible, whose responsibility is it to push for reform?

BACKGROUND

Since the middle of the twentieth century the concept of disability has, with gathering momentum, gradually become so complex that it now includes every kind of disorder of body or mind which lasts for more than a very short time and may cause some disadvantage to the person concerned. The growth of the concept can be traced to a political commit-ment that the State should recognise and compensate people who have acquired disabling injuries in the service of their country or as employees in industry, followed in due course by ever-widening pressures that the same should be done for everyone with similar needs no matter what the cause (Topliss, 1975; Blaxter, 1976; Stone, 1984). This means that the numbers of disabled people have apparently become very large, which in itself may be politically beneficial to them; a figure of one in ten of the population is sometimes quoted.

Ideas about disability and ways of accommodating different disabilities have also undergone profound changes and have received considerable public attention. One exam-ple has been the very significant change in the climate of opinion in favour of community care: voluntary organisations, active disabled people, specialists in community medicine, social workers, and public administrators are all talking about it, in very marked contrast to the mid-1970s when, for example, so many residential units for the younger disabled were being opened. A sequence of documents from one regional health authority has shown that the transition there took place around 1978 and 1979, which is compatible with more fragmentary information from Britain as a whole. The precise and lasting effects of this new policy emphasis, however, remain to be evaluated.

During the same period, the public expression of consumer views of disability has become increasingly effective. The range of approaches has extended from an open desire to collaborate with professionals and service planners on the one hand, to a direct challenge and confrontation with professionalism on the other. Finkelstein (1980) has argued that the real problem lies in the social relationships of an able-bodied world which takes little account of other ways of living and is therefore in that respect itself disabled. On a personal level there have been many detailed accounts of what have amounted to battles for independence, sometimes with the active help of all concerned but sometimes in the face of bureaucracy, inertia, and above all disbelief (La Fane, 1981; Shearer, 1982; Armstrong, 1985). Disabled persons' carers have publicised their experiences, too (Briggs and Oliver, 1985). The independent living movement, according to which people with disabilities plan and organise their own campaigns, services and physical resources, was born and developed in the United States in the 1960s and 1970s and has been imported to Britain: its recognition, evaluation and accommodation appear to be important contemporary tasks (Brechin *et al.*, 1981; Oliver, 1983, Goldsmith, 1984).

The concept of rehabilitation has also been extended well beyond physical medicine, remedial therapy and even well-planned hospital discharge, to a full consideration of the psychological, social and economic consequences of disabling disease (Brechin and Liddiard, 1981; Aitken, 1982). It has even been argued that 'real' rehabilitation begins when even the best hospital teams think they have finished; it is to do with the problems which follow hospital discharge, the establishment of a new way of life, ensuring that necessary equipment and services not only arrive but continue to be available, and preparedness at all times to troubleshoot if things go wrong. Rehabilitation teams certainly have continuing responsibilities to those disabled people whose condition is not only unlikely to recover but will almost certainly deteriorate; for this reason a recent report has preferred 'disability medicine' to 'rehabilitation' as a description of the medical profession's share of the task (Royal College of Physicians, 1986a).

As a result of all these trends the options have widened, and people with even the severest disabilities have found opportunities and fulfilment which at one time could scarcely have been imagined. Exciting as some of the developments have been, however, in general they have been uneven and individually isolated. Justifiable enthusiasm for disabled persons' rights as integral members of society has to some extent diverted attention from some of those who are most dependent: people who are, for example, unable to express an opinion clearly, or whose behaviour discourages others from helping them, or who are approaching but have not yet reached old age. To a large extent this book is about those who are in that kind of predicament, but it is also about the whole group of people whose physical disabilities have caused (or may in future cause) the help of residential establishments to be considered or accepted, and about the responses of the British public and voluntary services and institutions to their needs.

CLASSIFICATIONS AND NUMBERS

Within the public services, for a long time it has been administratively convenient to divide people with continuing special needs into certain groups. Children are the obvious example, with the educational, paediatric and child-care services dedicated to them, and among adults the principal groups are the mentally handicapped, the mentally ill and the elderly.

People with physical disabilities are commonly regarded as forming a fifth major group (Department of Health and Social Security, 1976 and 1977), although the emphasis is usually on a minority of them: those who are aged between 16 and 65. The lower of these limits is the statutory school-leaving age in Britain; the upper is the age at which men become eligible for a state retirement pension (women are eligible at 60). It has become widespread practice to identify dependent older people in terms of ageing rather than disability, so that 'the physically disabled' are, in fact, a kind of residual category, variously referred to as young or younger, and as physically disabled, physically handicapped or chronically sick. Although they make extensive use of health and social services, there are usually too few formal arrangements for dealing comprehensively with their needs.

Depending on the limits that are set to the concept of disability, people with disabilities are thought to make up some seven to eleven per cent of the total population in Britain (Knight and Warren, 1978). The principal source of information so far has been the government's National Sample Survey which was carried out in 1968 (Harris, 1971), one of the main purposes of which was to estimate the number of people in private households who might qualify for an attendance allowance. People with all levels of disability were included and classified according to an eight-point severity scale, but it was particularly necessary to identify those who were so severely limited that they needed someone to supply most of their wants. No account was taken, however, of people who were already in hospital or other forms of residential care, and the survey almost certainly gave too low an estimate of the numbers who were deaf, blind or mentally impaired but had no problems of mobility or personal independence.

Table 1.1 contains data derived from the National Survey which put the various age groups and levels of disability into perspective. Within the whole group some 15 per cent were described as severely disabled; rather less than half of that 15 per cent (around 1 in 250 of the total population) were thought to require special care, which was defined as the need for help by another person for living activities which occur more than once a day. Little more than a quarter of this special care group (around 1 in 1000 of the total population) were adults under the age of 65. Other government sources suggest that the number of younger physically disabled people in hospitals and residential homes is around 0.3 per 1000 total population (Table 2.5, Chapter 2) and it can be presumed that most of them are in the special care category. Valuable new data will become available when the results of a second government survey are published in 1988: unlike the earlier one, it is to

Table 1.1 *Data derived from the 1968 national survey of 'handicapped and impaired' in private households in Great Britain: estimated numbers per 100,000 total population, by age*

| | Age group 16–64 | | | | Age group 65 + | |
Category of disability	16–29	30–49	50–64	Total		Total
Needing special care (categories 1–3)	10	30	70	110	290	400
Severe handicap (categories 4–5)	10	70	230	310	560	870
All other disabilities (categories 6–8)	200	830	1820	2850	3670	6520
Total (all categories)	220	930	2120	3270	4520	7790

Table 1.2   *The components of dependency*

Personal, requiring special care
   1. Loss of use of both upper limbs
   2. Unreliability

Social, requiring formal provision of care
   3. Living alone
   4. Household inadequacies
   5. Poor personal relationships

Predisposing to residential care
PERSONAL
   6. Inability to communicate
   7. Unstable or progressive disability
   8. Socially unbearable behaviour
   9. Personal preference
SOCIAL
   10. Inadequate community services
   11. Expectations: public, informal, professional

include children and institutional residents, but at present there is no reason to expect that a radically different picture will emerge.

Table 1.2 outlines the factors that are associated with a need for special care. First among them are two quite distinct groups of disabilities: loss of both upper limbs and loss of reliability. The first of these obviously makes the help of other people necessary for basic living tasks. Unreliability, usually but not always due to impaired brain function, is likely to require regular or even constant supervision, as with the care of a child. Loss of mobility, as for example because of paraplegia, is deliberately not included because it is entirely compatible with independent living if there are no serious disabilities otherwise. Then there are factors which prompt demand for care from agencies outside a disabled person's household: they include personal isolation, family inadequacies, and poor personal relationships. These factors are exacerbated if a disabled person cannot communicate, or if his or her health or disability is unstable or liable to deteriorate, or if socially unbearable behaviour is for any reason a complication; whether or not the disabled person is in favour, the result may be a strong demand for residential care. Social factors of the utmost importance are the availability of services and the prevailing expectations. Four of the personal factors listed in Table 1.2 – loss of upper limb function, unreliability, inability to communicate and intolerable behaviour – are especially likely to be associated with disease or injury of the central nervous system, and several studies have shown that up to 90 per cent of the people in residential care are disabled for this reason (Miller and Gwynne, 1972; Bloomfield, 1976; Scott, 1984).

Despite all the systems of classification, it is of the utmost importance to remember that because severe disability affects people's whole lives and has so many different dimensions, each person's disability is an integral part of the total collection of attributes that makes him or her an individual. It also matters very much how long a person has been and expects to be disabled, and whether the disability can be expected to worsen or improve; in particular, there is a world of difference between the lifelong or near-lifelong disabilities of, say, cerebral palsy or spinal injury, and the much commoner but relatively short-lasting disabilities of later life. Each 'case' of disability is therefore genuinely unique: not only that, but every individual's personal situation, requirements and aspirations are likely to change with the passage of time, perhaps because of changing disability but also for a whole variety of other reasons.

SOME MATTERS OF TERMINOLOGY

At this stage it is essential to define certain terms because disability in its statutory sense is such a broad concept, with so many different aspects, that clarity of thought and language are essential if facts and ideas are to be clearly conveyed. The complexity has led to the proposal that there should be three separate but related concepts: *impairment* (loss of function), *disability* in a relatively narrow sense (loss of ability to perform specific tasks) and *handicap* (social and economic disadvantage). These terms were discussed in the National Survey report, were later elaborated, and have formed the basis for an international classification of impairments, disabilities and handicaps (World Health Organisation, 1980). Although the tripartite scheme has helped to make thinking more precise and to extend it beyond mere medical diagnoses and their immediate consequences, the classification has proved unwieldy in practice (Leading article, *Lancet*, 1986) and the terms themselves are not widely used in this precise way.

A word is still needed which embraces all three concepts; to avoid ambiguity *disablement* is sometimes chosen for the purpose but the more common usage is for 'disability' to retain this second, more general meaning, and that is the way in which it is principally used in this book. Moreover, because 'mental handicap' is such a widely recognised issue, 'handicap' also retains a similar general meaning but is associated in the public mind with mental and not physical disability (Weir, 1981).

It is usually accepted that *mental handicap* itself only refers to conditions which date from birth or very early childhood. To complicate matters still further, the Mental Health Act 1983 defined 'impairment' in quite a different way (see footnote, p. 105, Chapter 6). *Mental disability* is therefore perhaps the most acceptable term to describe non-physical impairments which have been acquired during later childhood or adult life.

As already mentioned, another important dimension of disability is that of time, and in this context the concept of a disabled person's *career* has been usefully introduced (Roth, 1963; Safilios-Rothschild, 1970) to define the sequence of events which mark each individual life, and the personal aspirations which accompany them.

A further pair of terms is still quite widely used despite being often very inappropriate: they are *chronic sick* and *chronically sick*. They imply that a person has an active disease process which may or may not require medical treatment, but they do not necessarily imply severe disability or even any disability at all; conversely, many people with even the most profound disabilities are quite without active disease. To use either term on the grounds that someone requires special care (as described above) is therefore simply misleading.

It is also worth mentioning *prevalence*, which refers to the proportion of people with particular characteristics who are to be found within a population at any one time such as those, for example, who would be discovered by a census. Prevalence may be related to the whole population or only a part of it: for instance, disabled people within a particular age group may be related to the whole population, as in Table 1.1, or to that section of the population which is of the same age. By contrast, *incidence* refers to the number of newly affected people who join a given population within a particular time: the numbers of new head or spinal injuries occurring within a year are examples.

The concept of care requires a number of definitions. *Care and caring* usually describe any task performed by another person for, or on behalf of, someone who cannot perform that task independently. They also describe a particular concern, motivation, commitment or personal relationship, unrelated to the performance of any specific task. Another meaning is to imply a certain protectiveness which is quite inappropriate for many disabled people, and in this book they are not employed in that narrower sense.

Caring can itself be divided into three separate groups of tasks. *Personal care* is the help that is required with all the personal obligations of daily living such as washing, dressing and eating. *Household care* is the business of ensuring that all necessary household tasks are undertaken. The third component is sometimes called *social care* but is frequently referred to as *enablement* in this book: both terms imply help that actively encourages a disabled person's personal potential and greater diversity of experience, including, for example, assistance with writing and reading, helping with mobility, and providing opportunities for social contact. Another word sometimes used is *support*, which can be taken to imply both household and social care.

Residential care itself describes care for which the recipient does not take ultimate responsibility, and which does not take place in a private household. Strictly the term should be *institutional* residential care, in the sense of a total institution as defined by Goffman (1961): a place of residence and work where a number of like-situated individuals together lead a formally administered round of life. Throughout the book, residential care is considered to include hospital care for any reason other than medical or surgical treatment or rehabilitation, and also residence in any hospital-based unit for disabled people or in a conventional residential home. The contrast is with *private households*, which may in turn be defined as independent and informal living units of one or more persons. *Community care* is care provided in private households.

Residential care as defined above includes programmes of short stay, although very frequently it is discussed in the much narrower sense of what is usually called long-term care or continuing care: residence for more or less prolonged periods of time, without intention or prospect of moving anywhere else. When necessary to avoid ambiguity, that particular arrangement is described as *committed residential care* in this book.

Finally, there are words which describe the people who have to make use of the resources and services with which this book is concerned. One of the essential features of disabled living is the need to become and/or remain a participant member of society, not a passive recipient of other people's attentions. For this reason the word 'patient' is unacceptable: 'client' is better but still implies supplicant status. I have therefore preferred to use the terms *customer* or *consumer*, which can apply to carers as much as people with disabilities. I have tried to avoid expressions such as 'the disabled' almost completely, and to use even 'disabled people' as sparingly as possible: *people with disabilities* is widely accepted as the most appropriate of these three alternatives, but sometimes the shorter ones have to be used to avoid clumsiness. *People with special needs* is also suitable, but of course there are many whose needs do not arise from disabling injuries or disease.

THE PROFESSIONAL ROLE

No second person, no matter how well trained and qualified, can ever know an individual person's experience and aspirations better than that person herself or himself, and no onlooker or even carer can do more than inadequately outline a few aspects of other people's disabilities. Medical students are taught to listen without prejudice to what their patients tell them and when necessary to what their patients' families and close acquaintances tell them too, and both practices are especially necessary when disability is severe. Professional people are always in a learning situation, but on the other hand our duty is also to face a whole range of human predicaments, many of them unexpected, unpredictable and unpleasant, about which we are usually expected to use our professional training and to exercise judgement in the process. But when we are working with severely disabled people, when we have to understand a person's whole career, we may well need to understand and be familiar with matters which are usually the business of other agencies and professions.

Professional people are trained to be detached emotionally from the tasks they have to do, no matter how unpleasant or potentially involving the circumstances may be, and this is easy enough in the separate world of a hospital or with problems which become self-limiting after only a short time. It is very much more difficult, and may at times not even be desirable, when a disabled person's problems continue and contact becomes closer, especially in the environment of residential care. Professionals find themselves slipping gradually into the role of family members, often indeed as substitutes for them, and for hospital staff in particular this may not seem appropriate to the role which they normally have to fill. One response, perhaps the usual one – and quite legitimate and logical in its way – is for the hospital-based professions to opt out and leave such matters to others no matter whom they may be. The alternative response, becoming involved and committed, both challenges their conventional thinking and almost certainly demands some adjustments to it.

Apart from countless examples of personal and voluntary initiative, much of the responsibility for helping disabled people lies in the field of social work, but there is a sizeable Health Service component too. Tradition has it that doctors tend to be consulted about severely disabled people when things go wrong, even if the immediate problem is not itself of a medical nature. Ordinary hospitals from time to time find themselves actually providing residential care, either because a disability has developed as a direct result of an illness that brought a person to the hospital in the first place, or because the hospital was resorted to in desperation as the only available institution with an open door. Because the provision of personal care is conventionally perceived as a task for nurses, when high levels of input are needed, the Health Service is commonly considered the appropriate agency to provide them. One result has been a form of residential care which is strongly influenced by traditional hospital practices and, in that respect, may well be unsuitable both for the customers yet unsatisfying for the professional staff who have to provide it. Under circumstances such as these it is even more important that professionals, while maintaining the highest possible standards of practice, should do their utmost to respond to the realities of the demands upon them and, whenever appropriate, re-learn their roles.

THE AIM OF THIS BOOK

This book is principally about adults who are young or at least are not yet old, and are severely physically disabled. It therefore concerns less than two per cent of the disabled population, one person in every thousand of the population as a whole. As explained in the Preface, it was prompted by an initiative of the Royal College of Physicians of London to which I was commissioned for a 15-month period during 1984 and 1985. The task was essentially to review the provision of residential care for such people, a resource which was seen to be expensive, poorly understood, and frequently either unavailable or inappropriately used. The study would, however, extend beyond a straightforward appraisal of the care provided, to other issues, including alternative facilities and the extent to which the requirements of people with severe disabilities were being met. Details of the programme are set out in Appendix 1.

I have also drawn on experience since 1975 within a Health Service geriatric department and also what was then a newly opened 'younger disabled unit'. The experience has allowed first-hand contact with severe disability at all ages from 16 onwards, including both sides of the reference age of 65. It has shown up most of the faults of hospital-based care as well as some of its better aspects; especially helpful has been a broadly representative council for disabled people which was loosely attached to the younger disabled unit and gave a balanced, outward-looking and sympathetic perspective to the principal issues of disability generally. Very recently, the experience gained in producing a first report of the Royal College of Physicians project (Royal College of Physicians, 1986b) has had a natural bearing on the preparation of local plans and policies for disabled people generally. Although this activity is still at an early stage, the experience of converting somewhat ideal recommendations into practical politics has already provided useful information.

Very little reference is made to practices outside Britain; a major reason was the limited time available for the research project, but there were more positive reasons too. First, an important feature of the enquiry was considered to be direct contact with residential establishments and the opportunity this gave to talk freely to staff and the people who live there; elsewhere in Europe, for example, this would have been much more difficult because of language barriers. Second, it was felt essential to give time to exploration outside the narrow field of specialised residential care itself, so that any extra time available should be spent examining the full range of possible services and approaches to disability. Third, if there was a danger of too superficial an approach at home it would have been a near certainty anywhere else: only isolated examples of good practice could have been briefly reported without any opportunity to relate them adequately to the needs of the communities they served. Fourth, social and political priorities and systems of public administration are notoriously different in detail and often in substance from one country to another, and there was no intention of embarking on a comparative study of social policy.

The contents of this book should therefore be seen as an attempt, from an admittedly medical perspective, to explain something about the dimensions of very severe disability, some of the ways of providing care, support and enablement, and what the response from those of us whose wish or business it is to be involved might ideally be. A simple catalogue of facts is not presented, nor a simple set of instructions for good practice, but instead an account of the evidence from which readers may form their own opinions as far as that evidence permits. It will be shown that very often there is no single best way of proceeding and that value judgements are frequently inescapable even though the range of options may be narrow. Social, economic and political affairs have moreover changed constantly during the past century and will continue to do so, and the same applies to the prevalence and nature of disabling disease, so that at least some ideas and courses of action which are appropriate now will become inappropriate quite quickly if not in years to come. Nevertheless, having set out a framework of facts and concepts the book ends with an agenda for further discussion, followed by some recommendations for good practice, new developments, and government action.

2
How provision for special care was established in Britain

The complex, patchy and unsatisfactory pattern of care for physical disability in Britain has its roots in a succession of social changes, new initiatives and consequent legislation, all set against a background of increasing longevity and changes in the pattern of disabling disease. Understanding something of the sequence of events helps to understand the existing situation, besides on occasions providing lessons for decision-making in the future. The two most important legislative events in the twentieth century were the National Health Service Acts of 1946 and 1947, whereby nearly all the hospitals were brought under one national administration, and the National Assistance Act of 1948 which gave the elected local authorities new responsibilities which had previously been adminis-tered under the Poor Law or had not existed at all. Some of the details of the story are different in England, Wales, Scotland and Northern Ireland but the essential components have been the same in all parts of the United Kingdom.

EARLY HISTORY

The public sector

The Poor Law itself originated in the sixteenth century following the demise of the church as a separate political and social influence, through a series of enactments – at first permissive and finally compulsory – which ended in 1601 (Checkland and Checkland, 1974). With sickness and infirmity (the 'impotent poor') usually secondary considerations, the Poor Law provided for 'indoor and outdoor relief' on the basis of each parish as a unit which levied its own special rate. The system lasted essentially unchanged until in 1834 a Poor Law Amendment Act, in response to unprecedented demands due to unemploy-ment, stipulated indoor rather than outdoor relief whenever possible (that is, admission to an institution rather than payment of benefits), and also the formation of unions of parishes for greater efficiency. The result was a network of workhouses all over the country, some of them very large, which as far as the able-bodied were concerned would be less desirable as residence than the homes of the lowest class of labourers. It was, however, recognised that such stringent conditions should not apply to children, the old or the infirm if help were sought on their behalf.

Long before 1834, however, what would now be called disturbed behaviour had produced its own pressures for residential care which presumably the old parish workhouses had not been able to meet. Alarming standards in the private madhouses of the eighteenth century became a matter of national concern: one solution, made statutory by Act of Parliament in 1774, was a programme of inspection by local magistrates or members of the Royal College of Physicians, but a second was to provide an alternative system of provision at public expense. Modelled on a successful charitable venture at York, the new county asylums were recommended in 1808 and made compulsory in 1845. Initially at least, they were envisaged in idealistic terms, as country estates where the residents would be treated as individuals, their minds constantly stimulated, with regimes which demanded kindness and forbearance from the staff and whose medical superintendents would foster an intimate and benevolent environment (Scull, 1979).

With the Poor Law providing workhouse accommodation rather than relief to families in their own homes, and with public funds available for the asylums for the insane, the stage was set for the big institutional expansion of the nineteenth century. Whether or not the increasing scale of industrial production was a contributory cause, many of the new institutions were astonishingly large. Grandiose architectural schemes proliferated (Thompson and Goldin, 1975) and most of the buildings are still in use, creating an image which has become inseparable from 'institutional care' in the public mind. The work-houses did, however, gradually lose parts of their clientèle as the public sector also began to provide fever hospitals, children's homes, hospitals for infectious diseases and colonies for the mentally defective; many Poor Law unions built their own medically controlled infirmaries as well. Especially after the inception of the State pension scheme in 1911, almost the only residents of what had once been the pauper workhouses became those who were described as chronically sick or infirm.

In 1930 the administration of the Poor Law was taken over by Public Assistance Committees of the elected local authorities; Aronovitch (1974) gives an intriguing account of life as a resident in one of the infirmaries during the period of transition. Most of the workhouses continued as 'general mixed institutions' and, although by 1948 the local authorities had appropriated more than half of them as hospitals (Abel-Smith, 1964), nearly all the establishments were seen to be providing, partly or wholly, long-term accommodation for the chronically sick. The medical profession therefore became responsible in a more complete way than before, and it did not discharge its responsibility well. Admission to the chronic sick wards was on demand from medical colleagues; there was usually a waiting list but there was hardly any screening procedure; beds increased in number, residents were mostly kept in bed, and the reputations of the hospitals sank.

The older charities

The history of charitable accommodation dates back at least to the religious foundations of the Middle Ages, most of which were destroyed in the sixteenth century and whose services were progressively supplanted by provision under the Poor Law. Only a few survived but during the succeeding centuries they were joined by many more, including hundreds of groups of almshouses and a growing number of infirmaries and hospitals. Perhaps because they were not obliged to serve everyone who might ask them for help, but no doubt also because there was no statutory limit to the funds they could raise, the charitable hospitals eventually became the principal base for medical education and innovation. Their emphasis therefore became intervention and cure rather than the more general relief of distress, but a few foundations nevertheless chose to serve 'incurables'.

Of these, two of the best known were and are the Royal Hospital and Home for Incurables at Putney, founded in 1854 and opened on its present site in 1864, and the British Hospital and Home for Incurables which seceded from it in 1861. (The founder of the Putney home had previously started no fewer than four public charities: three asylums for orphans and an asylum for 'mental defectives'; Stokes-Roberts, 1972.) Among the spa towns, the Royal Midland Counties Home was built in Leamington in 1874 and a similar establishment at Harrogate some years later. Another Home for Incurables was founded on Tyneside in 1894 from the surplus revenue of a twelfth-century charity for leprosy. A handful of religious foundations (at Haslemere and Pinner in the Home Counties and at Scorton in Yorkshire) developed an interest and a service along similar lines.

Records at the Putney hospital show that, in the 1870s, the commonest conditions accommodated were arthritis, paraplegia, hemiplegia and tuberculous disease of the spine: multiple sclerosis had not yet been recognised as a medical entity. There was also widespread contemporary concern about crippling disease among children. For example, John Grooms Association began in 1866 as a Christian mission but in 1879 opened an industrial training home for girls who were too crippled to go into domestic service; the institution, soon to be known as the Crippleage, was described as neither a hospital nor a home for incurables, and the disabilities catered for included tuberculous disease of the spine, tuberculous arthritis, absence of one or more limbs, blindness, rickets and kyphocoliosis (Martin, 1982). Examples of much more therapeutically-orientated ventures included the first convalescent home for cripples which was opened in 1900 and later became the Robert Jones and Agnes Hunt Orthopaedic Hospital, Oswestry (Cruttenden, 1975), the Lord Mayor Treloar Hospital for cripples at Alton and the Heritage Craft Schools at Chailey, both of the last two being founded in the early years of this century. People with epilepsy formed another specially identified group: residential care was and still is provided by the Maghull Homes near Liverpool, founded in 1888, the Chalfont Colony (1893), and the David Lewis Colony in Cheshire (1904).

Casualties of the 1914–18 war provided the next stimulus. During the war two village settlements for the disabled were started at Papworth and Enham, and the Royal Star and Garter Home for Disabled Soldiers, Sailors and Airmen was established at Richmond. There were similar but less ambitious ventures at such places as Rookwood in Cardiff and Ellerslie House in Nottingham. A voluntary group entitled the Central Council for the Care of Cripples was established in 1919. Both before and after the 1914–18 war, several charities had also become involved with rehabilitation and residential care for people who were blind and people who were deaf. A key feature of many of these establishments, as at John Groom's Crippleage, was the provision of occupation in the form of workshops which, whenever possible, were operated on a commercial basis or with a view to industrial training. In 1934 a workshop was opened in Leatherhead which later became the first component of Queen Elizabeth's Foundation for the Disabled, and 1937 saw the opening in Exeter of St. Loye's Training College for Cripples, now known as St. Loye's College for Training the Disabled for Commerce and Industry. The British Polio Fellowship was established in 1939.

Legislation

During this period the legislative background for disability as such was very limited. The first provision to be specially identified was elementary education for special groups: blind and deaf children in 1893, mentally defective and epileptic children in 1899 and all handicapped children in 1918. There was legislation for training centres for the war disabled in 1919 and for blind civilians in 1920. Provision for industrial rehabilitation, training and employment was made statutory in 1944.

FROM 1946 TO 1970

The National Health Service's inheritance

The new Health Service took over nearly all the charitable hospitals which had a therapeutic role, but only a proportion of the tiny minority which was mainly concerned with long-term care. The Poor Law institutions became its other major responsibility: all the hospitals, and a fair number of the general mixed institutions too (*Report of the Ministry of Health*, 1948). Altogether the service acquired some 55,000 beds which were designated for the chronically sick (*Report of the Ministry of Health*, 1949), of which between 80 per cent and 90 per cent were occupied by people beyond the age of 65 (McEwan and Laverty, 1949; Lowe and McKeown, 1950).

The definition of a hospital in the National Health Service Act 1946 was

> any institution for the reception and treatment of persons suffering from illness or mental defectiveness, any maternity home, and any institution for the reception and treatment of persons during convalescence or persons requiring medical rehabilitation. (Section 79.)

A special section of the Act dealt with mental illness but outside that section nothing was stated about long-term care. The local authorities were, however, given back this responsibility in Part III of the National Assistance Act 1948 in the form of an obligation to provide

> residential accommodation for persons who by reason of age, infirmity or any other circumstances are in need of care which is not otherwise available to them,

and to provide on those premises

> such health services, not being specialist services of a kind normally provided only on admission to a hospital, as appear to the authority requisite. (Section 21.)

At that time, however, because most of the old Poor Law institutions had passed to the Health Service, the fact was that far more hospital beds were available than accommodation according to the 1948 Act.

Those who knew and cared about the situation recognised that people were living in the chronic sick wards who did not need hospital services and might not even need institutional care at all (Warren, 1946). It was generally agreed that better accommodation was required but some doubt whether it was a Health Service or local authority responsibility to build it. It was also agreed that better systems of assessment and, if possible, rehabilitation were essential to prevent even greater accumulations of people in the hospitals as the numbers of elderly people grew during the rest of the century. The initiative was taken by a group of doctors who believed that a medical specialty was necessary and that, since by far the majority of the long-stay patients were old, it should be concerned with ageing and should be called geriatrics. This new specialty, by now an established part of the British medical scene, at first had a chequered career: a mixture of idealism and innovation with the sheer weight of the chronic-sick-ward tradition and all the stigma and cynicism with which it had come to be associated.

Up to this point it had seemed that the 'residual group' left behind by the Poor Law comprised the elderly infirm, but as geriatrics developed it became clear that there was yet another residual group: the 10 or 20 per cent of chronically sick hospital patients who were below retirement age. A report to one Regional Hospital Board in 1954 stressed a need to group the young disabled together in small special units (*British Medical Journal*, 1955), an idea which was developed further in an investigation funded by the Nuffield Foundation which concluded that particular attention should be given to neurological disorders and the provision of a community-based resource (*British Medical Journal*, 1960). Another leading charity recommended, at least for people under 35 years with the prospects of many years of residential life before them, accommodation in units which would be 'purpose-built, well equipped and homely' (Guthrie, 1968). A group was formed which called itself the National Campaign for the Young Chronic Sick, to press for action along these lines (La Fane, 1981).

Voluntary initiatives

One voluntary organisation, however, had already almost stumbled on the same residual group and was setting up a national network with aims of the same kind. In 1948 Leonard Cheshire, whose original interest was in supporting ex-servicemen, took a man with terminal cancer into a house he had recently bought in Hampshire, followed by a small succession of people of all ages with a variety of disabilities. The ideal of a domestic residential home had been re-born; two years afterwards the Cheshire Trust (later the Leonard Cheshire Foundation) was formed, and a second Cheshire Home (the name by which the first had become known) was opened in Cornwall in 1952. The committee of the new trust soon decided to restrict entry to their homes by excluding epilepsy, the old, people who were mentally unstable, and tuberculosis, although it is on record that Leonard Cheshire himself was opposed to quite such selectivity (Spath, 1977).

Nevertheless, much of his idealism was picked up and retained by the Foundation which at the same time found that there was a market for its endeavours, because of the fact that the public authorities were willing to fund the costs of care and maintenance for people for whom living in what were now geriatric departments was manifestly inappropriate, and for whom they had no resources themselves. Most of the funding was made possible by Part III of the National Assistance Act, so in effect this was a new opportunity which had not existed before. The number of Cheshire Homes grew steadily, and shrewd central administration ensured that they were evenly distributed across the country but with management almost entirely delegated to the individual homes.

The Cheshire Foundation has come to dominate the provision of residential care for younger disabled people in England, but other charities took important initiatives too. Some were older ones which diversified their interests: John Grooms Association, for example, enlarged its Crippleage, changed its name and improved its facilities so that it could accept much more severely disabled people. The Shaftesbury Society, founded like John Grooms Association as a Christian mission, but still earlier in 1840, adapted one of its children's homes so that it could be used by disabled people, and later opened others which have specialised in muscular dystrophy. Two branches of the British Red Cross

Society established homes specially for disabled women. For all three of these charities, however, residential care for physically disabled people remained only part of their work. As a new and independent venture, Sue Ryder set up a number of homes which took in people with a wide variety of needs, including physical disability but also mental illness and terminal disease.

The same period saw the growth of several new charities dedicated to the support of particular disabling conditions, some of which developed resources for residential care. The Spastics Society has become the largest: it was founded in 1952 and has expanded to an annual turnover approaching £30 million. Although its interests do not extend outside cerebral palsy, its activities are very varied and residential care is currently a substantial part of them. The Multiple Sclerosis Society, established in 1953, spends a high proportion of its income on the support of medical research but has also developed several short-stay homes. The National Fund for Poliomyelitis Research helped finance Mary Marlborough Lodge, an assessment unit which opened in Oxford in 1960 and is now part of the National Health Service. Other national support groups included the British Rheumatism and Arthritis Association (1947), the Muscular Dystrophy Group (1959), the Friedreich's Ataxia Group (1964), the Association for Spina Bifida and Hydrocephalus (1966) and the Parkinson's Disease Society (1969). There were also numerous local charities, a handful of which developed resources for residential care.

Public sector initiatives

Meanwhile, in the public sector the elected local authorities were having to face their new responsibilities for the elderly and chronically sick. A government-commissioned report in 1957 concluded that the number of beds for the chronic sick in England and Wales was about sufficient if they were properly used and better distributed; this in turn would depend among other things on the 'sufficiency of welfare accommodation for the infirm' (Boucher Report, 1957). Between 1948 and 1960 the elected welfare committees opened over a thousand new homes for old and handicapped persons of which 200 were newly built. The first one to be specially designated for younger physically handicapped people was opened in 1958 and, although the majority of authorities took no such initiative, gradually a small number of these special residential homes began to accumulate.

The National Health Service for its part had acquired some of the old charitable homes for incurables in the Midlands and North, and a small home in a converted residence which Guy's Hospital had opened in 1945. Again out of recognition that there should be some kind of segregation for younger people, the first new ventures by the Health Service either consisted of developments like that of Guy's or were just segregated wards within geriatric departments. By 1964 in England there were beds for 'young chronic sick patients' at 15 hospitals. Shone (1968) described the early experiences of one of these wards, and although they had not been altogether happy he outlined plans to set up another one. It is also relevant to note the establishment of units aimed at the rehabilitation of all grades of physical disability but excluding residential care: most of them were in the south-east of England, and examples include Camden Road, London, in 1945; Garston Manor, Hertfordshire, in 1950; and the Wolfson Centre, Wimbledon, in 1967 (Mattingly, 1981).

By this time another sort of medical consensus about the care of the younger disabled was emerging, expressed in a leading article (1969) in the *British Medical Journal* and then in an internal memorandum issued by the Ministry of Health under the number HM(68)41.

The solution recommended was unashamedly a medical model: to build new units situated within the environment of general hospitals, with full consultant cover (whatever that meant) and unrestricted access to remedial therapy services. At the same time, it seemed, rehabilitation was not to be expected but long-term care was, together with emphasis on diversional activities, provision for day places, the use of volunteers and a hope that holiday relief admissions would prove practicable. The memorandum was backed up with a paper on suggestions for the design of units and a model plan: it was considered that 'lineal plans wrapped around a courtyard onto which the communal recreative and therapeutic activities also look', would combine a requirement for external views and 'internal activities'; and 'the combination of the activities with the entrance [would enable] relatives and friends to take an active part'. The optimum size was thought to be some-where between 25 to 50 beds; small 'day spaces' in the corridors were recommended besides the 'communal space', a quiet room and a workroom. The proportion of single rooms was left vague but a roughly equal mixture of beds in single, double and four-bedded rooms seems to have been implied.

The Chronically Sick and Disabled Persons Act 1970

This Act of Parliament was regarded as a significant achievement at the time it was passed, and in retrospect it can be seen to have made a real contribution towards improving opportunities for disabled people (Topliss and Gould, 1981). A list of its contents is displayed in Table 2.1, showing that only four sections (2, 3, 17 and 18) were clearly applicable to the provision of personal care for the most severely disabled. Section 2 undoubtedly paved the way for a whole range of facilities including practical help and care, housing adaptations, the provision of meals, and also diversional activities, transport, holidays and the provision of telephones. Sections 17 and 18 were the only ones to deal with residential care and were restricted to one issue only: the separation of younger from older people with reference to the age of 65.

In the Bill that was first placed before Parliament, however, the corresponding section recommended that it should be unlawful for any health authority or local authority, or any

Table 2.1 *Contents of the Chronically Sick and Disabled Persons Act, 1970*

1	Local authorities' duty to inform themselves about local need
2	Provision of welfare services
3	Duties of housing authorities
4–7	Premises open to the public: access and facilities, provision of public sanitary conveniences, notices and signs
8	Access and facilities at university and school buildings
9–16	Advisory committees: housing, national insurance, industrial injuries, youth employment, disabled persons' employment: co-option of chronically sick or disabled persons
17	Separation of younger (under 65) from older patients in hospital
18	Information about accommodation of younger with older persons 'under welfare powers'
19	Information about chiropody services for younger persons
20–21	Use of invalid carriages on highways; badges for motor vehicles used by disabled persons
22	Annual report on research and development
23	War pensions appeals
24	The need for an institute of hearing research
25–27	Special educational treatment for the deaf-blind, and for children with autism and dyslexia

other institution, to admit to 'geriatric accommodation' anyone who was receiving long-term care for a chronic disability or illness and was under the age of 45. Exceptions were only to be with the authority of the Secretary of State, and 'geriatric accommodation' meant any building or section of any building which was wholly or mainly used for the accommodation of 'geriatric patients'. At the Report stage it was agreed that this was one of the most sensitive and difficult issues in the Bill and that any age criterion was liable to be arbitrary and unsatisfactory (Topliss and Gould, 1981). The Bill was finally amended in the House of Lords' Committee in an ambiguous form of words which removed the word 'geriatric', raised the age bar to 65 in hospitals but made it only advisory, and made no recommendations about residential care elsewhere. The ritual of an annual report to Parliament of people 'unsuitably placed' in relation to the age of 65, however, became a statutory requirement. An almost immediate consequence was a building programme announced by the Secretary of State during the following year, which would include new residential homes and new day centres for chronically sick and physically disabled persons, and a capital allocation by central government for the development of new units within the Health Service. Memorandum HM(68)41 was going to be implemented.

AFTER 1970

Public sector administration

Further important changes were enacted in public service administration at about this time, and in this context it is worth noting the differences between the four parts of the United Kingdom. Departments of social work were established in Scotland in 1968, and of social services in England and Wales in 1970, combining the previously diverse welfare and child care functions (and in Scotland the probation service) under the management of a director answerable to each elected local authority. Except in Northern Ireland, in 1974 the National Health Service reorganised and took over those few medical services (principally public health, community nursing and the ambulances) which had remained with the local authorities, and it also took over responsibility for the registration of nursing homes. The social services/social work departments were now on their own, financed and managed quite separately from the Health Service with the medical and nursing professions excluded. In Northern Ireland however, top-level administrative responsibility for health and social services had already been combined in 1972.

The movement towards community care

By the time these developments were taking place the desirability of institutional care had already been strongly challenged, most notably in respect of mental illness in the United States. Scull (1979) describes the social scientific research on the mental hospitals as amounting to a full-blown assault on their therapeutic failings, and a particularly well-known account was that of Goffman (1961). Anticipated in the Mental Health Act 1959, the response to the challenge has been progressive reduction in the number of hospital beds and increasing reliance on community care for mental illness and mental handicap, fuelled in England by public scandal at conditions in certain mental handicap hospitals from 1968 onwards (Martin, 1984). In particular the medical model of residential care was increasingly criticised, whether it was provided for children (King *et al.*, 1971) or the mentally handicapped (*Report of the Committee of Enquiry*, 1979; Ryan and Thomas, 1980). Similarly in hospital geriatric departments, there was concern about standards (Royal College of Nursing, 1975; Wells, 1980) and a new emphasis on change towards policies of short-term admission, family relief and community care.

Indeed the rapid growth of the very elderly population was enforcing the development of community services, especially because British social policy until the late 1970s had prevented the open-ended development of residential care at public expense which the policies of other countries had allowed. The local authorities' home help services, for example, expanded by a third between 1966 and 1979, and the community nursing service by the same amount between 1974 and 1984. People with physical disabilities were able to benefit from these trends, but they also began to develop a consumer view of their own. So, for instance, Davis (1976) attacked the whole concept of institutional care and described how a severely disabled couple had organised their discharge into purpose-built housing: the housing association which worked with them had itself been set up in 1960 to provide wheelchair users' accommodation. In 1981 a policy statement from a group called the Union of the Physically Impaired Against Segregation took the extreme view, calling not only for conditions which would allow all physically impaired people the means to choose where and how to live, but also for the phasing out of segregated institutions maintained by the State or by charities and the suspension of plans to build any more of them (Oliver, 1983).

In the United States, exasperation with conventional approaches to support and care, or the lack of any help at all, had led first to the disabled students' programme at the University of Illinois in the 1960s, and then in the 1970s the first Centres for Independent Living. In an account of these in 1979 De Jong wrote:

> The dependency creating features of the medical model and the impaired role are most pronounced in institutional settings. Institutions are self-contained social systems that allow house staff and various practitioners to exercise a substantial measure of social control with little outside interference . . .

> Severely physically disabled persons and their advocates are latecomers to the deinstitutionalization thrust. This is understandable. Unlike mentally impaired persons or ex-offenders, their disability is more difficult to conceal. Moreover, the deinstitutionalization of the severely physically impaired requires substantial environmental or architectural modifications not required by others . . .

With the helpful stimulus of the United Nations' International Year of Disabled People in 1981, the Independent Living Movement became known and to a limited extent established in England. In a general introduction to a totally revised Open University source book on disability published that year, the authors referred to the far-reaching changes which had been taking place in the field of handicap – not only technology, legislation, personal finance and availability of services, but also fundamental assumptions and the direct political challenge presented by disabled people themselves (Brechin, Liddiard and Swain, 1981).

It is true that cautionary noises, sometimes quite hostile ones, were also being made about community care – principally that it presented considerable problems of organisation and finance and that without adequate provision the burden on carers within families could be intolerable. Nevertheless, besides the increases in home help and direct meals services provided by the local authorities, there were also new national social security payments to compensate for disability (see page 21).

New initiatives also took place in the voluntary sector. A purely local enterprise in 1974, sponsored by a television company, soon mushroomed into a national network of Crossroads Care Attendant Schemes, of which there were about 90 by the end of 1986 (Crane and Osborne, 1979: see page 92). The same idea was implemented by the Leonard Cheshire Foundation (Inskip, 1981b) and was taken up by at least a few local authorities. New national groups for the support of particular disabling disorders were also founded: the Association to Combat Huntington's Chorea in 1971, the Spinal Injuries Association in 1974, and in 1979 the Motor Neurone Disease Association and Headway, the national head injuries group. In 1974 Action Research into Multiple Sclerosis was established as a rival to the Multiple Sclerosis Society; in 1976 the Chest and Heart Association (which could trace its ancestry to the National Association for the Prevention of Consumption and other forms of Tuberculosis, founded in 1898) became the Chest, Heart and Stroke Association. The Royal Association for Disability and Rehabilitation was formed in 1977 by the amalgamation of the Central Council for the Disabled and the British Association for Rehabilitation of the Disabled.

Among a very considerable literature on the difficulties of community care one might select a succinct survey of carers' responsibilities by the Equal Opportunities Commission (1980), a good commonsense account of the organisational problems of community care published by the Department of Health and Social Security in 1981, a detailed description of day-to-day problems by Cantrell and his colleagues (1985), the anthology of personal accounts edited by Briggs and Oliver (1985), and a first-rate review of the issues and principles from the House of Commons' Social Services Committee (1985). None of these particular accounts challenges the desirability of community care at least for those who want it, but they do point out the costs, difficulties and tensions which it necessarily incurs.

New perspectives of residential care

In 1972, under the sponsorship of the Ministry of Health, Miller and Gwynne published their detailed study of residential institutions for the physically handicapped and young chronic sick. Their description of two models of care – 'warehousing' and 'horticultural' – has since been widely quoted: while arguing that the latter allowed the residents more freedom, the authors were critical of both. They were harsh too in some of their judgements, for example in remarking that people taken into these institutions were seen to be incapable of occupying any role that was positively valued by society and in that respect were, in effect, socially dead. Hospitals, they considered, were inevitably dominated by the medical structure and culture, and the split between the various hierarchies denied the person in charge of a hospital-based unit the authority that the head of an institution needs. They commented that government advice had been predominantly concerned with the physical environment, and they believed that much more emphasis was needed on opportunities for independence and choice in the realms of personal development and quality of life. Put another way, two types of specialist service seemed to be required: an 'engineering function' concerned with physical handicap, and a second one concerned with ameliorating the psychosocial environment.

Partly as a result of the reorganisation of services, gradually a distinct social-work perspective of residential care began to emerge. The impact of the whole succession of legislation from the nineteenth century onwards was reviewed in a discussion document (McCoy, 1978), which among other recommendations suggested a general review of the legislation to remove some of its complexity, imprecision and omissions; research to establish more information about younger physically disabled people – who they are and what they really require; and more attention to admission processes so that the full range of options for every individual would always be properly considered. Brearley and his colleagues (1980) reviewed the procedures surrounding decisions to admit to a residential home. An experiment in resident-directed care was set up in two local authority homes in London (Dartington *et al.*, 1981). The Leonard Cheshire Foundation published an excellent handbook of good practice (Inskip, 1981a), and Clough (1982) gave a commendably clear account of the principles of residential care based on both personal experience and academic analysis. Oliver (1983) discussed some of the principal issues in a social-work context and also from a disabled person's point of view. The jointly published booklet *Home Life* (1984) is a further version of recommended practice with special reference to the growing private sector in old people's homes.

The new Health Service units

Meanwhile, in the National Health Service the initiatives rightly or wrongly taken during 1968–70 were coming to fruition, and in due course a number of papers describing the new 'units for the young chronic sick' began to appear. First off the mark were senior staff of the South East Metropolitan Region (Denly, 1972; Hardwick, 1974), describing a policy which anticipated residential, short stay and day care in the units that were being built but assuming that rehabilitation would not only be unnecessary but positively undesirable. Of the various planning documents produced at the time, one of the most committed was clearly dedicated to the idea of special hospital-based units while equally aware of the many uncertainties that existed at the time, not only within the Health Service but within the newly formed social services too (Sheffield Regional Hospital Board, 1973). The document envisaged that the units would accommodate people of 'all degrees of mental and social competence and mobility', did not recommend they should accept people for day care, and only hinted at rehabilitation; it included what would now be regarded as an overestimate of the requirement, based partly on the existing division of responsibility between hospital wards and old people's homes, and partly on the naive assumption that all very severely disabled people would accept residential care if it were offered them.

From the units themselves Prinsley (1973), in the North of England, wrote with undisguised enthusiasm about the new developments and the improved standards of living from which patients (*sic*) would benefit. Later reports from elsewhere were more cautious (Brown and Sutcliffe, 1976; Pelatt, 1976) and at one unit in particular a deliberate mix of functions was planned, with decision-making responsibility for admissions firmly delegated to the sister in charge (Bowman, 1977). A description of a unit in an adapted building appeared at about the same time, intended to be a comprehensive community service but evidently with a long-stay flavour to it (Wilson, 1978). Against this background a vigorously argued policy of rehabilitation came as something of a surprise (Benson and Williams, 1979) while at yet another unit a rehabilitation programme based on five-day admissions was under way (Owen-Smith, 1982). After an interval of several years there were two further accounts, one stressing the value of short-term admission (Pinder, 1984) but the most recent one a frank admission of failure, declaring that in future these units should concentrate on short-term assessment, holiday relief and rehabilitation, to the exclusion of continuing care (Critchley, 1985).

Criticism of the Health Service units had in fact been expressed almost from the outset. Shearer (1974) delivered a scathing attack based partly on a visit to a pilot unit which had been opened in 1968, partly on opinions expressed by disabled people at a seminar on the subject, and also on the publicity given to a Swedish system of housing with a personal care service which was then being developed by The Spastics Society, although only on one site. Two early surveys were also critical: one was included in a general review of residential accommodation for disabled people (Symons, 1974); the second was unpublished and was carried out by a senior nurse who had responsibility for one of the new units herself (Bloomfield, 1976). Another nurse with a similar responsibility wrote about her own misgivings (Davis, 1976). Much more recently Scott (1984) obtained 46 answers to postal questionnaires; he concluded that the 'younger disabled units' – as they had by now generally come to be known – could not expect to operate in isolation but only as part of a spectrum of services for the disabled, and that they should certainly try to avoid long-term care. Close liaison with local authority departments, the local geriatric service and voluntary organisations, he considered, was vital.

More legislation, and the support of residential care by social security payments

Not only was 1970 the year of the Chronically Sick and Disabled Persons Act and the establishment of the social services departments; in the National Insurance Act of the same year the attendance allowance was introduced. It was the first State benefit in Britain to recognise the costs of incapacity caused by anything besides warfare or industrial injury: it was to be paid to anyone so severely disabled as to require frequent attention in respect of bodily functions, or continual supervision to avoid substantial danger (Baldwin and colleagues, 1981). It does not require a contribution record or a means test, it is not taxable, and disabled people of any age are eligible to receive it. Its purpose is simply to make some financial compensation for the consequences of severe disability, with no restriction on how it should be spent.

The mobility allowance, also awarded on the basis of disability and nothing else, was introduced in Section 37 of the Social Security Pensions Act 1975 as a substitute for the much criticised issue of 'invalid vehicles', which was originally established for disabled war pensioners. A person who received the allowance must be unable or 'virtually unable' to walk, and this disability must be thought likely to persist for at least a year. There is, however, a lower age limit of five and an absolute upper limit of 75, and people who become unable to walk after the age of 65 are ineligible. It is not taxable although at first this was not the case. Other relevant (and taxable) social security payments were introduced at about the same time, for people who would otherwise be in employment: the invalid care allowance in 1975 (payable to carers), and the non-contributory invalidity pensions in 1975 and 1977 which were converted to the severe disablement allowance in 1984 (payable to disabled persons).

Meanwhile, in some areas the practice had grown of allowing means-tested social security benefit payments to be awarded, and in many cases to be substantially increased, in order to pay for places in residential care. This informal and unplanned development allowed an almost explosive growth in the private sector, mainly in residential care for old people, gathering momentum from about 1979 onwards: it also attracted a small but appreciable number of people below the age of 65. In 1983 the government's first attempt at regulating the growth in effect turned the discretionary payments into a system of entitlements with no budgetary limitation (Challis, Day and Klein, 1984). Horrified by the financial implications, two years later the government limited the per capita entitlements according to a four-point scale, depending on whether an establishment was registered as a nursing home or a residential house, and on whether the applicant was under or over the age of 65. Despite the restrictions the amounts payable, though admittedly means-tested, were still nearly twice the value of the benefits to which most applicants would have been entitled as occupants of private households (Table 2.2), and total cash limits were still not applied.

The private and voluntary residential homes have also been more formally regulated by a sequence of recent legislation. The Nursing Homes Act 1975 defined such homes as 'any premises used or intended to be used for the reception of and the providing of nursing for persons suffering from any sickness, injury or infirmity': the Act also covered maternity homes and mental nursing homes. Five years later the Residential Homes Act 1980 reviewed procedures for registration with local authorities but was less specific in its requirements. The rapid proliferation of old people's homes provoked the Registered Homes Act 1984 which was intended to make the 1975 and 1980 Acts compatible and also tightened the regulations. Because the health and local authorities were no longer the sole source of subsidy for residence in private and voluntary homes, not unnaturally they began to withdraw from that responsibility: as a result, some of the long-established homes then faced a drop in their income (Peaker, 1986).

Available evidence also suggests that hardly any of the new generation of private homes has chosen to specialise in accommodating the younger disabled: in particular, in the course of the survey described in Chapter 4, only one such home was discovered. On the other hand, the higher payments made for residents under the age of 65 provides an incentive for old people's homes to admit such people so that the intentions of Section 17 of the Chronically Sick and Disabled Persons Act have in effect been reversed. At the time of writing the situation remains unsatisfactory, with many of the issues mentioned in these last three paragraphs still contested and unresolved.

THE PROVISION IN 1985

The legislative and financial arrangements for residential care in the United Kingdom are summarised in Figures 2.1 and 2.2. Figure 2.3 shows that special residential homes and units for younger disabled people together amount only to a tiny fraction of total residential provision, especially in comparison with homes and hospital wards for elderly people. The government publishes annual figures for handicapped people aged 16–64 in hospital geriatric and psychiatric wards (but not those who have become long-stay patients in ordinary wards) and in all other forms of residential care; Figure 2.4 shows that whereas the number 'inappropriately placed' in hospital has diminished during the 15 years since 1970, as has the total number in the local authorities' own residential homes, the overall numbers have changed very little because of a marked increase in the numbers in voluntary and private homes. This increase has been coincidental with the new eligibility

Table 2.2 *Social security payments to severely disabled people in the United Kingdom (weekly rates from 25 November 1985)*

	In private households	Weekly rate £	In residential care	Weekly rate £
Non-taxable Not means-tested	Attendance allowance – lower rate[1]	20.45	(Attendance allowance may be payable to residents of some residential homes)	
	– higher rate[1]	30.60		
	Mobility allowance	21.40	Mobility allowance	21.40
	Severe disablement allowance	23.00		
	Invalidity benefit[2]	38.30		
Means-tested	Supplementary benefit ceiling rates		Supplementary benefit ceiling rates	
	clothing (extra wear and tear)	Extra cost only	onset of disability[3] after retirement age { residential care homes	120.00
	laundry	Negotiable	{ nursing homes	170.00
	heating	8.80	onset of disability[3] before retirement age { residential care homes	180.00
	domestic help	44.90	{ nursing homes	230.00
	for blindness	7.15		

[1] Depending on need for attendance at night.
[2] Dependent on previous employment until a ruling of the European Court of Justice in 1986.
[3] 'Substantial and permanent'.

(Further information on these allowances is given in Table 5.5, Chapter 5)

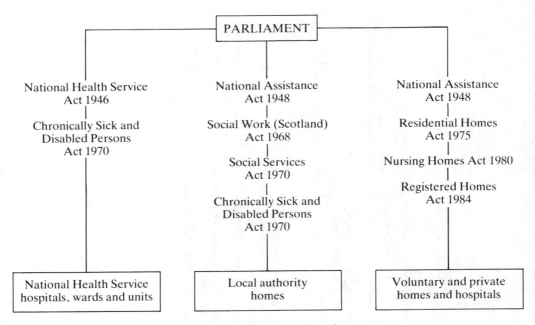

Figure 2.1 *National responsibility for institutional residential care*

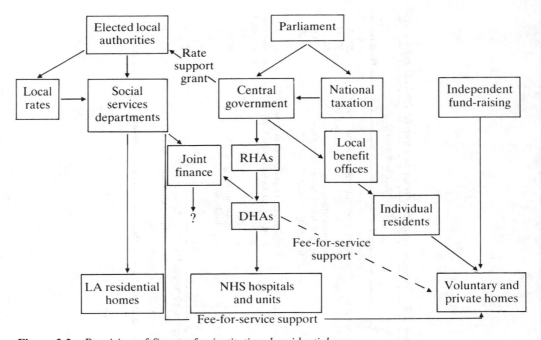

Figure 2.2 *Provision of finance for institutional residential care*
(RHA: regional health authority; DHA: district health authority; LA: local authority)

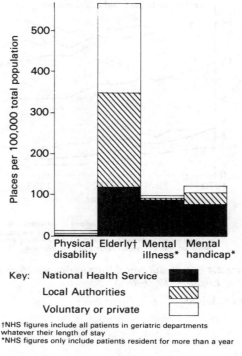

Key: National Health Service   ▉

        Local Authorities   ▧

        Voluntary or private   ▢

†NHS figures include all patients in geriatric departments
whatever their length of stay
*NHS figures only include patients resident for more than a year

Figure 2.3   *Residential care in England, 1984*

Source: DHSS

for social security payments, and can be presumed to have been largely in homes for the elderly, but it is uncertain whether the people concerned would otherwise have been in private households or in ordinary hospital wards. Using data from the survey described in Chapter 4, Figure 2.5 shows the successive development of special homes and units for younger disabled people, classified according to the four main agencies which manage them.

Figure 2.6 gives a further breakdown of the total distribution of younger disabled people in residential care according to the largest management agencies. The composite picture is based on several different sources of information and requires some comment. The diagram is in fact concerned with England: Wales and Northern Ireland have a rather similar profile, but Scotland has a much smaller local authority sector which does not provide residential care specially for the younger disabled. In Chapter 4 it will be shown that some 15 per cent of the special residential care provided by the four main agencies is occupied by people who have passed the age of 65. The outstanding fact, however, appears to be that less than half of the total group are in places that are intended specially for the younger disabled.

Of those that are accommodated elsewhere, some (reported annually to Parliament) are 'unsuitably placed' in hospital wards which cater mainly for the long-term care of old people, decisions about the inappropriateness being left to the judgement of hospital staff;

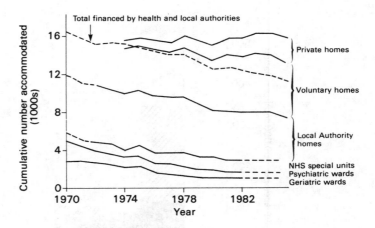

It can be presumed that most residents in voluntary and private homes who are not financed by local authorities are supported by social security payments instead. Data for nursing homes registered with the Health Service are not available.

Figure 2.4 *Physically disabled people aged 16 to 64 in residential care in England, 1970–1985*

Source: DHSS

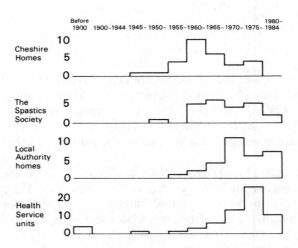

Figure 2.5 *Numbers of designated homes and units for younger physically disabled people, by year of opening*

Source: RCP survey

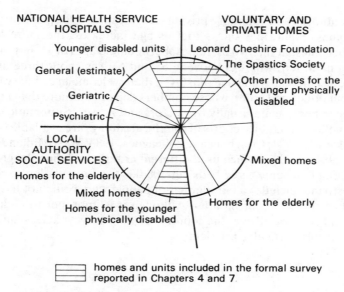

Figure 2.6　*Physically disabled people aged 16 to 64 in residential care in England, 1983: distribution by managing agency and type of accommodation*

Sources: DHSS, RCP survey

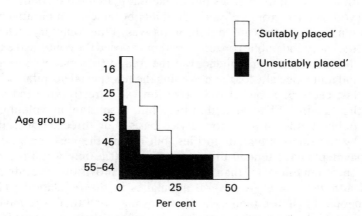

Figure 2.7　*Physically disabled adults below retirement age in residential care*

(Estimate of proportions based on returns to Parliament under Sections 17 and 18 of the Chronically Sick and Disabled Persons Act 1970, and on the Royal College of Physicians' survey) in the local authority and voluntary/private sectors, most of the places are likely to be in old people's homes. Figure 2.7 shows that as age increases, the more likely 'unsuitable' placement becomes: at the two extremes, between the ages of 16 and 24 the proportion is only about one in ten, whereas between 55 and 64 it is about three in every four.

There are also people who have outstayed their welcome in ordinary hospital wards, an important but ill-defined group whose numbers depend far more than any of the others on personal judgement, again usually by doctors and nurses. Systematic information about them is not collected but the reports of four local surveys are available (McAndrew, 1984; Swithinbank et al., 1984; Coughlan and colleagues, 1983; West Midlands Regional Health Authority, 1984), each of which used different criteria to define the group but produced data suggesting that some three beds per 100,000 total population were occupied in this way. This estimate includes a fair number of people who would not have been in hospital for more than three or four months. Although it is improper to deduce that the same findings would be made all over the country, the four surveys at least give some idea of the likely scale of this particular problem.

CONCLUSIONS

The British tradition of providing institutional care for dependent people, and therefore of expecting it to be provided, goes back many generations and probably many centuries even though most people with similar kinds of dependency have been and continue to be supported by their own families. The practice seems to have been given a powerful boost in the early nineteenth century for a mixture of punitive and altruistic reasons, and it has always relied for nearly all of its support on public funds. As life expectancy, social conditions and the patterns of disease and disability changed over the years, and as new ways of dealing with different problems were devised, the people who still went to live in the institutions were in most cases old or mentally disabled or both.

Among younger age groups physical disability became a comparatively unusual reason for admission to residential care, but the initiatives of the voluntary sector, the creation of a geriatric specialty and public concern together exposed the continued existence of people in that predicament. One consequence was the creation of a modest but significant number of homes and units specially for them, joining the few special hospitals which had survived from the last century. Some of this provision was directly financed and administered through the health and local authorities, but a substantial voluntary/private sector attracted public funds on a fee-for-service basis. For three decades these funds were provided by the same public authorities, but during the past ten years national social security payments have tended to replace them. At a time when there has been more emphasis on community care than ever before, the provision of residential care has also increased although there are several anomalies in the regulations. Opportunities for disabled people to choose their own life styles may well therefore have increased.

It is against this background of history and provision that current practices in residential care have to be evaluated, and the contemporary case for 'de-institutionalisation', independent living and community care. But first it is necessary to take some account of the client group itself, and the pressures which cause admission to an institution to be considered.

3
Physically disabling diseases and injuries, and their influence on individual careers

Available evidence suggests that most people with disabilities not only know but want to know why they are disabled, which inevitably means knowledge of their medical diagnostic labels. Members of the health care professions need no persuasion that diagnosis is essential to the understanding of a disabled person's predicament, but with the growing involvement of other professions and the growing consumer voice there has been a noticeable trend towards suggesting that the cause of a disability is unimportant. Partly this is to escape the categorising and dismissive labelling which many people associate with medicine, but it is also to draw attention to two obvious facts: the impact of most conditions can vary from mild to very severe, and people with different medical diagnoses can have many problems in common. The details of an individual's capacity and incapacity are what matter in relation to issues such as the need for help and equipment at home, access to a building, ability to drive, and ability to hold down a job.

On the other hand, whereas there is no convenient shorthand to describe impairment, disability or handicap which at the present time at least is generally accepted and understood, medical diagnoses can convey a great deal of information without the need to itemise each component. Although most disabled people would be hard-pressed to give their position on any disability scale, for most of them their diagnoses not only help to explain their own personal circumstances but also help towards explaining these circumstances to others. The same is true for everyone involved in their support and care. Perhaps most important of all, the diagnosis says something about a person's career – his or her experience of disability and the likelihood of what is in store – in a way that straightforward measurement of impairment or disability by its very nature cannot. So for these reasons it is desirable to have a clear understanding of the principal physically disabling conditions which cause help to be sought by or on behalf of the people we are considering.

Information about the commonest causes of very severe physical disability may be obtained from a number of sources including the survey described in this book (Table 3.1). The diversity of purpose of the original investigations, and a degree of uncertainty among the diagnostic categories used by the authors, together mean that no two of the reports are strictly comparable: there is consequently some need for interpretation. Nevertheless, the data confirm that disease or injury of the nervous system account for at least half of all severely disabling disorders, and for a noticeably higher proportion among those who are in hospitals or residential homes. Stroke is the commonest condition unless the population over 65 is excluded; even then it figures prominently in every group except those in psychiatric wards. Multiple sclerosis usually takes precedence in the 16–64 age group;

Table 3.1 *The commonest diseases and injuries among different samples of disabled people*

Author	Population studied	Age group	Most frequent conditions			Approximate proportion (%)	
			1st	2nd	3rd	Total nervous system[1]	Total 'brain'
Harris (1971)	National sample: very severe disabilities, needing special care	All above 16	Stroke	Arthritis	Senility	(49)	(46)
Agerholm (1981)	Attending rehabilitation centre	All above 16	Stroke	Multiple sclerosis	Spinal injury	77	(66)
Bristow (1981)	Care attendant schemes	All above 16	Stroke	Multiple sclerosis	Osteo-arthritis	64	(52)
Lovelock (1981)	Care attendant schemes	Mainly 15–65	Multiple sclerosis	Stroke	Cerebral palsy	(65)	55
Swithinbank et al. (1984)	Ordinary hospital wards, longer than 3 months' stay	15–65	Stroke	Multiple sclerosis	Trauma	(74)	(65)
McAndrew (1984)	Non-psychiatric hospital wards, longer than 3 months' stay	16–64	Multiple sclerosis	Stroke	Trauma	(79)	(70)
McAndrew (1984)	Psychiatric wards, longer than 3 months' stay[2]	16–64	Alcoholic brain damage	Alzheimer's disease	Epilepsy	92	(89)
Harrison (1987)	Special homes/units for the younger physically disabled	Mainly 16–64	Cerebral palsy	Multiple sclerosis	Stroke	89	79

[1] Nervous system and 'brain' indicates the principal location of disability. By 'brain' is meant all those conditions which can involve the brain but have not necessarily done so in every case; multiple sclerosis is the chief example. By definition, all 'brain' conditions are also disorders of the nervous system. Figures in brackets are by inference from the data provided.
[2] Only disorders which cause physical disability were included.

arthritis only appears conspicuously among people living in private households and when the elderly age group is included. Cerebral palsy is only prominent in the context of services intended specially for younger people. Trauma can be presumed mainly to include head injury and perhaps spinal injury. The physically disabled population in psychiatric wards is, from the evidence of one study, quite different from the others.

Because one of the main purposes of this book is to review those kinds of disability for which residential care may at one time or another appear to be an option, and to concentrate on people who cannot yet be considered old, it is appropriate to form a general picture of the disabling diseases and injuries to be found in residential homes and hospital units which cater specially for younger disabled people. Figure 3.1 displays a profile

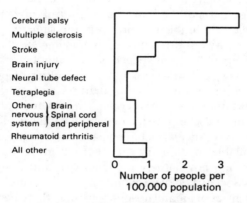

Cerebral palsy
Multiple sclerosis
Stroke
Brain injury
Neural tube defect
Tetraplegia
Other } Brain
nervous } Spinal cord
system } and peripheral
Rheumatoid arthritis
All other

0   1   2   3
Number of people per
100,000 population

Figure 3.1 *Medical diagnoses among patients and residents in homes and units for younger physically disabled people*

Source: RCP survey

representing the combined population of the Health Service's younger disabled units and of homes belonging to the local authorities, the Leonard Cheshire Foundation and The Spastics Society, and it is the framework on which the rest of this chapter has been constructed. The account is not intended to include detailed conventional medical descriptions of disease and it is not a complete catalogue, still less a discourse on medical treatment: instead, after very brief descriptions of the salient features of the chief disorders, short reports of individual people are given in the contexts of their life styles and with special reference to residential care. Briefer mention is then made of certain less frequent but important diseases; the chapter concludes with a system of classification.

A word must be added about the significance of injury or disease of the brain. The brain's anatomical complexity means that the variety of disabilities which can be encountered is bewilderingly large, regardless of the cause: the importance is that outward and visible signs, especially paralysis, may divert attention from disturbances which are far more profound. Broadly speaking, these can be divided into disturbances of posture and movement; of speech and comprehension; of visual and spatial recognition; of awareness and orientation; of concentration and motivation; of memory and recall; and of emotional and social control. Only a proportion of these disorders is arguably within the bounds of mental illness; the others are not, yet in many cases any associated physical disability can be relatively inconspicuous or even absent altogether.

CEREBRAL PALSY

Although this is not the commonest cause of very severe disability in the population as a whole, it is the most frequent among children and young adults and in the residential homes which are described in Chapter 4. By definition, it produces lifelong disabilities which date from birth or very early infancy. According to The Spastics Society's literature it comprises a group of disorders of posture and movement due to damage or failure to develop normally in those parts of the brain which control movement. It takes so many forms that no two people are disabled in precisely the same way. Some are so lightly affected that they have no obvious problems but others may be clumsy at walking and/or have difficulty with their upper limbs or speech; some cannot even sit and may be almost totally helpless. There may be deafness or other difficulties of perception; many have learning difficulties which make them slow to mature, and some are frankly mentally handicapped. Intelligence may also be very high however, and uncontrollable facial movements may give a quite false impression of mental handicap. The physical disabilities are broadly classifiable into spasticity (including partial or complete paralysis of any or all of the limbs), uncontrollable involuntary or 'athetoid' movements (usually caused by severe jaundice at birth and now largely preventable), and unsteadiness of voluntary movement. The Spastics Society believes that too many older cerebral palsied people who are today in residential centres or mental hospitals are only there because they did not have the early treatment and training that could have helped them live independent lives.

Because of the wide range of symptoms and severity the ascertainment of incidence and prevalence is not easy, but widely quoted figures are about 1 in every 500 live births and about 2.5 per 1000 children of school age. Extrapolated to adult life and allowing for higher mortality among the most severely disabled, a prevalence of 200 per 100,000 has been estimated for the population as a whole (Bowley and Gardner, 1980; Pharoah, 1985). No good actuarial figures exist however, nor a national register of cerebral palsy although one or two local registers have been established. These uncertainties help to explain why, for example, the National Sample Survey reported only about 40 people with cerebral palsy living in private households per 100,000 total population, of which about nine were severely handicapped with six of these in the special care category. The data in Figure 3.1 suggest that at least a further 3 per 100,000 are in residential care, but it does not follow that all of them are in the severely handicapped group. Information on prevalence trends is still unreliable; it is likely that improved obstetric techniques have reduced the overall incidence, but the increased survival of very premature infants may have caused an increase in the numbers of very severely disabled children, especially those whose cerebral palsy is combined with absence of vision or hearing.

In the past at least, it seems, adult residential care has been sought particularly when children leave special residential schools (when the decision that they should leave their family homes may already have been made years previously); as the result of discharge programmes from mental subnormality hospitals; and when ageing parents die or are perceived to be no longer fit enough to provide the necessary care. Of those known to The Spastics Society for whom residential care becomes an issue, 70 per cent have mental as well as physical disability though only some 5 per cent or 10 per cent have troublesome behavioural problems. Cerebral palsied people with even the severest degrees of paralysis and special disorders have also been able to reach impressive degrees of independence, fulfilment and attainment; all too many have, however, remained dependent, frequently to the extent of remaining wholly dependent on residential care.

A young woman of 21, whose disability was due to fairly mild paralysis of the right arm and leg, lived in a local authority home. She explained that she had decided to go there because she really did not want to be with her parents. She had attended several schools including a special school for the physically handicapped and a residential training college where she said she had learnt such things as confidence in going out and the ability to do simple housework and cooking. Her great interest was riding, to which she had been introduced at the age of seven by the charity called Riding for the Disabled. Eventually, she agreed, after I had asked her to think about it, that she would like to move out to a flat of her own; if she were to take a job, more than anything she would like it to be with horses.

In another local authority home was a man in his late thirties with very indistinct speech who had to use a wheelchair. He had once lived in a Spastics Society hostel, but then got married and moved to his own flat not far away. Not long afterwards he became ill and there was some question about a diagnosis of multiple sclerosis. Later his marriage broke up and he went to a local authority home which he disliked: five years before I met him he had moved to the home he was in at present. Now he was in a rehabilitation flat in that home, being given every encouragement and nearly ready to move into a newly-built flat of his own, very much looking forward to being able to run his life the way he wanted to.

A woman in her forties, yet again in a home belonging to a local authority, told me she had never lived on her own. At the age of 16 she had gone into a mental hospital: she left it many years later to go to a succession of places including a training centre run by the National Society for Mentally Handicapped Children, a residential home run by a private charity, a home belonging to The Spastics Society, and then the place where I met her, which was closest to her remaining relatives. She was a wheelchair user but not severely physically disabled and did not give the impression of significant mental handicap either. Whatever attempts may have been made in the past to help her to consider living in a private household, certainly no such encouragement was being given at the present time.

A man of about 60, living in a Cheshire Home, was fully ambulant and talkative although his speech was indistinct. He had spent most of his life with his father and sister in a village about ten miles away, until a few years ago when they both died within the same week. It seems that he was thought incapable of caring for himself, came to the residential home and had been there ever since. He liked the place because it had a lot of historical associations in which he said he was very interested. He used to enjoy walking everywhere but felt less able to do that kind of thing now, which he attributed to his age. Again it seemed that he could almost certainly have managed in his own home given appropriate encouragement and help, but now no plans were being made in this direction at all.

As an example of the severest kind of disability, a boy of ten was a recent arrival at a residential school. He had the physique of someone far younger, needing a corset to help him sit up, and he was troubled with bouts of considerable spasm in his legs. Often he would just flop. He could only make noises, not speak at all. His attention was easily distracted by someone's presence when he would grin and laugh in a way that is character-istic of severe cerebral palsy: otherwise he seemed lost inside his own world. One could only guess what his thoughts might be. He was due to start a programme of conductive education but at that stage the outcome was by no means certain. Even if it proved successful, the staff at the school were concerned that the initiative might be wasted unless there was some way it could be maintained when he was no longer a child.

Descriptions of far fuller and involved lives, characterised by determination to challenge any obstacle and make use of every opportunity, are for example to be found among the papers written by Brett (1978 and 1979), the personal histories recorded by Berwick (1980) and Waller (1984), and the semi-autobiographical novel by Brown (1970).

MULTIPLE SCLEROSIS

This disease has three features in common with cerebral palsy: it is one of the most frequent reasons why residential care is sought; it may produce disabilities which to an onlooker mimic the spasticity and tremor of cerebral palsy almost exactly; and the disabilities vary at all levels from trivial to profound, and in their nature according to the parts of the central nervous system that are involved. But there of course the similarity ends: cerebral palsy is for life and from the onset of life, whereas multiple sclerosis is always acquired (nearly always in adult life) and either steadily or intermittently and unpredictably progressive. Life expectancy in all but the most severely affected cases of cerebral palsy is normal or nearly so, but life expectancy with multiple sclerosis is not. It is right that (for example) literature produced by the Multiple Sclerosis Society emphasises an optimistic view because a sizeable proportion of people who acquire the disease do not ever become very severely disabled and live on into old age. It is also undeniably true, however, that others become very dependent indeed, and one of the most difficult aspects of the disease when advising, planning and arranging systems of support and care is its unpredictability. A very good account of the disease, partly based on personal experience, has been written by Burnfield (1985).

Again, because of the wide range of symptoms and severity, the true ascertainment of prevalence is not easy, but the most usually quoted figure for England and Wales is about 60 per 100,000 total population (Kurtzke, 1980) although some recent evidence has suggested a figure nearer 100 (Williams and McKeran, 1986; Swingler and Compston, 1986). A higher prevalence in cooler climates is generally recognised, for example in Northern Ireland and Scotland and especially in the islands of Orkney and Shetland. In contrast to cerebral palsy, the National Survey data are fairly compatible with this range of estimates and they show, moreover, that among the people of all ages with multiple sclerosis who live at home, about 30 per 100,000 are severely handicapped and 20 of these are in the special care category. The data in Figure 3.1 suggest that nearly three people with multiple sclerosis per 100,000 population are in special residential care, and from Table 3.1 it seems likely that many more are in hospitals and residential homes of other kinds. The figures altogether help to confirm the impression given by clinical practice that multiple sclerosis dominates severe disability between the ages of 16 and 64. Examination of national mortality figures shows also that life expectancy has extended by at least ten years since 1952 (the period for which records are available).

Clinical experience suggests that the issue of long-term care is most likely to be raised when the ability to walk is finally and/or suddenly lost, leaving a major mobility problem for which a household may be ill-prepared; when non-motor disabilities such as deterioration of personality, memory, awareness and/or intellect become very prominent; when complications develop such as febrile illness (very often due to infections of the respiratory or urinary tracts) or a rapidly developing pressure sore; or when family support is suddenly or seems likely to be withdrawn, sometimes due to ill-health but very often because a marital relationship is disintegrating. With cerebral palsy the major caring responsibility at home rests with parents; with multiple sclerosis it is with a husband or wife.

A man in his forties had had multiple sclerosis for at least five years and was very pleased to have been able to move into a residential home eighteen months before I met him. He liked it because it gave him many more opportunities than had been available once he had been forced to give up his job: he then lived in lodgings with a landlady, having been separated from his wife for quite some time. Now he was able to pursue a number of pastimes including outdoor sports and social events and games within the home, and he went out shopping in his wheelchair whenever he wished. He had done his turn as chairman of the residents' committee too. His speech had already become indistinct, and he knew of course that his abilities generally were continuing to decrease.

A woman in her mid-sixties was living in a Health Service unit composed of nineteenth-century buildings. She had become a wheelchair user two years after the onset of multiple sclerosis 20 years ago and had been in hospital for most of that time. At first this was because her husband was at work, and she became one of the first residents in one of the first of the newly built hospital units. She moved because her husband retired and moved, but still she did not return home even though he was able to lead a full and active life: she did, however, regularly join him at home for a few hours every Sunday. She was in no doubt that she preferred this second unit; within a few weeks she had done more and seen more than ever in the previous one, and she mentioned regular physiotherapy, regular sessions in the big occupational therapy room, and regular outings. She felt she was very fortunate in not having been moved to a geriatric ward even though her bed was in a dormitory and the day room would win no prizes at all. Quite simply, she deeply appreciated the genuine kindness and warmth she had been shown and she described the unit as 'just fantastic – this is our home'.

In a local authority home I talked to a man in his fifties whose wife worked on the care staff of an old people's home. Until fairly recently he had been able to propel himself in an ordinary wheelchair but he had now completely lost the use of his upper limbs. He also had visible difficulty breathing and said he could only take shallow breaths. He had a pressure sore too, and had found that the best way to deal with it was to sit on a particular cushion and let the community nurses dress it. He told me at length about his illness, its complications, the attention he had received at the local hospital, and the frequent discomfort he now had to endure. He was critical of some of the things that had been said and done by the hospital staff but he greatly appreciated the home he was now in, which he had entered two months ago. He was sure it was not reasonable for his wife to have to care for him at home any more although he did admit that the community services could have been better. He planned to go home occasionally for a week or two at a time but otherwise his wife and children visited regularly – they only lived a mile or two away. He had been allowed to choose his own wallpaper for his room, and he reckoned he was settling in for the last phase of his illness, however long or short that might turn out to be; in fact he died less than six months later.

Another young woman in her thirties was dreadfully incapacitated by tremor; she lived with her two young children and her husband who had a full-time job. Her multiple sclerosis was clearly advancing quite fast and it was not long before she began to alter in appearance and became almost inarticulate. Paralysis, spasticity and fixed deformities of her limbs increased and it was only these which began just a little to limit the tremor. The statutory services were good, but perhaps the key factor was the extended family; her parents were able to support her husband and the services whenever their help was needed. Added to this a regular programme of short stay in a Health Service unit, eventually adjusted to one week in every six, proved a stable arrangement which helped keep the family together despite her continued deterioration. Towards the end she and the family preferred that she stayed entirely at home, which was where she died three years and three months after the unit had first been introduced to her.

The effect of multiple sclerosis on one woman in her thirties had been serious enough to impair her personality, memory and intellect. She and her husband had three young children; he cared for her personally with the help of community nurses but refused all other offers of help including equipment and adaptations to the house. She ceased to be able to do much that was useful but severe physical disability came late: eventually, when she became wheelchair-dependent rather suddenly, her husband had already begun to neglect her. At this point he asked for more help, but not in their own home; day centre attendances and a respite care programme in a Health Service unit were arranged but during the second of these he announced that his girl friend was expecting a baby and he was seeing a solicitor about a divorce. After a good deal of discussion it was decided not to send his wife home when the second period of respite care had ended, because to do so would have had very unpleasant consequences and a bed in the unit happened to be available. She seemed partly aware of what had happened, not greatly upset or surprised about it, only vaguely concerned about her children and more or less content with the place where she now was. Her condition remained unchanged for six months until a terminal illness which lasted no more than a few hours.

A number of descriptions of multiple sclerosis from personal experience have been published, examples including the account by Burnfield (1985) which has already been mentioned, an American book by Birrer (1979), and an idiosyncratic autobiography written in England during the 1914–18 war and recently reprinted (Barbellion, 1984); reference might also be made to a formal study of the self-perceived problems of multiple sclerosis sufferers, conducted in the 1970s in Kent (Cunningham, 1977).

STROKE

The disability which everyone recognises as stroke is paralysis on one side (hemiplegia) associated, if it is right-sided, with a high probability that speech will be affected. It is by definition a disease of the brain, caused by spontaneous 'vascular accidents' which can affect any part of it, and one person may suffer more than one of the them. Moreover these accidents, whether due to ruptured blood vessels or to obstruction of the blood flow, are wholly unpredictable except that certain risk factors are known. Some individuals therefore undergo a succession of strokes and their downhill progress may be quite rapid, in some ways like that of multiple sclerosis. Others only ever have one episode and in that way are more like people who have sustained a head injury – as indeed the term 'vascular accident' implies.

Although a person severely paralysed by stroke can be very helpless, it is not usually the paralysis that disables most. Almost all varieties of organic mental symptoms can occur, depending on the site or sites of the damage: apathy, uninhibited behaviour or more subtle loss of social awareness if the frontal lobes of the cerebral cortex are affected; problems of positioning in space, initiating purposeful movements and associative reasoning of all kinds with damage to the parietal lobes; problems of vision and recognition in association with the occipital lobes; impairment of memory if the temporal lobes are involved. Speech defects (the left temporo-parietal area) can be intolerably frustrating and occasionally very bizarre, and disorders of posture and body awareness (the right temporo parietal area) can be very disabling. Damage deep in the cerebral cortex can profoundly affect pathways from all these areas besides often being responsible for emotional lability. Urinary or faecal incontinence can be very troublesome. The result of whatever non-motor changes have taken place is often described as a change in personality, and a close relative (usually a wife or husband) may find this very hard to live with, especially if relationships previously have been a bit shaky and/or (s)he is expected to do most of the caring.

For some people the result of a vascular accident may be a number of non-paralytic disabilities with relatively slight hemiplegia, or paralysis without a typical hemiplegic pattern, or no paralysis at all. The term 'stroke' is often not imagined as including this group, in which the pattern of disabilities can be very like those produced by head injury. One particular variant, which is not infrequent as a reason for residential care, is for spontaneous bleeding around the base of the brain (subarachnoid haemorrhage) to cause damage to that highly critical part of the nervous system: the resulting impairment of mental and physical function can be very severe indeed.

Although particularly associated with old age, stroke can occur at any time of life but begins to be noticeably frequent from, say, the age of 50 onwards (subarachnoid haemorrhage is associated with somewhat younger ages); it is now believed that its incidence, at least among people in late middle life and the early retirement years, is very slowly on the decline. One English estimate of the prevalence of stroke in the 16–64 age group is 125 per 100,000 total population (Weddell, 1980) with a figure for all ages of about 500. The National Sample Survey's estimate for all ages was more than 300 per 100,000 in private households, of whom about half were severely disabled and about 100 needed special care. Putting these figures together, the number of severely disabled stroke victims under the age of 65 is perhaps around 60 per 100,000 total population. Figure 3.1 shows that the special homes and units for younger disabled people only provide beds for them at the rate of about 1 per 100,000; on the other hand, the number of people of all ages who are in hospitals and residential homes because of stroke is of the order of 50 per 100,000 with some five to ten per cent below the age of 65 (Wade *et al.*, 1985; data from my personal clinical practice). Expressed another way, for every stroke victim under 65 who is in a home or unit for younger disabled people, some three to five of similar age are in geriatric wards or old people's homes.

As an example of that, a man of 57 had a sudden spontaneous cerebral haemorrhage. He immediately underwent surgery: the blood clot was successfully evacuated and his survival was ensured, but he was left with a profound left-sided hemiplegia and has never walked again. His rehabilitation had to be in a medical and then a geriatric ward; he finally returned home after eight months but only with the understanding that for three days and two nights in each week he would be in the geriatric ward, not at home. Whereas he had been in normal full-time work up to the day of his haemorrhage, he now needed help with all basic activities of daily living. He was dependent on community nurses and on his wife (who herself had rheumatoid arthritis) for almost everything while he was at home: they had no children or close relations. He put on weight, but the problems of lifting were eased by a portable hoist which just about fitted into their small flat. Perhaps the most distressing feature however was his new, almost apathetic personality; because of this and his wife's worsening arthritis, after three years his hospital stay was extended to four nights in each week with occasional but regular longer breaks. It was an uneasy compromise.

A somewhat younger man, who had severe hypertension and had been treated for it, had two strokes within a few months of each other on opposite sides. He was sent home from hospital to his wife, who was a nurse, with inadequate rehabilitation. She got him walking again with the help of a community physiotherapist and gave up her job to be able to care for him properly. He remained fairly helpless but his speech returned and most of the time he was pleasant and appreciative of all that she did. Unaccountably, however, at times he would lose his temper and his reason and would then become very difficult to manage. In spite of her distress he refused to go away from home again, until after about eight months and at the third attempt he was persuaded, very reluctantly, to accept regular short stay admissions to a Health Service unit for younger disabled people. His bizarre and at times violent behaviour then deteriorated further, needing drug treatment which helped at first but soon made him even more dependent. In spite of it all his nearly exhausted wife was determined to stand by him; with psychiatric advice, the support of a community mental nurse and attendances at a geriatric day hospital besides his short-stay admissions, he improved considerably and her task, three and a half years after his strokes, became much more tolerable.

A West African man of 60 had a mild right-sided stroke followed less than a year later by another one on the left side. For a time he was quite helpless but gradually he recovered his speech and his ability to walk. He was, however, left with two very troublesome disabilities: a tendency to both faecal and urinary incontinence unless he was reminded (or he reminded himself) to be careful about it, and a degree of uncontrollable clumsiness in both hands that made even the simplest tasks difficult. If this were not enough, he lived in lodgings in a large and somewhat disreputable household. After two attempts to resettle him there his landlord finally sent him to hospital complete with a suitcase of clothes: an emergency placement in a voluntary hostel proved impossible because of profuse incontinence and he was finally admitted to a geriatric ward. There he was an obvious misfit and looked neither ill nor old, wanting to get out yet having nowhere to go. The problem remained unsolved until about six months later he suddenly died.

A 28-year-old woman woke one morning with a bad headache and within a very short time she had become unable to speak or to move any of her limbs. She had a full-time job and was living with a flatmate. From the district general hospital she went first to one Health Service unit and then, in order to be nearer her mother, to a second one. Three years later she had limited use of her right arm and could use a communication aid with which she slowly spelt out her share of perfectly normal conversation. As with anyone who relies on that method of communication, time had to be set aside in order that she could tell people what she really thought. Her view of the place where she had to live was that it was too clinical, but she appreciated the personal interest and expertise that everyone offered. The plan was that she should eventually manage 'in the community' once more, perhaps in her own flat with intensive input from statutory services and volunteers, or perhaps living with her sister.

Wade and his colleagues (1985) have written an excellent comprehensive review of stroke. Among published personal accounts of different kinds of experiences, including recovery, are those of Ritchie (1960), Wint (1965), Griffith (1970) and Law and Patterson (1980).

BRAIN INJURY

Just as with the three other conditions which have been discussed so far, severe 'closed' head injury (caused by a blow to the head without penetration of the brain) produces a very wide range of disabilities in different people – different in their nature and complexity as well as in their severity. After a severe impact any part of the brain may be damaged although there is some evidence that the frontal and temporal lobes of the cerebral cortex and the mid-brain are most vulnerable. Although the permanent areas of brain injury can be quite localised, usually the damage appears to be diffuse; this is almost invariably the case with other causes of brain injury such as encephalitis, the effect of poisons and, for whatever reason, prolonged deficiency of oxygen supply. Penetrating head injuries also occur of course, when the damage can be expected to be localised. The resulting disabilities are often hard to describe, though the physical disabilities are usually fairly clear-cut: hemiplegia, unco-ordinated and/or uncontrollable movements just as in cerebral palsy. Mental disabilities can include any or all of the components listed on pp. 36–37; noisy and even violent behaviour is frequent during the early recovery phase. Speech disorders and slowness of reaction are also common. Severe though the outcome can be, however, the trend towards recovery is undoubted; presumably because the damage is truly permanent with no underlying active disease process, there is good evidence that even very severely head-injured people can continue to learn, with no certainty about any time limit to the process.

These ongoing mental and physical disabilities may co-exist but the more common outcome is for the physical disabilities to become slight or disappear altogether, leaving someone with 'a changed personality' but physically able-bodied. For this reason the prevalence of persisting brain injury in any community is difficult to estimate with any reliability. Two recent estimates put the figures as high as 100 or even 150 per 100,000 (Leading article, *Lancet*, 1983; Bryden, 1985); the National Sample Survey only reported 30 per 100,000, however, only two or three of whom were severely disabled while 20 were reported to have disability which was 'minor, non-motor'. Much more is known about the *incidence* (see p. 6) of traumatic head injury – the fact that it is commonest among young men, commoner in some parts of the country than others, and most frequent among unskilled workers and most often caused by road accidents. It is also known that very severely affected people cannot be expected to live long whereas those who are mildly affected can expect a normal length of life. There is evidence that changes in practice in hospital accident/emergency departments have reduced the number of very severely disabled survivors, and that the peak incidence of head injuries in the 1960s has been followed by a slow decline which may have been helped by seat-belt legislation (London, P S, personal communication). The inference from these various pieces of evidence must be that the number of people who are permanently and very severely disabled from head injury may still be increasing very slowly but is likely to remain limited, while the number with milder, mainly mental consequences continues to grow appreciably. I have been unable to obtain similar information about persisting disability due to other causes of injury to the brain.

Set against this background the small number of people with severe physical disability, perhaps four or five per 100,000 in the community if the National Sample Survey figures are anything like correct, are just one part of a much larger and complex group: it is debatable whether they have more in common with others who are similarly disabled no matter what the cause, or with their less severely affected peer group who have also had head injuries.

Certainly the small numbers are compatible with the figure of 0.7 per 100,000 in special residential care for physically disabled people (Figure 3.1), but an additional, similar number of people are also long-term residents in psychiatric hospitals. In one survey of this 'psychiatric' group, 45 per cent were found to be victims of road accidents, 20 per cent had had other forms of head injury, 16 per cent had brain damage due to toxins, encephalitis, anoxia or hypoglycaemia*, 10 per cent had had subarachnoid haemorrhage and a few had been operated on for cerebral tumours (Eames, P., personal communication). The 'brain injury' component of Figure 3.1 can also be divided into categories: head injury (all forms) 55 per cent, postoperative 25 per cent, and subarachnoid haemorrhage 19 per cent.

A young man in a residential home had had a road accident which had clearly been some years previously, and his rehabilitation had included a spell in one of the few specialised brain-injury units after which his progress there had not been maintained. He was hemiplegic but only his left arm was completely paralysed and the movements of his right leg were probably not normal. When I met him he was sitting slouched in his wheelchair, looking uncomfortable; obviously he had found eating his midday meal difficult and the traces of it still showed. Two back numbers of some magazines were stuffed beside him and one of the residents left him a paperback thriller as she passed. His left eye was closed during most of our conversation although he could open it, and his eye movements were dissociated and almost continuous. His speech was slow and indistinct; he could not remember the accident and seemed to have rather indistinct memories of all that had happened since. He could not tell me where he was nor why he was there but said he would like nothing better than to return home to his wife. On the other hand he explained where his home was, and the names he gave to places there were all quite correct. He said he could read and did indeed read a newspaper headline for me, but when asked questions about it he obviously had not been following the events to which it referred. When copies of his magazines were put in front of him he simply seemed to gaze at them uncomprehendingly. The care staff complained that he was liable to messy habits, interfering with other residents' property, and getting himself into awkward situations while attempting to leave the building. It seemed that he was bored beyond endurance, and yet clearly his capabilities were quite limited. He certainly gave the impression of wanting more appropriate input than the home could provide, but it was not conventional nursing that he needed.

A divorced woman in her late thirties underwent general anaesthesia for a minor procedure and was in a coma for some days afterwards. At three months she could still not use her limbs properly and had virtually no control over her posture; she was only incompletely aware of what was going on. At six months she went through a stage of noisy, demanding, almost uncontrollable behaviour and needed sedative drugs; at nine months she was walking though she needed guidance and had the hunched posture and gait of an old lady. One of the psychological scales gave her a mental age of two and a half; her speech had remained fluent but conversation was very difficult because of her inability to concentrate on what was being discussed. Two years after the injury she was no longer paralysed but still had great difficulty initiating certain actions such as climbing stairs, getting into a car or even eating. She had virtually no family – her children had been formally adopted – and only one friend had remained good enough to visit her regularly. By the time four years had passed, she was still resident in a Health Service unit; she enjoyed going out when she could, to a day centre for example, or 'swimming' with

---

* *Anoxia, hypoglycaemia*: periods during which the blood concentrations of oxygen or glucose (respectively) are dangerously low. Such periods need only be quite short for obvious, lasting brain injury to occur.

someone's help, or an occasional group holiday with other disabled people. She retained a good memory for names, places and faces; some aspects of her private, personal life still made her very emotional; her conversational ability had improved a little and she could show a sense of humour, describe her various outings and make the point that she hated doctors because they kept her cooped up. Those who knew her best were no longer certain that she was improving; the unit where she lived was too unnatural a social environment and did not have the skills to re-educate her further.

In another Health Service unit was a young man who had been run into by a car when he was on his way to help with the Christmas post. He never regained consciousness, and after two years in the local general hospital he went to a hospice many miles away until the local unit found him a bed. When I met him fourteen years after the accident he was still being fed by a nasogastric tube, unresponsive to any kind of stimulus or conversation. His parents visited every day and had made a new life for themselves in taking responsibility for the unit's social activities; they did some modest fund-raising and kept up a regular programme of events in which everyone could join. Emotionally and practically they remained wholly involved in their son's continued life, insubstantial as it was, and in the fortunes and welfare of the unit as a whole. They continued to hope that one day he would show an improvement.

An excellent general review of the consequences of closed head injury has been edited by Brooks (1984). Headway, the National Head Injuries Association, issues a series of booklets and pamphlets: inevitably directed at carers rather than the people with the disabilities, they include not only a descriptive account by Torrens and Cummins but also a personal story of recovery (Keirs, 1986). Another of Headway's papers includes the following quotations from relatives:

> 'I have had two daddies, haven't I?' (A four year old girl who could not recognise her father after his accident).

> 'You have to try and forget the child you had to be fair to the child you now have.' (Mother of an eight-year-old seriously injured boy).

> 'It's like making love to a stranger.' (Husband of mother with two children).

Two recently televised documentary films (Elers-Jarleman, 1984; Dollar, 1986) each describe a personal story in intimate detail.

SPINAL INJURY

The stereotype of a disabled person is a wheelchair user, and the people to whom everyone else can relate most easily are those whose general appearance, demeanour and conversation remain within the limits of what are accepted as 'normal'. This is not to understate the difficulties which people with paraplegia experience: the sudden need to adapt to a new, more limited way of life; the frustrating and often unnecessary problems of mobility and access; lack of true understanding by the able-bodied; the hidden and variable problems of impaired sensation, continence and sexual performance. The fact remains that uncompli-cated paraplegia allows continued full though maybe modified participation in the worlds of work and recreation and in private life; people with paraplegia rarely need to consider institutional care unless there are serious complicating factors, or on a very temporary basis as for example while waiting for wheelchair-suitable housing to be created by adaptation or newly built. The point of course is that such people retain full use of their arms and hands.

Tetraplegia (loss of use of all four limbs) is another matter, especially in its severer forms. Like paraplegia it is due to injury or more rarely disease of the spinal cord, in this case in the neck; the damage may be complete or incomplete, and sharply localised or spread over a certain length of the cord. Once stabilised, if it is at the level of the seventh cervical vertebra ('C7') there is little difference from paraplegia; at C6 level the disabled person has some problems with manual wheelchair propulsion, transfer to and from the wheelchair, dressing and eating; at C5 these difficulties are all more severe; at C4 there is little or no use in the arms and at C3 or C2 there may be breathing problems too. Postural control is likely to be more exacting than with paraplegia, and the invisible disabilities may be much more tiresome: liability to pressure sores, poor body temperature control and instability of blood pressure, although all of these tend towards improvement after the first few critical months have passed.

Extraordinarily, for such a well-defined group of people, most of whom go through a period of rehabilitation in specialised spinal injury units, the prevalence of spinal injury in the community is not known. Partly it is because a proportion become disabled for other reasons than trauma, sometimes as a complication of an existing disabling disease such as rheumatoid arthritis. Not all such people go to the spinal injury units and they may also present problems of definition, but this is not the whole explanation. Spinal injury is not a notifiable condition and there is no obligation on British spinal injury units to report or monitor the people they have treated. Estimates therefore vary vaguely between 15,000 and 30,000 in the United Kingdom (30 and 60 per 100,000 population) with no certain knowledge how many have paraplegia and how many have tetraplegia though a 2.5-to-1 prevalence ratio currently seems likely (8–17 per 100,000 for tetraplegia). Figure 3.2 shows that damage at C5 level and above is likely to account for just over a quarter of all tetraplegics at present, so that for each 100,000 population there are perhaps 2–4 tetraple-

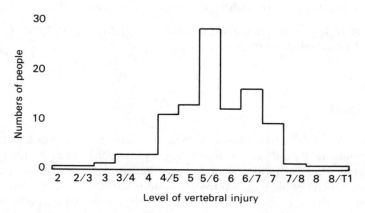

Figure 3.2 *Levels of cervical cord injury: indicative figures of prevalence*

Source: membership of The Spinal Injuries Association, November 1984. The data do not necessarily represent the population as a whole.

gic people who, if they are not in residential care, would be candidates for it if domestic support networks were not available to them; Figure 3.1 shows that the number of 'residents' with spinal injury is in fact some 0.5 per 100,000 population, and nearly all of these have tetraplegia. Life expectancy is nearly normal after spinal injury even, it seems, with damage at high levels in the spinal cord: new injuries occur at the annual rate of about two per 100,000 population, more than half of them now causing tetraplegia, so that the prevalence of this condition may be expected to go on growing slowly for at least the next couple of decades.

As an articulate group, people with spinal injury are far more able to describe their experiences, symptoms, hopes, fears and achievements than any outside observer, and many have already done so. The fundamental feature of their predicament is that it combines an unchanging disability of sudden onset, in a few cases amounting almost to helplessness, with previous experience of able-bodied living which is unimpaired by injury to the brain. Some of them have been in the forefront of those disabled people who are campaigning for change: initiating and organising plans for independent living and publicising them, becoming involved in policies and planning procedures, and contributing to teaching and an academic understanding of disability. Not many physically disabling conditions share these features to such a degree, although poliomyelitis is one of them and the impact of total deafness or blindness can be very similar. In comparison with the brain, the spinal cord is a relatively simple structure, so that the range of possible disabilities is comparatively limited; for this reason, people with spinal injury demonstrate very clearly how the differences among individuals have as much to do with personal, social and economic factors as with differences in the severity of impairment.

In respect of residential care, I feel able to record the following impression which people with tetraplegia have given me. Some were enthusiastic, like the man who felt a degree of personal freedom in the large community which had been impossible in all the years he had spent in the confined circumstances of his own small family home. Another had been allowed a degree of luxury and independence in a hospital unit which did not cost him his compensation award and which he was sure he could not achieve in the world outside. One or two had 'given up' and became fatalistically resigned. Others had moved out and some of these had grievances: that the rehabilitation units had simply assumed that if family support was not available, residential care was the only option and a Health Service unit would do nicely; that getting the wheels in motion in order to settle into a new home was a tremendous battle; that society's whole approach to disability is wrong and underlies all the difficulties. One resident confided her thoughts in writing: her public face was light-hearted, mostly cheerful and bantering, but her private feelings at times were those of suicidal despair. Another person spoke of a need, immediately after the injury and the initial period of rehabilitation, to withdraw and decide one's principles before coming back as an active citizen; the process could take a number of years, and some people find residential care an appropriate environment in which it can happen.

In 1984 the Spinal Injuries Association carried out a survey of its tetraplegic members, reporting its findings in catalogue fashion. The following selection of quotations is taken from answers to just a few of the questions that were asked

> Being a tetraplegic has made me totally dependent on my mother; my social life is limited. At the moment I can't think of any good thing.

> Tetraplegia has deprived me of my independence, loss of high income and pension. Nothing good.

I had led a very active life and the frustration I still feel when unable to take part in sports etc. is no easier to bear almost 17 years on.

Good things: I have thought very hard: none. Problems: dependency on others.

Tetraplegia's worst effect is its destruction of spontaneity of action.

Good effects: there are none. It might be claimed that one has a more sympathetic insight into the world of the disabled, and of the caring (or carelessness) of our helpers. Closer inspection shows that this is not a personal advantage at all – you don't have to break your neck to get it anyway.

The first thing I would like to say is that it sorts out who are your good friends and relatives.

My disability has taught me to appreciate the simpler things of life and the value of friendship rather than the value of material possessions. It does seem a pity that a tragedy has to occur to me for this realisation to make manifest.

I think in many ways becoming a tetraplegic has made me a better, happier person. Before my accident I had a very active life but I was rather selfish. Now I can understand people more and I am a lot more considerate.

Tetraplegia was the best thing that ever happened to me. For, had I not become paralysed, I would not have achieved most of the things I have.

Of the many general accounts of spinal injury, the very comprehensive review from a psychological standpoint by Trieschmann (1980) and the matter of fact description based on personal experience by Rogers (1978) are particularly helpful. Personal accounts have been written by Hearn (1972), Ellis (1981), Coe (1982), and at second hand by Hurley (1983), and a formal study of the personal and social implications has been reported by Creek *et al.* (1987).

NEURAL TUBE DEFECT

This condition is perhaps better known as spina bifida and/or hydrocephalus. Congenital but not inherited, it produces one or more of four related disabilities: a defective part of the spine which, if uncovered at birth, may leave the spinal cord exposed and if so, requires surgical correction to ensure survivial; paraplegia; distension of the brain and skull (hydrocephalus) which may be prevented by surgery; and mental handicap which only occurs where there is hydrocephalus. Paraplegia may vary from mild spasticity of the legs to complete wheelchair dependence, and it is almost always associated with incontinence. At its mildest the disorder produces little or no disability, whereas the severest forms are incompatible with life. Some of the people affected by it who are now in residential care were admitted many years ago, when they were likely to have been among the more severely disabled natural survivors. Although there were quite marked geographical variations, the incidence until recently was of the order of two in every 1000 live births.

New surgical techniques in the 1960s allowed the preservation of many more infant lives but often at the price of formidable difficulties and a need for repeated surgical operations in the ensuing years. The result was also a population 'bulge' or cohort of such people who were thought to be a potential cause of a great increase in demand for residential care. In practice, however, that has not happened, for several reasons: the present practice of encouraging parents to keep their disabled children at home, the limited life expectancy of the most severely disabled people despite all the surgical intervention, and a decline in the incidence of the condition which is partly spontaneous but has certainly been aided by diagnostic procedures which allow suspect pregnancies to be terminated. The result is that the incidence during the 1980s has fallen to about six for every 10,000 live births, although there are still geographical variations (Lorber and Ward, 1985). As far as adult prevalence is concerned, a survey of spina bifida in Scotland in 1980–81 suggested a figure of about six per 100,000 total population, of whom half were completely independent and only five per cent were 'totally dependent'. Another survey in 1981, however, revealed two school-leavers per 100,000 total population, of whom 24 per cent were substantially reliant on wheelchairs and 22 per cent were wheelchair dependent beside having major urinary, bowel and other problems (Castree and Walker, 1981). They were born when surgical intervention was at its height; the figures in future years will be far lower.

A woman in later middle life had always had some disability because of spina bifida although she was without hydrocephalus, and she had always lived with her parents until the age of 42 when rapidly increasing paralysis necessitated an orthopaedic operation. She was quite ill and very disabled for some time afterwards; her recovery lasted two years and was incomplete. Six years later she was still in a Health Service unit of which she had been one of the first residents; by then her parents were both still alive but in their eighties and she had not seriously contemplated returning to them. Her disability had in fact become tetraplegic, and she considered she would need far too much attention to live on her own. In a single room which she had made quite homely, despite the restrictions of an institutional building and hospital regulations, she seemed set on staying for a good long time.

A couple in their twenties had been married for about a year and lived in a disabled persons' flat, one of several specially built and grouped together by a charitable housing association. Each had required surgery at birth, and one of them in particular had had numerous operations during childhood; then there was a long gap until the last surgical intervention which was a 'urinary diversion' – reorganising the kidney drainage into a piece of bowel which was separated and made to communicate with the outside world by means of an abdominal stoma, to which a drainage bag had to be applied. Both partners had made use of a local day centre and workshop, run by the Association for Spina Bifida and Hydrocephalus; they had also been helped at a local rehabilitation centre where one of them had lived for eighteen months while a flat was found for them. Both of them until then had been very dependent on parental support; even with continued family help and good statutory services, they had not found marriage easy, but they were still willing to do their best to make a go of it. They had however both been unwell, one with a resistant infection and the other with a pressure sore; the result was admission to hospital and several months' separation.

RHEUMATOID ARTHRITIS

In the residential care context, rheumatoid arthritis in a way presents a contentious problem; some people whom the disease afflicts severely can receive advice to give up their homes which others would challenge, despite the undoubted difficulties of pain and disability when associated with social isolation. Usually characterised by onset in wrists and hands, the disease more often than not remains localised to only a few joints but in a small number of cases progresses with varying speed to involve almost all of them except perhaps the hips and some joints of the spine. The onset, too, can be literally at any age from childhood to very advanced years; complications can ensue in the severer cases but the disease rarely shortens the expectation of life. Severe pain and inflammation in the early stages leads eventually to joints with restricted movements or which become altogether fixed, and often to obvious deformities.

The total prevalence is of the order of 2000 per 100,000 population but it is probable that only some five per cent are very severely disabled, so that in this category of disability the prevalence is somewhat similar to that of stroke. On the other hand, the bed occupancy in homes and units for younger disabled people is of the same order as for much rarer conditions, and the occupancy of geriatric hospital beds is correspondingly low. The combination of physical disability and unimpaired brain function means that people with rheumatoid arthritis resemble those who have spinal injury, although the progressive yet unpredictable nature of the disease makes comparison with multiple sclerosis more appropriate.

A woman of 58 with long-standing rheumatoid arthritis had moved into a new bungalow just over two years ago in order to live close to her son. Within three months of the move she had a very severe gastric haemorrhage for which an abdominal operation was required, after which her knees became fixed in a bent position. She said the medical opinion at the time was that she could not go home and she doubted whether she could manage, so after a few months she was moved to a residential unit. She did not, as she put it, find 'instant companionship' there but soon settled down and became very happy. She did not mind the five-bed dormitory but much preferred the single room she was eventually given. She had become the secretary of the residents' committee which had given her extra interest. Despite (or in her view because of) almost no physiotherapy, her strength had gradually returned. She still owned her bungalow and, given the option, she would have preferred to be back there. She told me that no-one had accompanied her there at any time since the operation, to assess how she might manage. She remarked that it was 'the hardest thing' to persuade people that living alone did not mean being lonely. Paradoxically, the issue might have to be properly faced because at the age of 60 she expected to be transferred to a geriatric ward, and her resistance to it might initiate the rehabilitation and discharge which was surely worth a trial.

Locker (1983) has written a detailed description of the implications of physical disability, relating them to the experiences of people with rheumatoid arthritis.

OTHER NERVOUS SYSTEM DISEASES

The seven conditions which have been described are those which are found most frequently in residential homes and hospital units for younger disabled people, accounting for some 80 per cent or more of all the residents. A further 10 per cent or more have other diseases of the nervous system, of which potentially there is quite a long list: five in particular merit brief mention.

Parkinson's disease is a common, progressive and, in its advanced stages, extremely disabling condition; although some people develop it during middle life, in terms of numbers the principal impact is in old age. Like all other diseases it is variable, for example, in age of onset (though hardly ever before 40), precise pattern of physical impairment, rapidity of progress and also the extent of mental disability. The physical problems include stiffness, tremor, facial immobility, dribbling and difficulties with speech, although the worst feature is often the one which to an observer is least apparent: the inability to initiate simple body movements such as walking, manual tasks or turning over in bed. With the arrival of levodopa treatment, however, the picture has changed; the stiffness and disabilities of movement are capable of almost complete alleviation, and speech can return to normal, but some people treated in this way are surviving into a state in which their mental disabilities are more troublesome than their physical condition. Especially in older age groups, a proportion show mental disorientation from the beginning. The population prevalence is about 200 per 100,000 of whom about 10 per cent are very severely disabled, and in one city less than 20 per cent were under the age of 65 (Mutch and colleagues, 1986).

A woman in her late fifties had been successfully treated with levodopa for some years, and if for any reason the drug was stopped she promptly developed florid features of Parkinson's disease once more: speechlessness, ridigity and helplessness. She was widowed and lived on her own, although her octogenarian mother lived next door; other members of the family were too far away to be able to help. The question of residential care began to be raised when she became increasingly liable to falls, following which she could not always be relied upon to be left alone. There was division of opinion whether she should be expected to remain in her home, though this was what she preferred to do; prolonged admission to a geriatric hospital was eventually necessary because of a large pressure sore. During the time it was healing she presented a curious mental state: apparently fully aware, resentful of her confinement, able to manage her financial affairs, but frequently unable to converse because of what appeared to be blockage of thought. She also became finally incapable of walking and her mobility was restored by an electrically propelled wheelchair. The eventual decision, to which she reluctantly agreed, was that she should reside in an old people's home.

Huntington's chorea is an inherited condition which starts in middle life and runs a characteristic course lasting some ten years until death, but again there are people who fare better or worse than this. The first features are uncontrollable, purposeless bird-like movements which may affect limbs, trunk, face or speech: as the disease progresses these become increasingly troublesome so that an exhausted sufferer can find it impossible to keep still, as well as being liable to frequent accidents, spillages and falls. Speech becomes difficult and a curious mental state develops, consisting of short-term memory loss and repetitive patterns of behaviour but only mildly diminished awareness. Noisy and occasionally violent outbursts are only displayed by a minority. Terminally the victims become weak, quiet, helpless, bedridden, frightened, speechless, and last of all unable to swallow.

Only about 6000 people in Britain are affected (12 per 100,000) but the disease deserves special consideration because of its pattern of inheritance, and because those who are responsible for residential care often take the view that people with Huntington's chorea fit oddly into a community of those who are disabled for other reasons. The children of every affected person have a 50 per cent chance of developing the same disease; the emotional consequences within families can therefore be profound. Certainly the uncontrollable movements and behaviour patterns make the physical ability very conspicuous and unusual; conversely, the mental disability is usually too mild to justify admission to a mental hospital. The sufferers and their families therefore, with all their understandable problems and anxieties, have all too often become pariahs of residential care, unable even to obtain temporary respite. It is not a satisfactory state of affairs.

Motor neurone disease is also progressive and rarely begins before the age of 40. Again there are variants, some causing difficulties with speech, swallowing and breathing at a fairly early stage so that fatal pneumonia may occur within a year or two of onset. Others, and these are the ones who may present major problems of support and care, steadily lose their muscle power throughout the body and finally become wasted, helpless and speechless; in these instances the course can be very much longer. Strictly, the disease involves the brain because all the nerve cells concerned with voluntary movement are affected, including those which originate in the cerebral cortex. The only external evidence of brain involvement is, however, an occasional tendency towards too easily laughing and crying: otherwise the striking feature is the full preservation, not only of mental function but also of bodily feeling, and considerable problems of discomfort and pain can therefore arise. The fairly rapid sequence of events has allowed terminal care hospices to find a role in the care of people with motor neurone disease, and at least in some cases it can be more appropriate than residential care of the kind described in this book.

Poliomyelitis had long been a cause of disability when its incidence reached almost epidemic proportions during the 1950s, since which time the vaccination programme has made new cases very rare. As with spina bifida there is therefore something of a cohort of people, now mostly in later middle age, whose disabilities range from relatively trivial to the devastatingly profound. The nature of the disorder suggests comparison with spinal injury, but in some important respects disability is much less; people with poliomyelitis retain full control of bowels and bladder, and they retain normal sensation so that their liability to skin damage and pressure sores is negligible. On the other hand the most severely afflicted of them became permanently dependent on artificial ventilation; in the early 1980s the national centre for 'responants' in London had about 100 such people on its books, all but a handful of whom were living in private households. Only a very few people with poliomyelitis are, in fact, in residential care.

Alzheimer's disease deserves brief mention: it is hardly ever accepted as a reason for residential care intended for physically disabled people, but it is especially prevalent (as 'senile dementia') in old age and is arguably the biggest single cause of pressure for residential care if all age groups and disabilities are considered. Certainly it is one of the principal reasons for committed residence in geriatric and psychiatric wards and old people's homes. In all but the late stages however, the disabilities are almost entirely behavioural: loss of social behaviour patterns and awareness leading to progressively severe memory loss, disorientation, disturbed behaviour, and then disorders of speech and balance. Terminally, the disabled person becomes almost inert, death being caused by an incidental infection or by loss of appetite and ability to swallow. Only if a person is referred in these late stages might he or she 'fit' an environment of care for physical disability, and by then most such people are beyond the age of 65. Tragically, however, younger people are occasionally the victims.

OTHER DISABLING DISEASES AND INJURIES

The muscular dystrophies are a complex group of different, mostly inherited disorders of which the commonest, Duchenne's dystrophy, is transmitted by women but develops only in boys. Relentlessly progressive, it is usually fatal by the mid or late teens although survival well into a young man's twenties is becoming less uncommon. Other disorders in the group give much better expectation of life including one which, like Duchenne's, also affects only boys and men. As far as residential care is concerned, an important aspect is that some people with muscular dystrophy have entered it in anticipation of rapid deterioration and a fairly short life, only to find that the outlook was in fact far better; some very long-term residencies have arisen as a result.

A young man of 16 had spent his adolescence and much of his childhood in a local authority children's home. He had developed the signs of Duchenne's muscular dystrophy by the time he was 11 but continued to live there happily; it was a modern purpose-built home on a municipal housing estate and had eight residents altogether. As he grew older he would in due course have had to move elsewhere, but the more important fact was that his weakness was progressing so fast that he could no longer easily be cared for, or withstand the rough and tumble of the home. There was a Health Service unit for younger disabled people nearby, so he went to live there instead; his time there was a happy one, just living with the residents and staff, enjoying the company and still able to go to the special school which he had been regularly attending. He was by far the youngest resident however, and after a couple of years it was thought that the community of a Cheshire Home several miles away would suit him better. After a trial stay he agreed, but he was only able to live there for a few months before he died at the age of 19.

A woman in her sixties had become a resident of a new Health Service unit when she was just past 50. At that time she was still able to walk with a frame, and she had been living with her parents and brother in a bungalow which suited them quite well. Her admission was prompted partly by the death of her mother but also by the opening of the unit. Twelve years on, the unit had long since become her life and her home and she enjoyed playing a considerable part in deciding how it should be run. Now a wheelchair user but otherwise quite well, she was aware that in the 1980s she could have expected community services to be able to continue supporting the family without the need for admission to residential care.

The muscular dystrophies closely resemble nervous system disease but there are other disabling diseases and injuries, including of course rheumatoid arthritis, which do not. The total list is a long one and the conditions are very varied, but together they account for a very small percentage of the residential places for younger disabled people and the proportion among long-stay residents in geriatric wards is not dissimilar. In particular, among the younger ages three of the commonest groups of disabling disorders are very thinly represented in residential care: osteoarthritis, heart disease and chronic chest disease. They constitute more than ten per cent of the people helped by care attendant schemes however, among whom the total without nervous system disease is about a quarter (Bristow, 1981). Other conditions that should be mentioned include osteogenesis imperfecta (brittle bones disease), phocomelia (deficient limb development) and disability due to limb amputation.

'Multiple pathology'

It is important to remember that a few people are disabled by more than one condition; they comprise about five per cent of the residents in homes and units for the younger disabled, but a considerably higher proportion in geriatric departments. Examples I have encountered among younger people include muscular dystrophy with asthma; rheumatoid arthritis with tetraplegia; long-standing paralysis due to poliomyelitis with recent paralysis due to stroke; and the combination of stroke, heart disease, and limb amputation because of gangrene. Diabetes, in particular, can be responsible for this last combination and not infrequently adds blindness to it. Some of the disabilities arising from multiple causes can be devastatingly severe.

Summary of prevalence data, and changing prevalence patterns

Table 3.2 summarises some of the statistical estimates in the foregoing accounts, together with some of their implications for residential care; it also gives an indication of prevalence trends. At present, some conditions are apparently becoming commoner. The incidence of cerebral palsy at birth is probably increasing a little, and more children with severe multiple handicaps are thought to be surviving. Stroke is generally considered to be gently on the decline. The incidence of severe head injury may be falling but the total population of brain-injured people is probably growing because of survival. Survival is also the reason why the number of people with spinal injuries is still rising, and there are more people with tetraplegia than ever before. Poliomyelitis and spina bifida have dwindled dramatically, at least partly because of effective prevention.

CONCLUSIONS: A SYSTEM OF THINKING ABOUT PHYSICALLY DISABLING DISEASES AND INJURIES

The various diseases and injuries that go together to make up the full range of severe physical disability can be classified in three ways, providing a system of thinking about them in terms, as it were, of three dimensions: anatomy, age of onset, and course.

Anatomy

As already explained, the most important consideration is whether the brain or the rest of the nervous system is involved, so that in this respect there are three categories:

1. *Disorders involving the brain*, which include cerebral palsy, stroke, multiple sclerosis, brain injury, neural tube defect, Parkinson's disease, Alzheimer's disease and Huntington's chorea, as well as many other conditions not described in this chapter. The total population of people with one or other of these conditions is about 50 per cent in those served by care attendant schemes, 80 per cent in homes and units for younger physically disabled people, 80 per cent in hospital geriatric wards, and 90 per cent of the physically disabled people who are in the wards of mental hospitals. Brain disease or injury is important not only because of the paralysis it produces but because for a variety of reasons it frequently causes unreliable or unsociable behaviour, or what is loosely described as personality change.
2. *Disorders involving the nervous system but not the brain*, which include spinal injury, spina bifida without hydrocephalus, poliomyelitis and, for practical purposes, motor neurone disease; a minority of people with multiple sclerosis also contribute to the list. Rarer conditions not described in this chapter include Friedreich's ataxia and polyneuritis. The proportion of residents in this category in homes and units for

Table 3.2 *Comparative estimates of the prevalence of twelve disabling conditions (all ages: various sources)*

Prevalence per 100,000 total population

	All cases	At home needing special care	In homes/units for younger disabled people	Trend	Where residential care might be provided, *apart from homes/units for younger disabled*
Cerebral palsy	200	6	3.3	uncertain	mental handicap hospitals
Multiple sclerosis	80	20	2.5	living longer	—
Stroke	500	100	1.2	lessening	geriatric units/old people's homes
Brain injury	100	5	0.6	accumulating	mental illness hospitals
Spinal injury	45	3	0.5	accumulating	—
Neural tube defect		(cohort)	0.4	lessening	—
Rheumatoid arthritis	1000	60	0.3	—	geriatric units/old people's homes
Parkinson's disease	200	~20	0.1	modified by drugs	geriatric units/old people's homes
Huntington's chorea	10	3	0.1	—	mental illness hospitals
Motor neurone disease	10	3	0.1	—	hospices; ordinary/geriatric hospital wards
Muscular dystrophies	20	2	0.2	living longer	—
Poliomyelitis	80	3	0.1	disappearing	—

younger physically disabled people is about 10 per cent, and the proportion served by care attendant schemes is about the same.

3. *Disorders not involving the nervous system*, of which those described in this chapter include rheumatoid arthritis and the muscular dystrophies. The possible list is, however, a very long one and includes conditions such as osteoarthritis, chest disease, heart disease and limb amputations, as well as a whole variety of diseases which are uncommon or rare. People disabled in one of these ways account for nearly 40 per cent of those who are served by care attendant schemes, but only a very small proportion of residents in homes and units for the younger physically disabled.

Age of onset

This is the second way of considering disability, the most important distinction being between those whose disabilities begin at birth or in early childhood, and those who acquire them later.

1. *Onset at birth or in very early childhood*
   In this group disability and personality are indissolubly linked, because each individual is without personal experience of able-bodied life. Such people accept their disabilities in ways which are hard for those who acquire them later, but their educational and social careers often cause them to be far less socially mature than is within their capabilities by the time they reach adult life.
2. *Onset during childhood or adult life*
   People in this category have to adjust to their difficulties and this is often a long and complicated process, although the exact way in which each person does so depends on an infinite variety of personalities and personal circumstances. Adjustment is also dependent on the *mode of onset*: if it is *sudden*, as with most of the acquired stable conditions (see below), the process is necessarily acute and painful. If the onset is *gradual*, as with most of the progressive conditions, adjustment can take the form of slow adaptation to increasing limitations, but even in these cases there can be periods of acute awareness of deteriorating function.

Course

The third 'dimension' of severe disability is its course, with its consequent effect on a disabled person's career; there are three categories.

1. *Stable conditions*, which include cerebral palsy, spina bifida, hydrocephalus, brain injury, spinal injury, poliomyelitis, some cases of stroke, and many cases of neural tube defect. The most severely afflicted people are, however, liable to develop complications which may cause their disabilities to be unstable, and very long-standing impairments are subject to changes associated with ageing which in most instances are poorly understood.
2. *Unstable conditions*, which include most cases of multiple sclerosis, stroke and rheumatoid arthritis, besides the complications of stable disorders to which reference has just been made.

Table 3.3 *A three-dimensional classification of some of the principal diseases and injuries which cause severe physical disabilities*

	Involving the brain	Involving the nervous system but not the brain	All other conditions
Onset in infancy or early childhood			
stable	Cerebral palsy Hydrocephalus (neural tube defect)	Spina bifida (neural tube defect) Poliomyelitis	Phocomelia
unstable	Severe cases of hydrocephalus	Severe cases of spina bifida	Osteogenesis imperfecta
progressive			Muscular dystrophies
Onset in later childhood or adult life			
stable	Brain injury	Spinal injury Poliomyelitis	Limb amputation
unstable	Multiple sclerosis Stroke		Rheumatoid arthritis Osteoarthritis Heart disease Chest disease
progressive	Parkinson's disease Huntington's chorea	Parkinson's disease Multiple sclerosis Motor neurone disease	Muscular dystrophies

3. *Steadily progressive conditions*, which include many cases of multiple sclerosis, together with Parkinson's disease, Huntington's chorea, motor neurone disease, Alzheimer's disease and the muscular dystrophies. Even these progressive conditions can however sometimes arrest for a time, although the ultimate outcome is almost universally fatal.

Table 3.3 summarises the three dimensions of severe disability with reference to the diseases and injuries which have been discussed. The main components of the practical challenge they present have already been outlined in Chapter 1 (Table 1.2). With all these issues in mind, consideration may now be given to some of the realities of British institutional responses to the challenge of care.

4
Working and living in residential care: the results of a survey

The disabling diseases and injuries described in the last chapter are responsible for about nine tenths of the disabilities found in the residential homes and hospital units which are provided specially for the younger disabled. In Chapter 2 it was explained how these establishments came into existence in Britain and how they supply barely half of the total residential care taken up by physically disabled people aged between 16 and 65. In Chapter 1 it was suggested that in private households the number of very severely disabled people in the same age group is at least three times greater than the total number in residential care, from which it would follow that the special homes and units accommodate less than an eighth of that particular population.

For some three decades at least, however, these homes and units were regarded with idealism: at a time when comparable levels of care could otherwise only be found in hospital wards, they were considered the best possible option for severely disabled people who were in difficulties in their own households. Even though much of the idealism has now been transferred to the development of community care, residential care still has its enthusiasts; and with the best will in the world, few believe that all disabled people can be entirely supported by families, friends and community services all the time. Moreover, the special residential establishments are still very much with us, consuming perhaps some £90,000,000 of public funds, and their residents and staff do not deserve to be put on one side and ignored; unless the work that they can (or should) undertake is clearly understood, inappropriate decisions at both personal and planning levels will continue to be made. Yet although the homes and units are readily identifiable and collecting information from them is fairly straightforward, no really broadly based survey has previously been reported.

DISCOVERING WHERE THE SPECIAL ESTABLISHMENTS ARE

To stay for a moment with published statistics and following on from the information for England and Wales given in Chapter 2 (Figure 2.5): Figure 4.1 displays similar data for Britain on the basis of Health Service regions (reckoning Wales and Scotland as one region each), although without data on the use of ordinary hospital wards and again with uncertain information about private nursing homes. As in Figure 2.5, there is the complication that homes for people with epilepsy or sensory impairment are also included.

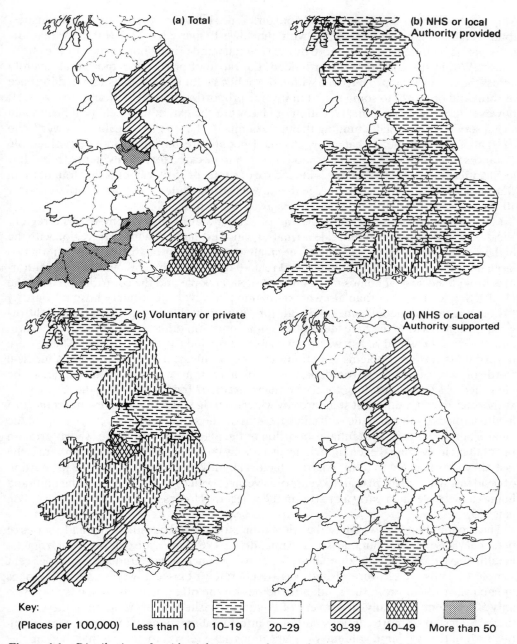

Figure 4.1 *Distribution of residential accommodation of people with disabilities aged 16 to 64 in Britain, by National Health Service region*

Sources: DHSS/Welsh and Scottish Offices. (The data include accommodation for people with epilepsy and sensory handicap, and those who are unsuitably placed in hospital geriatric and psychiatric wards.)

Map (*a*) shows that there is about a twofold difference between the regions with the highest total number of places and those with the lowest; maps (*b*) and (*c*) show that the unevenness is influenced much more by the voluntary and private homes than by the public sector. Within the voluntary sector indeed, the range of provision is more than fivefold across the country (map *c*) but even within the public sector the extremes show a difference of threefold or more, to some extent in inverse proportion to the voluntary provision. If, however, not the geographical location of places but the extent to which local health and social services are actually funding them is examined, the spread is again narrower (map *d*). This may well mean that many disabled people are having to move considerable distances from their own neighbourhoods in order to be cared for, and evidence from a few local authorities suggests that this is indeed so: of a total of 75 placements that four of them were supporting, less than half were in their own districts while more than a third were over 30 miles away and a fifth were 100 miles away or more.

(The idiosyncrasies of two regions and of Scotland are worth comment. One region, Wessex, is at the bottom of the scale no matter which estimate is made. The region with the highest provision, Mersey, has one of the smallest populations but happens to contain two large homes for people with epilepsy and related disorders. In Scotland the local authorities provide no special homes for younger disabled people and the contribution from the Health Service is higher than elsewhere – mainly, however, in ordinary hospital wards.)

Locating the individual homes and units for younger disabled people is fairly straightforward, simply because they are identified as different from other forms of residential care, and the way in which a list was drawn up is explained in Appendix 1. There were nevertheless certain problems of definition: for example, is a reserved area in a medical ward, or a ward in a geriatric department, or a wing in an old people's home, to be identified as a special resource for the younger disabled? It does seem that the responsible authorities may use different standards by which to judge, and there are even instances of health authorities disagreeing with clinical teams on the subject. Moreover, in many of the Health Service units a substantial proportion of the places are reserved for short-term use (all of them in two units) even though the usual view is that committed long-term care is the task they are expected to fulfil. Another factor, already mentioned, is that the proportion of residents who are more than 65 years old averages well over 10 per cent in the units and homes as a whole and nearly a quarter in the Cheshire Homes in particular (Figure 4.5 on page 65).

The account that follows is based on the findings of a postal questionnaire and a series of personal visits, again as summarised in Appendix 1. A response rate of 80 per cent from the Health Service units gave a sound basis for drawing conclusions, although the 40 per cent sample of units which were visited was (deliberately) biased towards the newer ones opened since 1968. From the residential homes on the other hand the response rate was only 50 per cent, and only 20 per cent of them were visited; interpretation in these cases therefore has to be more cautious, although informal discussions with central administrative staff in the two large voluntary organisations gave reason to believe that the samples were fairly representative. It was also encouraging to discover reasonable correspondence with the findings of Scott (1985) who received a 50 per cent response from a similar enquiry among Health Service units, and with surveys of the Cheshire Homes conducted by the Leonard Cheshire Foundation itself.

The degree to which self-selection may have distorted the picture nevertheless has to be taken into account. People may have decided to respond because they were particularly proud of what they were doing, or particularly frustrated, or enjoyed completing questionnaires, or because of previous personal contact with myself. I have accordingly taken care not to draw far-reaching conclusions which depend on small differences in numerical data or which, for other reasons, would require a more complete sample. A more important reservation is that any survey can only give a picture of what is happening at one particular time: policies and practice are constantly changing and, whereas some units and homes appear to have altered little over the years, some can always be expected to be intent on innovation and reform.

Outside the four main groups the enquiry was frankly selective, and the fragmentary information that was obtained did not lend itself to formal analysis. It is by no means certain that the available list of homes and units was complete, particularly in respect of private homes which may have opened only recently. The information did suggest that this miscellaneous group may have provided some 2.5 places per 100,000 total population – about half the proportion shown in Figure 2.3, the remainder presumably being homes for people with sensory handicap or epilepsy, which were deliberately excluded from the survey.

The remaining contents of the chapter are therefore in two unequal parts, of which the larger is an account of the units and homes managed by the National Health Service, the Leonard Cheshire Foundation, the local authority social services and The Spastics Society. Not only do these four organisations provide about four-fifths of all the special residential care for physically disabled people; it also happens that the numbers of places provided by the first three of them are each of the same order although The Spastics Society is only responsible for about half as many as each of the others. The four groups' philosophies and managements are sufficiently distinct from one another, yet sufficiently uniform internally, to justify a formal comparative study. Besides making a fairly brief descriptive and statistical comparison, however, the account also includes short reports of a series of conversations with residents; not at all a systematic enquiry, they nevertheless give a flavour of different personal experiences and points of view, at least as far as the people concerned were prepared to divulge them.

The second, smaller part comprises descriptions of a few of the homes and hospitals which comprise the rest of the voluntary and private sector. Formal comparisons among them are scarcely possible because they are too disparate a group: instead, the intention is simply to show the variety of what is provided. Consideration of the use made by younger disabled people of other forms of residential care (hospitals and old people's homes) is deferred until Chapter 6.

THE FOUR LARGEST GROUPS OF UNITS AND HOMES

Before considering some of the detailed findings, it is necessary to give brief preliminary descriptions of the units and homes for which the four agencies are responsible. The descriptions are largely based on impressions from the postal survey and personal visits, together with information from social service departments and the national offices of the two major charities.

The National Health Service's Younger Disabled Units

As explained in Chapter 2, this category comprises units which have been developed in four distinct ways. There are a few separate institutions dating from the nineteenth century, and a few one-time private residences which were taken over by the hospital service in the 1940s and 1950s. There are ordinary wards more or less upgraded, which have simply been set aside for this particular client group. Finally there are the new purpose-built units, all of which were opened from 1968 onwards; most of them are on hospital sites, and in some cases it is necessary to run a kind of gauntlet between hospital buildings of every kind in order to reach them. Their design fairly obviously follows the advice issued by the Ministry of Health in 1968 (see Chapter 2), most of them being either L-shaped, U-shaped or forming a closed rectangle. They are all on ground level and in most designs single rooms are few. Whereas in some of them the most conspicuous feature is an enormous day activity area, often with the main entrance opening directly into it, in others the provision of living space away from the dormitories and bedrooms is clearly inadequate. One or two have been situated sufficiently apart from the parent hospital to look as if they do not belong to it. Health Service management tends to be obtrusive, with standard signs and notices, standard fitments, standard staff uniforms and sometimes a certain casualness which is not always inviting or friendly. Further descriptive detail is included in Chapter 7.

The Cheshire Homes

The organisation of the Leonard Cheshire Foundation is by maximum delegation to the periphery. Until fairly recently, residential care has been its only concern, and it is altogether responsible for a network of homes in many different countries. In Britain, where it started, there are 71 homes altogether, and several more are being planned; for physical handicap there are 53 in England with five in Wales, three in Scotland and a complex of flats in Northern Ireland. A small central headquarters is responsible for overall policy and organises a regionally based advisory and counselling service. In the past few years the Foundation has been encouraging the development of family support services as alternatives or at least complementary to residential care. Fund-raising for capital and physical amenities is done locally by each home's management committee, but the Foundation provides interest-free loans to get projects started. The committees have almost complete responsibility to negotiate fees with the registering authority, decide admission policies and manage their own homes, but they in turn usually delegate their authority partially or almost wholly to an appointed head of home.

About half the homes occupy old buildings and the rest are entirely purpose-built; many of the older properties have had modern extensions added and the new buildings tend to resemble those of the local authority homes (see below). The size and location of the properties varies from remotely situated country houses surrounded by parkland, to unobtrusive dwellings deep in the suburbs of a city or town. It is widely believed within the Foundation that the homes all differ from one another very markedly in character. As far as appearance, location, management style and the involvement of volunteers are concerned this is probably true, but the data reported in this chapter give the strong impression that they are all concerned essentially with the same group of disabilities and have very much the same admission policies. Depending on the building and to some extent on the management, the homes can give the impression of a fair amount of relaxed informality or on the other hand of orderly neatness – just like the differences among ordinary private households. In some cases the staff wear uniforms of the kind worn by nurses but other homes prefer to manage without them, which seems to have little to do with whether they are registered as nursing homes or not.

Local authority homes

Only 54 of the 115 local authorities in England and Wales have set up residential homes for the physically handicapped. Almost without exception these homes have been purpose-built, and although there are architectural differences which reflect the changing fashions of the past three decades the layout in all of them is very much the same. Nearly all of them are situated where the authority has happened to have land and in most cases this means that they are part of a housing development, perhaps in a cleared area in a town or city or well out in the further suburbs. The organisation within each home is accountable to senior departmental management, which in turn is responsible to the social services committee of the elected authorities. The precise administrative structures vary somewhat, as do the extent to which the details of policy-making and management are delegated to one level or another. Professional input is dominated by social work; uniforms are hardly ever worn by the staff.

The buildings themselves are very like the large number of homes for the elderly which were built at the same time, the main difference being that more concession has been made to wheelchair mobility. There are therefore usually at least two or three sitting rooms; most of the bedrooms are single, opening off corridors, each with a bed, washbasin, wardrobe, dressing table and room for just a little extra furniture. Residents are generally encouraged to personalise their rooms as much as they wish. In the first generation of buildings the usual arrangement is for one large dining area and in most instances a large recreational area as well; these are on the ground floor with perhaps a few of the bedrooms, and the remaining bedrooms are on upper floors. More recent designs have tended to group the bedrooms round smaller living rooms and communal self-catering facilities, all on the ground floor, to allow more personal independence and less regimenta-tion. Toilet facilities, however, mostly remain communal. A refinement is sometimes to put a number, a bell-push and a letter box on each bedroom door. Often there is a day centre alongside which serves the local community and may be managed as part of the home or quite separately.

The Spastics Society

Unlike the Leonard Cheshire Foundation, The Spastics Society is concerned with one group of disabilities only, but residential care is only one part of a wide range of initiatives with which it is involved. It has a more centralised administration which, as far as residential care is concerned, is responsible for (at least participates in) a majority of the decisions about admission, and is also directly responsible for the management of 70 per cent of its residential units. The others are run by local affiliated branches and in this respect are more like the Cheshire Homes. Altogether they occupy properties which are as varied as the Cheshire Homes, but the Society classifies them into three groups.

The residential centres on average possess 32 beds each; at least half of them aim to cater for the severer disabilities and one in particular provides very special input for the most severely incapacitated. Most of these centres have their own workshops and three have hydrotherapy pools. The house units and hostels are nearly all smaller and much more simply equipped although there is one with 80 places. There are also nine short-term centres or family help units, two of them catering specially for the severely disabled. Fees are determined centrally, and in some cases the running costs are considerably subsidised by the Society's own funds. The Society has not succeeded in distributing its residential care as evenly across the country as the Cheshire Foundation: although it provides facilities in most parts of England and Wales there is considerable concentration in the south-east, especially in Essex. The Society is not active in Scotland where there is a separate Scottish Council for Spastics.

Summary of information about locations and layout

Turning now to data from the postal questionnaire: some basic statistical information is set out in Table 4.1, and helps to give proportion to the descriptions in the preceding seven paragraphs. It is noticeable that all but a tenth of the homes and units provided between 10 and 40 places, with 20 to 29 being the most frequent number; the Cheshire and local authority homes tended to be larger than the others. In the Health Service units, even in the newest buildings, single rooms remained the exception but they were almost universal in the social services' homes, with the charities in this respect varying considerably.

Table 4.1 *Location and layout of units and homes*

| | Numbers of units and homes | | | | |
	Health Service: old and/or adapted	Health Service: new purpose-built	Cheshire Homes	Local Authorities (Social Services)	The Spastics Society
On own site:					
rural	2	—	15	1	31
urban	6	1	14	32	8
On hospital site:					
separate	10	28	—	—	—
attached	15	24	—	—	—
Purpose-built	—	32	8	31	5
Ex-private house	4	—	21	2	11
Ex-hospital	29	—	1	—	5
Beds provided:					
0–9	2	—	—	—	4
10–19	13	7	4	6	8
20–29	8	23	9	14	6
30–39	4	2	15	10	1
40 or more	3	1	2	3	2
In single rooms: (per cent)					
0–19	19	3	—	2	9
20–39	10	22	2	—	5
40–59	1	—	9	1	1
60–79	—	4	10	9	2
80–100	5	4	9	21	4

Source: RCP survey

Admission policies

The character and the work of the residential homes and units were both very dependent on their admission policies, and a summary outline of the factors which excluded admission is set out in Table 4.2. The most striking features are (a) the variability of the upper age limit for admission over a range from 45 to 65 in three of the groups, though most of the Health Service units would accept people over the age of 60 and The Spastics Society had no firm policy; (b) a general reluctance to accept people with mental illness or disability, often described in different and inexpert terms but often also with the explanation that this was only if the mental problem predominated or was otherwise very severe; (c) an apprehension about nursing in the local authority homes which again seemed to represent a lack of understanding – no doubt because many of them had no trained nurses on the staff. The list of excluding factors also conveys information about the different pressures to which the four agencies were subject, not to mention some of the staffs' specific apprehensions.

A summary of the selection procedures and persons involved is shown in Figure 4.2, and this information deserves careful scrutiny. There was, for example, a complete contrast in the nearly universal requirement for trial residence by the two voluntary agencies in comparison with the public sector, especially the Health Service units, although other procedures differed much less. Again in the voluntary sector and especially in the Cheshire Homes, the staff and residents were very much involved in the decisions; this was less so in the local authority homes, and in the Health Service units the staff and residents generally had to accept whoever was sent to them. All the homes and units relied on external input to

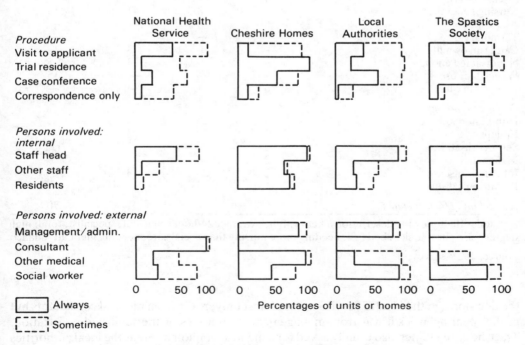

Figure 4.2 *Procedures used and persons involved in deciding about admissions*

Source: RCP survey

Table 4.2 *List of factors excluding admission to units and residential homes*

	Per cent of units or homes			
Factor	Health Service (N = 61)	Cheshire Homes (N = 30)	Local Authorities (N = 32)	The Spastics Society (N = 16)
Age				
No lower limit	14	7	6	10
Lower limit 16–17	71	20	66	48
Lower limit 18–19	9	60	22	42
Lower limit 20 or more	5	13	6	—
No upper limit	4	27	16	80
Upper limit 45–49	—	3	6	—
Upper limit 50–54	4	13	16	—
Upper limit 55–59	9	23	12	5
Upper limit 60–64	27	23	25	10
Upper limit 65 or more	57	10	25	5
Mental factors				
Mental handicap	18	53	22	5
Mental illness	43	30	22	—
Mental disorder unspecified	11	13	6	5
Behavioural disorder	38	17	9	—
Personality/'won't contribute'/not 'alert'	4	7	—	5
Senile/presenile dementia	14	—	6	—
Coma/'unaware'	14	—	—	—
Caring factors				
Intensive care	4	—	—	—
Nursing generally*	—	3	44	10
Acute illness	6	—	—	—
Terminal care	6	—	—	—
Can't run own life	—	—	3	—
Not disabled enough	9	—	3	5
Wheelchair user	—	—	—	15
Long-term care	6	—	—	—
Specific pathology				
Huntington's chorea	4	23	—	
Epilepsy	2	20	3	
Sensory disability	2	7	3	n/a
Malignancy	2	3	—	
Infectious disease	2	20	3	
Parkinson's disease	—	3	—	
No excluding factors stated	9	—	31	70

* includes the following descriptions: heavy, full, extreme, 24-hour, constant, specialist, total, high degree; also chronic sick, bed fast, needing more nursing than social care, needing night attendance

Source: RCP survey

the decisions; in the Health Service it was almost universally from medical consultants but in the other agencies it was from management committees or the senior administration. The Cheshire Homes also usually asked for a medical opinion whereas the local authorities and The Spastics Society preferred to seek social work opinions instead.

Another aspect of admission policy was that, whereas the public-sector homes and units tended to restrict their intake to their immediate localities, the voluntary agencies felt free to take residents from anywhere. This fits in with the regional statistics already quoted, and the information from local authorities: one example was provided by a remotely situated centre belonging to The Spastics Society where at least two-thirds of the residents used to live more than 50 miles away, half of them more than 100 miles away. Certainly nearly all the Cheshire Homes I visited preferred to look widely afield in order to be sure that they chose well when there was a vacancy, on whatever basis that choice might be made.

Overall, especially taking into consideration the patchy geographical distribution of the homes and units, these varying admission policies revealed all too clearly how tensions are likely to arise because no-one will show an interest, especially in cases of combined mental and physical disability, with awkward personalities and at ages much beyond 50.

Attributes of the people who are accommodated

On the basis of a few guidelines, senior staff were asked to make their own assessments of the disabilities for which they were catering, by classifying as mild, moderate or severe the individual physical and mental disabilities of the people who were resident on a particular date. Their opinions were necessarily subjective and cannot have been uniform, so the replies convey something about the staffs' approaches as well as the disabilities themselves. Moreover, no attempt was made to relate those categories to any of the published disability scales such as that of Barthel (Wade and colleagues, 1985) or the one that was used in the National Sample Survey, although it is likely that both 'moderate' and 'severe' were within the National Sample's special care category (see Chapter 1 and Appendix 1, Table A4). A similar question about 'social disability' proved unanswerable because it was related to economic and social relationships with the world outside, from which so many residents had become isolated because of their length of stay.

Accepting these limitations, Figure 4.3 shows that there were some fairly clear differences among the four agencies. There were more people with the severest physical disabili-

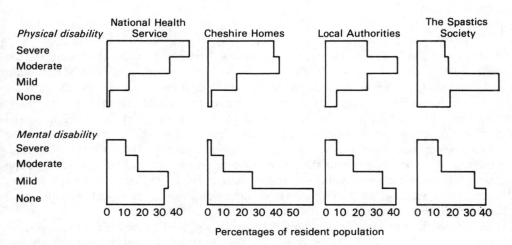

Figure 4.3 *Distribution of levels of disability in the units and homes*

Source: RCP survey

ties in the Health Service units than elsewhere. The highest proportion with severe mental
disability was in the care of The Spastics Society but the Health Service was close behind.
The Spastics Society did, however, accommodate a considerable number who were only
mildly physically disabled or even without much physical disability at all. The most
outstanding feature was the claim that in the Cheshire homes only 10 per cent of the
residents had moderate or severe mental disability, with only another 25 per cent whose
mental disability was considered mild. A most important conclusion, however, is that
disabilities at all levels of severity are to be found in the care of all the agencies: only the
proportions among them were different.

A similar conclusion applies to the medical diagnoses (Figure 4.4). The Spastics Society's
contribution (not shown in the figure) made cerebral palsy the largest category, and it

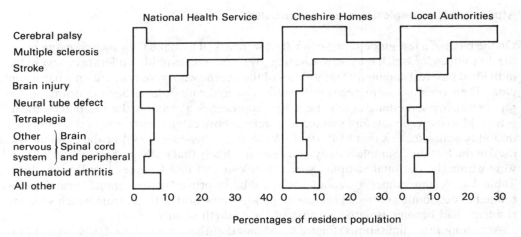

Figure 4.4 *Distribution of medical diagnoses in the units and homes*
(Note: in The Spastic Society's homes nearly all the residents have cerebral palsy.)

Source: RCP survey

was also by far the largest category in the local authority homes; in marked contrast, the
Health Service units were hardly involved with it. The other numerically dominant
condition, multiple sclerosis, was far and away the most prevalent cause of disability in the
Health Service units and the biggest single category in the Cheshire Homes, the local
authorities taking a much smaller share of that responsibility. On the other hand the
Cheshire Homes did not provide much accommodation for stroke disability which in the
16–64 age group was otherwise shared nearly equally between the Health Service units and
local authority homes. In the smaller diagnostic categories the differences between the
agencies were much less noticeable (except, of course, for The Spastics Society) but there
did seem to be a greater proportion with brain injury and a smaller proportion with neural
tube defect in Health Service care.

The age distribution again showed overlapping characteristics among the four agencies
(Figure 4.5). In the Health Service units there was quite a sharp cut-off at 65 which may
imply that people were being moved elsewhere when they reached that age. In the
Cheshire Homes, where there is a guarantee of a place for life, the resident population

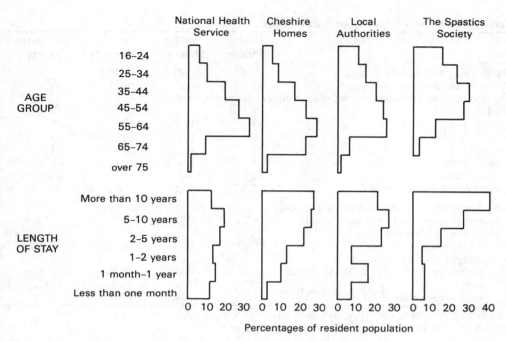

Figure 4.5 *Distribution of age groups and length of stay in the units and homes*

Source: RCP survey

beyond retirement age amounted to almost a quarter of the total. Residents in the local authority and Spastics Society's homes tended to be younger but, bearing in mind the relatively recent opening of so many of these homes and the young age at which cerebral palsied people have in the past been taken into residential care, the data may well have represented a cohort of people with normal life expectancy who were simply and slowly growing older. That aspect of the matter is clearly shown in the second part of Figure 4.4 which demonstrates the very considerable length of time residents can stay once their security has been assured.

Coming and going

The statistics discussed in the last three paragraphs are derived from census data and therefore give a static picture, but it is equally important to know something about admissions and discharges: a selection of relevant figures is displayed in Table 4.3. Clearly, whether a unit or home held a waiting list, and how long it was if it did, varied enormously and must have depended partly on the number of outright refusals that were given; the Health Service units were asked about these refusal figures but not the others. Figures for planned short stay (variously known as floating beds, rota beds, holiday relief, respite care or shared care, and defined as any period of stay of which the discharge date was agreed before admission) show that the voluntary sector has been rather tentative about this service whereas many of the units and homes in the two public sectors had become very much involved, with however a great deal of difference in the commitment given by individual homes and units in all the four groups.

Table 4.3 *Activity analysis of units and homes*

	Health Service	Cheshire Homes	Local Authorities	The Spastics Society
Numbers on waiting lists (range)	0–65	0–90	0–10	
Requests refused annually (range)	0–23	(n/k)	(n/k)	} n/a
Planned short-stay admissions, per year: numbers of units/homes				
nil	5	7	3	9
total 1–24	13	18	15	5
total 25–54	16	5	8	1
total 55–74	12	—	4	1
total 75–99	3	—	1	—
100 or more	12	—	1	—
average number per person	2.53*	1.25	1.72	(—)†
All other admissions and discharges, per year				
Admissions: proportion from hospital	42%	33%	28%	7%
Discharges and deaths				
total per bed	1.90	0.11	0.11	0.04
total per bed excluding net 'exchanges' with other residential homes	1.87	0.10	0.10	0.03
deaths ⎫ proportion of total	20%	70%	26%	17%
going to own home ⎭	66%	15%	49%	31%

* excluding two units with very high numbers – see Chapter 5
† too wide a scatter for the number to be meaningful

Source: RCP survey

The proportion admitted from hospital varied from one agency to another but was biggest in the Health Service units. On average, apart from planned short stay these units manage to admit nearly two people annually for every bed they possessed, but as will be shown in Chapter 7 this average figure reflected a very wide variation. Again apart from planned short stay, the corresponding figures from the Cheshire and local authority homes were almost identical with one another, although in the former they depended mainly on death whereas in local authority care there were nearly twice as many people who return to their own homes as there were who died. So, if one disregards not only planned short stay but also the net exchanges with other residential homes (discharges to other homes which were matched by admissions from other homes), the annual vacancy rate was almost exactly one bed for every ten in each of these two important sectors of English residential care. Given the long life expectancy of young people with cerebral palsy, it is not surprising that The Spastics Society seemed to need about thirty places for every annual admission once its places were all full.

Management

Most of the Health Service units had a chaotic system of divided management responsibility which is discussed in some detail in Chapter 7. In the residential homes on the other hand, management responsibility was usually much more clearly defined, although the details varied from one establishment to another. The Cheshire Homes had gradually evolved a policy whereby a head of home had overall administrative charge and a head of care, almost always a qualified nurse, was responsible for the care staff and the care programme. The head of home was answerable to the management committee, and between them they took full responsibility for policy, public relations and finance, as well as the details of running the home. Most Cheshire Homes also had a residents' committee, and residents' representation on the management committee.

The local authorities usually appointed an officer in charge of each of their homes, with similar responsibilities to a Cheshire head of care, supported by two or three senior care staff and answerable to senior management including the authority's finance department. In The Spastics Society's units the senior person in a home was usually called a manager and could be supported by up to six or more seniors, depending on the size of the unit, some of whom could have specific responsibility for organising residents' activities: accountability, except in the homes run by local committees, was to the Society's central management.

Care staff

Given that the residents' dependency levels differed significantly among the four groups of homes and units, the levels of care staff might be expected to have varied in proportion. Making comparisons is, however, not straightforward, for several reasons. For example, in reply to the postal questionnaire about half of the Health Service units could not say how many night nurses they had, usually because of separate management at night but also because night nurses were sometimes part of a larger pool which served the parent hospital as a whole. In the homes and units generally, the extent to which the seniors were directly involved with care was not consistent. The ratio of care staff to domestic staff in the residential homes averaged about five to one but there are some very wide variations; assuming that housekeeping standards were reasonably uniform, there must have been a considerable overlap of duties between the two groups as a whole. The Health Service units had uneven levels of domestic staff too, whose duties were, however, usually quite strictly limited.

These difficulties notwithstanding, for the purpose of crude comparison Figure 4.6 shows the range and mean levels of nursing in the Health Service units, and of care and

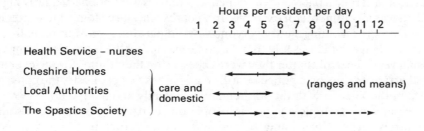

Note: one Spastics Society centre caters only for young people with severe/profound multiple handicap – on a five-day basis only

Figure 4.6 *Approximate staffing levels in the units and homes (ranges and means)*

Source: RCP survey

domestic staff with a notional addition for seniors in each of the groups of residential homes. The levels are expressed as hours of care per patient or resident per day without making allowance for absence on leave. The differences between the groups do seem to be what would be expected from the information on dependency levels, although it can reasonably be argued that since the Health Service figures did not include domestic staff, there were bigger differences between the Health Service units and the residential homes than could easily be explained by the declared differences in dependency alone. Nevertheless many of the Health Service units complained about difficulties due to shortage of nurses which, however, only happened when the total nursing input amounted to less than five hours per resident per day (patient/nurse ratio greater than 1.07 to 1), again making no allowance for absentees.

Part-time working varied among the nurses in the Health Service units from nil to 80 per cent, and among the care staff in the residential homes from nil to 100 per cent. Within these prodigious limits there was an even spread of part-time staffing proportions which could only reflect individual managerial preference and perhaps local demand for employment. The proportion of qualified nurses averaged 50 per cent in the Health Service units but the range was from 30 per cent to 80 per cent, which again must have been due to managerial preference. The impression is that qualified nurses perhaps filled up to 10 per cent of the posts in some Cheshire Homes but qualifications turned up only sporadically in the other residential homes, with social work and other forms of training just as likely as nursing. Within the Health Service units, apart from those which were on separate sites, only about an eighth had control over their own domestic staff and virtually none were responsible for their own catering.

Questions were asked about the use of equipment: in the Health Service units and local authority homes the care staff used lifting equipment for about a third of their residents, generally preferring movable hoists (90 per cent and 75 per cent respectively). In the Cheshire Homes on the other hand, hoists were used for half the residents with a 75 per cent preference for ceiling-mounted equipment. Here again was an example of managerial preference.

There is no doubt that the residential homes tended to be more domestic than the Health Service units. In some of them the senior staff, care staff and residents all ate separately but in many everyone sat down together. A young deputy officer in one local authority home talked with enthusiasm of their 'great big grown-up family' but it was a community in which there was a lot of cerebral palsy and the dependency levels were not particularly high – only one resident was incontinent, for example. In a nearby Cheshire Home one winter evening I briefly joined the incoming shift; everyone worked part time, most of them lived in the neighbouring village, and I was told that the home was in fact the largest local employer. In an atmosphere of cheerful chatter they were checking on their duties for the evening from the posted arrangements on a notice board. In a Spastics Society hostel the conversations took place in the kitchen with the warden and her family and a large dog. Two or three Cheshire Homes were employing young people on short-term attachments, some from other countries (especially Denmark) and some on government training schemes. In general it did seem that being out of uniform helped generate an informal atmosphere, but perhaps it was only that uniforms seemed obvious if the atmosphere was a little strained.

The self-determination programmes of a few local authority homes were interesting: the idea was that each resident should have not only the full authority but also the full responsibility to determine his or her daily programme, with the help of the care staff as required. This did not just involve basic activities like getting up, going to bed, dressing, and a few leisure pursuits; it included, for example, deciding what to eat and when to eat it, preparing all meals and shopping for them too. The residents therefore had to be competent and motivated to take these initiatives and they had also to learn the necessary social skills, but it did not matter how severely physically disabled they were. The regime was clearly not appropriate for every disabled person in residential care.

Yet in the Health Service units too, despite the management problems and the uniforms, the atmosphere could be pleasant and relaxed. For example, in one unit which had seemed rather formal, a member of domestic staff told me that it was a very happy place and by far the most agreeable of any she had worked in. An enrolled nurse in another unit had been employed by a nursing agency in the town for a year or so, had spent part of that time in the unit, had liked it and asked specially to join the staff when a vacancy arose. She described the work as frustrating at times and the patients as set in their ways and demanding, but there was job satisfaction too in the relationships which could develop with many of them. In contrast, a registered nurse in a third unit had a grievance that her job description referred to rehabilitation whereas she had found that her main responsibilities lay elsewhere. Then there was a unit which had big short-term admission and day care responsibilities and had changed its emphasis from long-term care to rehabilitation, where everyone looked overworked and tired. I was told how members of staff were always being withdrawn to help other parts of the hospital which seemed to be in a kind of perpetual crisis, but over an evening cup of tea some of the nursing auxiliaries told me how beneficial they though the change had been because the unit was now able to help so many more people.

Professional input, other than nurses

Whereas the Health Service units (with one exception) all had attached consultants and either general practitioners or junior hospital doctors as well, the residential homes relied on the general practitioner service for their medical input. The usual pattern was for a particular practice to be attached to a particular home, although some homes were able to allow at least some of their residents to choose any local doctor they happened to prefer. All the Health Service units had at least some service from physiotherapists and occupational therapists (OTs) but their input from other health professionals and from teachers was very limited, following no kind of pattern. Most Cheshire Homes had visiting physiotherapists but only about a quarter of them had trained OTs; most, however, had therapy aides and quite a number had art teachers.

The local authorities had to make do with less of everything in these respects; only a third had access to physiotherapy and even fewer had OT or recreational teaching. The Spastics Society presented a very varied picture, from simple living units with no formally organised activities to the large and well-equipped workshops which were a prominent feature of some of their larger homes. Virtually none of the residential homes had specifically attached social workers, a resource which more than a third of the Health Service units were able to enjoy.

Costs and charges

The issue of costs has to be related to the background of dependency levels and the input of special skills, and some basic comparative information is set out in Figure 4.7. One of the

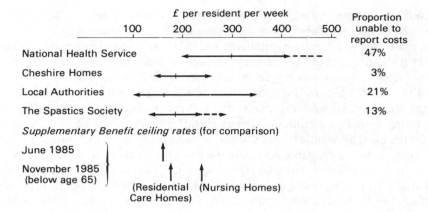

Note: several Health Service units reported costs in excess of £400 per week
which seemed incompatible with their reported staffing levels.

Figure 4.7 *Reported costs in the units and homes: ranges and means*

Source: RCP survey (1985 figures)

most notable features is that no fewer than half the people responsible for managing the
Health Service units did not know what their costs were.

There is a further problem: the four sets of data are not strictly comparable and in their
different ways are all probably incomplete. The Health Service costs were based simply on
the overall running costs divided by the number of available beds; when there was doubt
about the division about services and staff between a unit and its parent hospital, the wrong
figures will have been produced. This need not matter unless an over-high figure calculated in this way is used as evidence that hospital-based care is necessarily more expensive
than care in a residential home. In the homes themselves the figures stated usually
represented charges rather than costs, and in the voluntary sector would therefore not
have included any element of subsidy which there might have been from independent
funds. Perhaps for this reason too, the figures do not correlate well with the different levels
of disability with which the four agencies were involved. Figure 4.7 also shows how the four
ceiling rates of Social Security payment for residential care fit into the general picture.

At this point some general comment is necessary on the subject of charges, and on
personal allowances made available to residents. (To match the findings of the enquiry,
the figures to be quoted were correct for 1985.) The National Health Service offers all its
resources without direct charge to the consumer and committed residential care is no
exception, despite the fact that over a ten-year period, say, the commitment could easily
cost £150,000. Indeed, as the regulations stand at present the Health Service is quite unable
to levy a charge for living in its younger disabled units, even when a resident (through receipt
of an award in compensation for injury, for example) is well able to pay. Personal private
income is still available to a hospital resident of course, and so is the mobility allowance,
but after a year in residence all other forms of State benefit are reduced to £7.15 weekly.

Social services on the other hand are obliged to levy a charge on a sliding scale,
whenever weekly personal income is above £35.80 and/or personal capital (including the
value of a house) is above £1,250; if necessary, State benefits are continued to allow a
minimum personal income of £7.15 per week with again, mobility allowance excluded

from the calculations. Anyone entering private residential care is similarly allowed a basic small income and a basic reserve of capital, in this case £9.25 a week at £3,000 respectively; all other income except mobility allowance is taken into account when deciding what proportion of the maximum permissible board and lodging allowance shall be paid. It follows that for people who possess levels of income and capital of modest substance, there is a positive financial incentive to seek Health Service residence whatever the other disadvantages of that form of care may be.

A glimpse of the residents' experiences

The following series of short descriptive accounts is selected from notes made after about eighty conversations in some sixty units and homes, almost all with people who were receiving committed residential care. In more than half the cases a member of senior staff either accompanied me or advised me about the people I should meet; only with the remainder did I make my own arbitrary choices and talk with people on my own. The series begins with people who were obviously happy about their personal circumstances, and moves progressively to some of those who on the face of it were least content or were benefiting least.

Perhaps the best example of a person who felt very positively was a man who had been disabled since early childhood by poliomyelitis, with total paralysis of his arms but some use in his legs. He had been in residence in a local authority home for four years but usually returned to his family home from Friday evening to Monday morning each weekend. He said it was the first time he had lived 'alone' since leaving his residential school many years ago; he liked the home because it did not have 'a nursey atmosphere'. He had everything he needed in a remarkably well-equipped room and could call for help whenever it was necessary, which was not often. Recently he had become an Open University graduate, and when I met him he had just began to seek employment in the 'remote working' section of information technology, which he hoped to be able to pursue from his base in the home. He had also become a full participant member of a recently established local working group on disability. The support and help he was receiving in his personal daily life allowed him to be fully independent in these other outgoing ways: he was busy, constructively occupied, and asked for nothing more.

A young woman with cerebral palsy and very indistinct speech described the self-determination regime of the residential home in which she lived. She liked the layout, which consisted of groups of five or six self-contained flatlets grouped around a communal dining area and kitchen; she thought the way of life was both better than being at home and better than being 'in a home', but quite hard going as well. At home she had sat watching television all day while her mother was around the house, but in the residential home everything was 'thrown back on her': she was expected to go shopping as soon as she got there, for example, but she gave the impression that she enjoyed the new responsibilities. Her plan was to live eventually in a place of her own, and with the regime she had described there seemed every chance she would succeed.

Then there were the people who had become active in the running of their residential homes and had found fulfilment that way, even though their contribution could be fairly small: a man who had been paralysed for half a lifetime and had found the home offered great personal opportunities after more than twenty claustrophobic years with his wife and children; an ex-professional man with multiple sclerosis who felt similarly after the restriction of living with a landlady in a small flat; and several other residents' chairpersons in Health Service units and local authority homes whose business it was to introduce me as a visitor to the other residents and to show me round.

In one home the chairman lived in a double room with his wife; between them they had made it indistinguishable from the sitting-room of any suburban lounge except perhaps for the slightly odd shape and the sliding door on to the corridor outside. He had muscular dystrophy which had extended during the past two or three years to involve his hands and upper limbs, although these were not completely paralysed. He had originally been persuaded to enter the home because of the near certainty of progressive deterioration, and the assumption that if he deteriorated too far he would then not be acceptable as a resident. There was also the attraction of a woman resident to whom he was very attached until she died a few years ago. After that he partnered up with another resident who became his wife: she was only mildly physically disabled by cerebral palsy but seemed to benefit from the environment of residential care. It seemed a happy arrangement.

Several residents of local authority homes saw them as providing freedom rather than restricting it. The notes I made refer, for example, to a young man with multiple sclerosis who had previously lived with his sister until she got married, leading to the almost inevitable personality clash with his new brother-in-law; another young man with Fried-reich's ataxia and his family nearby, who was able to get out when he wanted to with an outdoor electric vehicle of his own; and an older woman with multiple sclerosis whose husband lived only half a mile away, who was convinced that she could not have been coped with at home and could not imagine anywhere nicer or more convenient than the place in which she was now living. All those people appreciated having their own rooms, the relaxed, kindly and informal regime, the freedom to do as they wished, and the opportunity to go out frequently for purposes of their own.

With a rather different perspective, a 39-year-old man in a Health Service unit had a fairly high-level tetraplegia of five years' duration; he had taken over the whole of a room which had been intended for four beds, making it his own living space complete with his own furniture and equipment. He had been able to do this because the unit's financial allocation had never allowed the use of more than half the beds it had been designed to accommodate. His marriage having broken up, he believed he was too dependent to live in his own household; he described the way in which he 'used to sit for days and days', but he had now developed a life style of his own, helped considerably by the income from the sum he had been awarded in compensation. He said that the residents did not 'all click together' as a group but he, too, very much appreciated the almost complete freedom he had been given to do as he liked.

The rights of people with disabilities to form personal attachments and satisfying sexual relationships, no less than any other member of society, have received a fair amount of attention (Greengross, 1976; Stewart, 1979) and I am unable to add anything of consequence to what has been written. Desires and frustrations are perhaps obvious when residents are around the usual marriageable age. Two members of staff of a local authority home described to me that they believed many of their (predominantly rather young) residents were sexually frustrated: 'the lasses all dream of a chap with a pair of legs', was the way one of them put it. There had been three marriages in that home; two of them had ended with the couples still resident but formally separated. The third pair had stayed very fond of one another but chose to sleep in separate rooms; together with the communal, waited-upon life during the day, this was hardly married life as most people might understand it.

A young woman of 22 had multiple congenital disabilities. Her home originally was in inner London but she had been admitted to residential care as a child and had then moved on to one of the well-known specialist institutions, where she had had several surgical operations to correct some of her deformities. She said she had great difficulty there with doctors and others who would not take the time to explain things to her – she was only one of 200, after all, and eventually she decided deliberately not to cooperate. In her late teens she had spent a year at an assessment unit, after which the next move was to the residential home where I met her. Before that she had not known anything about progressive disease, and on her first day she was upset by seeing an elderly resident asleep at the dining table. In order to be sure that she was still growing mentally and learning, as she put it, she had joined a number of outside associations including two directly concerned with disability, and a Christian Fellowship which she said gave some structure and meaning to her life after a childhood characterised by frustration and rebelliousness. She said she would also like a husband.

People can also be very content even though they are making do with much less than they might otherwise have expected. In a Health Service unit which occupied old buildings, I talked to a couple of women who were sitting side by side between their two dormitory beds. Each of them had multiple sclerosis, and one had been resident for over 20 years. The other had not been there so long but said she had nevertheless made the decision herself: her husband was still living many miles away with her daughter and grandchildren and was working in the senior post he had held for several years. As their fellow residents were being put to bed in the same dormitory at five o'clock in the afternoon, the two ladies described how they enjoyed playing Scrabble together, visits from those people who would come and talk to them, and excursions when the opportunities arose. They were both very cheerful and said that the unit was marvellous: when I asked if they would prefer more privacy they admitted that it would have been nice but of course they appreciated that it was not possible.

Back in another Health Service unit, a man in his early sixties with multiple sclerosis described his accommodation as 'fine', but its most annoying feature was the lack of things to do. His disease had begun over thirty years ago and his first marriage later broke up: after a period on his own he had remarried, apparently successfully, and had lived with his new wife in a flat which they liked. He had been attending the unit for some years, first as a day patient 'for physiotherapy', then for two weeks every three months, then for three in every five weeks, and finally for the whole time except for alternate weekends. He told me that his wife had preferred to care for him on her own rather than ask nurses or home helps to get involved. He did not think there was anything wrong with their relationship but 'nobody could cope with me at home', he declared. He admitted that the unit was like a hospital but 'you get the best treatment in a hospital, don't you, and it is warm'. He was fairly sure that he would have been less bored at home: of his fellow residents, some did not want to talk and some could not, the only diversion being when an occupational therapist came for an hour to organise some games. He could only make one comparison which was with another Health Service unit where he had stayed; he thought the food and the remedial therapy there were both better.

Sometimes, to an outsider at least, the living conditions seem almost ideal but are not what people really would have preferred. A young woman with muscular dystrophy and disabling chest disease was living in a beautiful room in a conventional residential home, with French windows out on to lawns, a reasonable amount of space and some delightful fabrics and furniture which she had chosen herself. She had spent much of her childhood in special education and had managed to go away from home for a while to live with a group of disabled people, sponsored by a charity, in a small artistic community more than a hundred miles away. Her health, however, had not allowed her to continue there and she rather ruefully had to accept the home as the best arrangement that could be made for her under the circumstances. She would have preferred to live in a house or flat of her own or perhaps in a residential home which was in or near a town centre, but she was certainly not complaining and accepted that people had advised what they had thought was best for her.

The question of one's fellow residents can often present problems. At one large residential home in the countryside, a widow in her late fifties had gradually lost the use of her legs because of a very slowly progressive spinal disease. After becoming an obligatory wheelchair user she had kept going at home for a year or so before agreeing to stay in rotation ('posted round') with her three daughters. With the birth of a granddaughter she came to the residential home and was pleased to settle down after this rather unstable life style. The number of residents had however expanded from its original sixteen, and she did not like that so much: many of the new ones had an unpleasant, rapidly progressive disability and she sympathised with them, yet she felt they should in some way have been segregated. There had at one time been a residents' committee but it had failed, and she thought this was a pity.

Then there are those who were much less satisfied. In another residential home I spoke to a bachelor in his sixties who had been obliged to give up his home because of a stroke. He could not remember how long ago that had been, and since becoming a resident his left leg had had to be amputated. He said life was boring: there was not much to do except wheel himself up and down the corridor and go on a very occasional outing to a pub. Perhaps he never did have much going for him, but he did seem to exemplify the familiar predicament of many older disabled people who have to live in geriatric wards.

Another woman in a Health Service unit felt she had been abandoned by her family: she gave the impression she would rather have been at home. Her speech, however, was very indistinct and the conversation revealed fairly evident mental deterioration and disorientation. It was hard to know how to evaluate her feelings. People with disorders of speech, awareness and behaviour are, of course, especially vulnerable because of their inability to put their point of view or work things out for themselves or, in the case of behavioural difficulties, even to be liked. If language is intact, they can communicate with devices varying in complexity from a finger-board to computerised technology and/or nothing more than eye movements, but if not only expressive language but also the ability to understand has been destroyed by brain damage, and especially if brain function is otherwise well preserved, the social difficulty can be extreme.

Residents' involvement in decision-making

To return to the formal written enquiry: an open-ended question was asked about the involvement of patients or residents in decision-making, and Table 4.4 outlines the commonest replies. The Cheshire Homes' nearly universal involvement of residents in committees illustrates the desire that their residents in general should be able to contribute something to the community of each home; it certainly contrasts with the apparently more casual arrangements elsewhere. Nevertheless, the efforts the other groups claimed to have made is by no means negligible, and only a handful of Health Service and Spastics Society units reported no involvement at all. It must be stressed yet again, however, that these

Table 4.4 *The involvement of patients/residents in decision-making*

Proportion of homes/units	Health Service	Cheshire Homes	Local Authority Homes	The Spastics Society
More than 85%		Represented on management committee(s) Residents' own committee		
50–84%				
25–49%	Patients' own committee Meetings with staff	Meetings with staff	Patients' own committee Meetings with staff Informal involvement	Meetings with staff Self-determination programme
5–24%	Informal involvement 'Staff approachable' Consulted Suggestions book	'Staff approachable' Help choose staff Given jobs	Self-determination programme Involved in own review Help choose staff	Residents' own committee Informal involvement Help decide admissions Help choose staff

Source: RCP survey

were the views of the senior staff; the opinions of the patients or residents themselves might well have been very different. During the visits, my impression was that the residents could show every variation from abject surrender through pleasant everyday relationships to imaginative co-operation and even, in one or two cases, a bid to take over the privileges if not the responsibilities of management itself. The self-determination programmes, already mentioned, were another aspect of the same issue, although their aim was primarily to encourage personal independence rather than participation in managing the affairs of the home.

Did the committed residents need to be where they were?

To the vexed question of how many of the committed residents really required residential care, there can be no conclusive answer. For many people, staff and residents alike, the issue is a sensitive one which they may prefer not to discuss; personal preferences and value judgments in any case are likely to vary widely. The material reported in this chapter certainly does little to help elucidate the matter but on the other hand I did form certain impressions which should probably be recorded, even though they were based on a non-random sample and (from this point of view) quite superficial conversations. Regardless of the management of a unit or home, the number of residents who were delighted with the place was about a quarter, and nearly twice that number expressed themselves as content. Rather less than a third were uncertain or unhappy or would frankly have preferred to leave. Bearing in mind the lower dependency levels in the residential homes, especially those which were managed by the local authorities, I thought that about half their residents could have lived quite well in private households, and quite possibly appreciably more, provided of course that the will was there and the community services were up to a reasonable standard. As will be discussed in Chapter 7, in the Health Service units with their (in general) high dependency levels, the difficulties of arranging alternative care would have been correspondingly greater.

Initiatives and outside contacts

To two enquiries asking for open-ended replies about the units and homes as local sources of information about disabled living and as sources of new initiatives, more than three-quarters of the senior staff gave at least some sort of answer. The highest response was from the Cheshire Homes, followed by the Health Service and The Spastics Society, with the local authority response the least positive; the greatest variety of replies was, however, from the Health Service units. Table 4.5 gives an indication of the most frequent activities that were mentioned.

Replies were also received to questions about the use of voluntary help and about contact with other services for disabled people. The amount of voluntary work in all four groups appeared to be much the same, whether the activities were taking residents out, helping with care, assisting with social events or just visiting. In the Health Service units and local authority homes, staff and residents' families were as likely to volunteer as outside persons. In the Cheshire Homes, outside persons contributed the greatest variety of effort but members of staff did a fair amount too, with families contributing less. In The Spastics Society units, residents' families contributed least of all. External contacts with

Table 4.5 *Ways in which senior staff believe their homes/units may have been sources of information and new initiatives (other than fund-raising)*

Proportion of homes/units	Health Service	Cheshire Homes	Local Authority Homes	The Spastics Society
25–50%	Working with district services	Giving talks Receiving visitors	Independent living	Giving general information Outsiders coming in Residents participating in local community Independent living Students working in Giving talks Media publicity
5–24%	Advice and help with equipment Rehabilitation Contact with voluntary groups Planned short stay Improvements in patient care	Giving general information Media publicity Family support service Independent living Students working in Social events Special projects (outsiders coming in) Residents participating in local community Day care service	Giving general information Social events Planned short stay	

Source: RCP survey

community nurses and social services were strongest within the Health Service units and local authority homes. All the establishments tended to have at least some contact with others within their own organisations. The amount of contact with rehabilitation services seemed limited but fairly uniform.

OTHER HOSPITAL UNITS AND RESIDENTIAL HOMES IN THE VOLUNTARY AND PRIVATE SECTOR

Within this group is a wide range of provision for younger physically disabled people, from very small homes on a domestic scale on the one hand to the Royal Hospital and Home for Incurables on the other. At least two-thirds of the resources are in the south-eastern part of England. Also included in the government's published statistics are residential workshops and commitments to disabled ex-servicemen, two specially created village communities which some might consider to be a variant of community care, and three very large centres for people with epilepsy and related disorders. Many within the group have little in common except a certain overlap in the nature of the disabilities they accommodate.

The Royal Hospital and Home is important because, although it takes residents from all over the country, it makes a big contribution to the London area and in particular supplies more than 100 beds to the Health Service region in which it is situated (3.5 per 100,000 population). As in the Cheshire Homes, a quarter of its residents are over the age of 65, but the patterns of physical disability, mental disability and medical diagnoses closely resemble those of the Health Service units for the younger disabled. Alongside a tradition of a century and a quarter of a frankly medical model of committed care, it has built new teaching, research, medical engineering and rehabilitation facilities which include a day hospital. About half the people so far admitted to its rehabilitation programme have been disabled by traumatic brain injury, with physical disabilities which are typically combined with severely impaired awareness. Wedgwood (1982 and 1984) described its philosophy as a 'dynamic approach' to the constantly varying demands which severe physical disability can present.

Another medically orientated unit is attached to a religious foundation which was itself established at the turn of the century. Developed by the charity in collaboration with the local health authority, the new unit had been expected to develop a policy like that of the younger disabled units in the Health Service elsewhere. Instead the commitment was given entirely to rehabilitation and was achieved by returning to the referring hospitals some 20 per cent of the people admitted on the grounds that their recovery was inadequate: otherwise about half moved on or returned to their own homes but more than 15 per cent moved to some other form of residential care. Old and young people were dealt with together, with more than 40 per cent between the ages of 60 and 74 and nearly half aged 65 or more (Agerholm, 1981).

Some voluntary homes have taken on other specialist functions. One example is the Shaftesbury Society's interest in muscular dystrophy, especially at three of their homes. There the residents are almost all male, almost all have Duchenne muscular dystrophy and are almost all under the age of 30. The mortality rate is between two and four per year but occasionally residents are discharged to their own homes. The care becomes highly specialised as the dystrophy becomes terminal – residents can call up to 30 times at night – but the buildings, the management model and the staffing input follow the social services pattern of residential care. Medical cover is from general practice but there are close working relationships with local hospital, neurological and urological services which are greatly valued.

The Sue Ryder homes collectively accept people with such a wide variety of problems, especially those with malignant disease and those past retirement age, that hardly any of them can be listed as homes for younger physically disabled people. One of them, however, does concentrate on this client group, and more by accident than by design has become expert in the management of Huntington's chorea. Here the specialism not only includes management of terminal care but also the sympathetic and expert understanding of the disease. Again the interest and support of a specialist medical team is much appreciated.

The Association to Combat Huntington's Chorea ('Combat') is indeed very concerned that so many homes and units refuse to admit people with this condition even for short-stay care, and has therefore set up a tiny home of its own. In some ways it provides a specialist environment to cope with the uncontrollable movements and unstable gait, but Combat is in no doubt that it would prefer the disease to be accepted in ordinary units so that help may be given with less disruption and nearer people's own homes. Other specialist short-stay homes are run by the Multiple Sclerosis Society; in one of them which I have visited, residents come for a fortnight's break from all over the country. It is very popular and in effect provides very severely disabled people with an enjoyable holiday. Yet other charities own and manage places which are frankly holiday homes, very often by the seaside.

John Grooms Association for the Disabled has gradually converted and extended its pre-war 'crippleage' estate so that it provides care facilities very like the other residential homes, except that the policy has been to restrict admissions as far as possible to school leavers: people for whom residential care is seen as a step forward to a more independent life. Some may well remain resident for a long time, perhaps for the rest of their lives, but others have moved on and will continue to do so; the Association's growing stock of specialised housing is intended to help them. Still in the home, however, is a group of now very elderly ladies who provide a fascinating glimpse of the previous regime. I met five of them, one with fixed hips due to tuberculous disease, two with rheumatoid arthritis which had been inactive for a very long time and who were not very severely disabled, a lady whose legs had both been amputated, and one with no evident physical disability at all. They had lived there for fifty years and had never been expected to cater for themselves; discipline was very strict in the old days but now, so the care staff told me, they were regarded as quite a handful, rather like children who had never grown up.

At least two charities have provided a combination of a purpose-built residential home with sheltered housing on the same site. Residents have much the same pattern of disabilities as in a local authority home, and the residential care part of one complex in particular accommodates 26 people with cerebral palsy out of a total of 39.

One small home was set up under a charitable trust in 1970 by two couples with a strong religious conviction, because of the special and unmet needs of a severely disabled young man whose fate otherwise would have been life in a hospital ward. At its peak of activity it was a small community of a few long-term residents matched by an equal or slightly greater number of people in programmes of short stay, together with the two couples and paid helpers during the day. It occupied a large suburban semi-detached house with very pleasant extensions occupying much of what had been the garden, and it was willingly supported by local social services departments. Now, however, it has closed: applications for the type of disabled person the home had set out to care for have fallen off, and the trust funds are to be used to buy small properties that can be adapted for disabled people to live in as independently as possible.

In 1986 it appeared that hardly any of the new private sector homes which had been developed to take advantage of the revised supplementary benefit rules (See Chapter 2, p. 22) had elected to specialise in physical disability among younger people. On the other hand, the higher payments made for people under the age of 65 certainly provide an incentive for proprietors to look favourably on this group, even though their homes' principal commitment is to the elderly; hospitals and Health Service younger disabled units are already taking advantage of this opportunity to discharge residents who might otherwise have to spend long periods in their own care, and the rising numbers of people in voluntary/private homes shown in Figure 2.4 are almost certainly due to this trend. Unlike the accommodation of younger with older people under the auspices of the health or local authorities, this particular practice does not have to be reported annually to Parliament; according to hearsay, the outcome in at least a number of cases has turned out to be quite satisfactory, but it will be a few years before the practice can be evaluated properly.

I did, however, discover and visit one new private residential home whose owners hoped to specialise in the care of younger disabled people. It had previously been a large private house next door to a hotel, surrounded by open countryside but only a few miles from the county town. The two proprietors had previously worked in the local social service department and they had decided there was a need for a home like this, because of the people with disabilities with whom they had come into close contact in their own families and in the course of their work. They had admitted eight people and were planning very shortly to expand, but not to more than sixteen or twenty. Their new residents included two physically disabled people (from head injury and multiple sclerosis) who were also blind, a young man who was more mentally than physically handicapped, a married couple in their sixties who were both disabled, and a man whose childhood disability had been complicated at the age of 40 by a stroke, after which he had spent nine years in a Health Service unit of the hospital-ward type. They said they had had some problems recruiting staff, but even so they had been able to provide night care; there was no doubting their enthusiasm nor the pleasantness of the environment.

WORKING RELATIONSHIPS BETWEEN HEALTH AND SOCIAL SERVICES AND THE VOLUNTARY SECTOR

One of the objectives of the visiting programme was to find out more about the way in which the two branches of the public service, both offering comparable residential care to a comparable client group, try to work together. In some parts of England (for example, Kent, South-East London and most of Essex) and in Scotland, it appears that the Health Service has been expected to provide almost all the residential resources; in others (many parts of the West Midlands) it is the other way round. A common pattern is, however, for Health Service units and local authority homes to have been built quite close together to serve similar populations.

In one county town, the two places were less than a mile apart. The medical consultant to the Health Service unit was involved in decisions about admission to the local authority home and had a regular weekly visiting session there, but none of the other staff nor the residents made any regular or even frequent contact. In another town a similar pair of establishments had opened within six weeks of each other and at first there was close liaison, but with staff changes the links soon broke and when I visited there had been no serious attempts on either side to re-establish them. With a third pair it was the reverse; relationships had been distant for many years but now the staff were beginning to get together and share problems and expertise with a view to working quite closely together in the future. There were Cheshire Homes in all three of these areas but they all operated very much in isolation.

In larger towns and cities the pattern was very much the same. In one of them the Health Service unit had established good community links through its planned short-stay programme and through the local Association for the Disabled, and the consultant was on the management committee of the local Cheshire Home. At the local authority home, however (only three miles from the Health Service unit), the staff told me they felt isolated and had very little contact with other residential homes of any kind. In another city, things were moving a little faster and an independent living group had been formed, although there was clearly a long history of little or no collaboration so that there was a lot of work to do. In the same city, the Cheshire Home had contacts with a different Health Service unit, whose advice on technical and nursing matters, such as mattresses and equipment, had been greatly appreciated in the past. Fifteen miles away there was a similarly good, though somewhat distant relationship, between another Health Service unit and its associated local authority home, both of which were committed to policies of rehabilitation wherever possible – but in that area the Cheshire Home seemed to be out in the cold, although it was seen as a useful long-stay resource to be called upon when necessary.

Two cities in conurbations offered interesting contrasts: in one, the rehabilitation function had largely moved to a social services home while the Health Service unit contented itself with family support and long-term care; in another, a full-time senior social worker had city-wide liaison responsibilities and a regular commitment to the local authority home, but was based at the Health Service unit. This was the only district where there seemed to have been some genuine attempt by top management in health and social services to get the two branches of residential care together, but there was not much liaison between other members of staff. Elsewhere, if there had been any serious attempts by the two services to collaborate at authority or senior level, the staff of the units (including the medical consultants) were mostly unaware of it.

As far as the voluntary sector is concerned, The Spastics Society seemed to be in a world apart from the Health Service units but clearly it had overlapping functions with the local authority homes and the mental hospital services. Some of the Cheshire Homes were happy to work closely with the Health Service but they were criticised too, especially from the hospitals, because of their apparently very selective admission policies; in some parts of the country they were being pressurised by the Health Service to help by admitting people whom they did not want to take. The two points of view seemed almost incompatible and the result was a kind of stalemate with neither party completely satisfied. On a more positive note, in one district where the local Health Service unit had deliberately pursued a policy of long-term care, the nearby Cheshire Home had developed a day centre, an interest in special training and a policy of rehabilitation with a view to resettlement in the community if the opportunity should arise.

An occasional experience in ordinary day-to-day practice has been to come across a desperate social worker, pressurised by a doctor or coerced by an apparently intractable family crisis into getting a younger disabled person into residential care by some means or other. The local hospitals and old people's homes will not oblige; such designated resources for younger disabled people as there may be are all full: there then is a series of letters and telephone calls directed all over the country to whatever establishment will agree to help, if that is the right word to use. It is not a satisfactory state of affairs. Early in 1985 the Leonard Cheshire Foundation and the Greater London Council jointly opened a computerised bureau as an attempt to help solve the problem by modern technology, the first of its kind in Britain in this particular field.

CONCLUSIONS

In Britain, residential homes and hospital units which are intended to cater specially for physical disability accommodate less than an eighth of all the people who might be suitable candidates for them and are aged between 16 and 64. Four large groups, including the Health Service, the local authority social services and two charities, together provide the majority of these special resources. Their admission policies are necessarily selective, if only on the basis of age; the exclusion factors represent different philosophies and reactions to external pressures, and some of the pressures demonstrate the fact that some kinds of disability are not well catered for.

The resulting residential populations are all similar to the extent that certain diseases and injuries of the nervous system are predominant, but they vary in such matters as the proportion of residents admitted from hospital, the overall levels of physical and mental disability, and the relative proportions of fixed, unstable and progressive disabilities. In mature establishments where residents have security of tenure, as many as a quarter can be over the age of 65. Regular programmes of short stay are most widely offered within the Health Service and by a few voluntary homes which have made them a speciality; residential homes otherwise seem to regard them as potentially disruptive.

In the Health Service the framework of care follows the medical model (Table 4.6), with emphasis on medical, nursing and remedial tasks and residents referred to as patients. In the social services' units the key note is domesticity, with staff and residents somewhat closer to being equal partners, even to the extent that residents can be placed in full charge of their personal lives. Homes and units run by the charities tend to be hybrids with features of both models, in proportions varying according to the individual establishment. There is a certain amount of disagreement about the role of staff with professional qualifications, especially nurses, but also others such as doctors and social workers. Costs do reflect residents' dependency levels but they undoubtedly reflect a variety of management factors as well.

The residents' views are as varied as their personalities and personal predicaments. Although the majority speak well of the care they receive, especially appreciating the kindness and hard work of the staff, their opinions of their own circumstances range from enthusiasm through contentment to a certain ruefulness, and sometimes profound depression; a few are quite unable to communicate. Whereas some residents have obviously been able to make good lives for themselves in agreeable surroundings, even perhaps to the extent of exploiting them, others, whose circumstances seem to an outside eye to be much less attractive, can be just as content. Both as individuals and as a group, their involvement in the running of their units or homes varies considerably, although ultimate authority always lies elsewhere.

Table 4.6 *The medical model and the alternative model of residential care: some distinguishing features*

	Medical model	Alternative model
Customer		
title	Patient	Client or resident
status	Recipient of care	Participatory recipient of care
Environment		
general layout	Emphasis on service given (nursing)	Emphasis on domesticity
bedrooms	Emphasis on ease of observation	Emphasis on privacy and personal choice
Decision-making		
management	Divided between medicine, administration and nursing	Delegated to person in charge
clinical/casework	Medical prerogative	Emphasis on social work and client's consent
Staff		
qualifications	Strong emphasis on nursing	Variety of special training or none
clothing	Uniforms	No uniforms
Occupying the customer's time	Centred on remedial therapy	Centred on diversional or workshop activity

Many establishments have become resources of value to their local communities and have generated new initiatives of one kind or another, although about a fifth admit to nothing at all in either respect. Outside the four main groups, some voluntary homes have developed special interests which include particular diseases, particular social groups such as school leavers, or particular approaches such as linked schemes of residential care and housing. Working relationships between the agencies in general, however, are discouragingly poor: overall it is easy to see how gaps in service can develop, initiatives can be discouraged and frustration and criticisms can arise.

Essentially, residential care can assume one or more of three different functions in a disabled person's career. It can be an *opportunity*, a step forward to new and wider experiences and chances for fulfilment, whether or not leaving the residential unit or home is ultimately to be part of the plan. It can be a *refuge* into which a person may withdraw from unbearable circumstances elsewhere, its help received with gratitude, and this too can apply whether the residence is to be short-term or committed. For some it is a refuge at first and an opportunity later on. Finally it can be a *prison* where people feel trapped by the apparent lack of any alternative and a lack of understanding of their real aspirations, for which simple kindness may not be enough of a compensation. A clear understanding of the alternatives to special residential care for younger disabled people is therefore required, as well as an understanding of the different strategies by which residential care can be put to wider use. These subjects are considered in the next three chapters.

5
The expanding options for living at home

During the 1980s a familiar experience has been to hear statements that ideas have changed, that nearly all disabled people want to live outside institutions, that to be concerned with residential care is rather out-of-date, and that not only are there new plans for community care but exciting things are being achieved. In most ways there is no reason to question such statements; I have myself participated in the change of attitude in ordinary clinical practice, especially in geriatric medicine. The new climate of opinion may not be universal but there can be no doubt about the quite dramatic difference in comparison, for example, with 1975 when twelve new Health Service units for younger disabled people were opened. Put very simply, whereas in that year to have suggested that a very severely disabled person could go home from hospital could easily provoke the shocked disbelief of one's colleagues, a similar suggestion in the mid-eighties is usually accepted as being in the natural order of things – even though the business of making sure that it happens may not be very much less difficult.

Yet this kind of optimism, if that is what it is, does need to be tempered. There is, for example, the generally expressed view that whatever happens there will always be a need for committed residential care; besides that, because people should be free to choose, there will always be some who prefer it to the isolation of their own homes. It is also recognised that many younger disabled people simply could not survive in private households without the care of their parents or other close relations, whom some of them can expect to outlive. Another objection is that, despite the change of opinion nationally and even internationally, in some localities matters are different and community services are as unsatisfactory as they have always been. I have also had my own experience of what have appeared to be utterly intractable problems in terms of family support and community care, or problems which could be only solved in these terms at the price of a great deal of apprehension, aggravation or anger, not to mention personal risk to the disabled people involved.

HARDWARE

Personal equipment and the domestic environment

The principle is straightforward: a person whose movements are limited may be given greater capabilities by appropriate equipment and by modifications to the physical environment (Goldsmith, 1976; Goldsmith, 1983). Benefits of three kinds may ensue: the disabled person may acquire a wider choice of activities, the need for personal assistance may be reduced or even abolished, and the element of risk may diminish. Any or all of these benefits may increase both the possibility and the desirability of living in a private household rather than residential care. Anyone with sufficient income may, of course, buy whatever item he or she particularly requires, but the purchasing power of people with severe disabilities all too often falls far short of their requirements. As a result they have to apply for resources in kind, and unfortunately the allocation systems and procedures in Britain are currently far from straightforward.

According to Section 29 of the National Assistance Act 1948, the elected local authorities are empowered to 'promote the welfare' of persons who are substantially and permanently handicapped by illness, injury or congenital deformity. Section 2 of the Chronically Sick and Disabled Persons Act 1970 states that if a local authority is satisfied that such people need works of adaptation in their homes, or the provision of any additional facilities designed to secure their greater safety, comfort or convenience, it shall be the duty of that authority to make those arrangements. In practice, the departments of social services or social work have assumed these responsibilities, in turn delegating most of the decisions to their own occupational therapy staff. Local authority housing departments have, however, also become involved, partly by accepting financial responsibility (under the Housing Act 1974 and the Housing Rents and Subsidies Act 1975) for substantial structural adaptations to their own properties, and partly by powers made available to them (by the Housing Acts of 1974 and 1980) in the form of Home Improvement Grants to private owners of property occupied by disabled people. The systems are cumbersome and slow, depending on good working arrangements between the parties concerned, and liable to continuing modification as government policies change. Nevertheless, they do work, and large numbers of disabled people and their families have benefited from the finance and expertise which have been made available.

Besides these responsibilities of the elected local authorities, other components of the public sector supply equipment too. District health authorities manage what is usually called a loan service with particular emphasis on personal appliances and hospital-type furniture. The main agents for issuing wheelchairs are the Artificial Limb and Appliance Centres, part of a separate government agency which is rather loosely under medical control, and environmental control equipment is issued by regional health authorities after assessment of need by a designated consultant. It is widely acknowledged that the arrangements are chaotic (Table 5.1), and hard to understand, and that the individual services frequently fail to deliver appropriately, on time or even at all. One of the most serious sources of difficulty is that necessary equipment or alterations may be refused because, for example, a social service department's budget has all been spent (and local authorities vary in the priority they give to this expenditure) or a health authority has devised no mechanism for allocating the funds. Concern about the administative muddle is widespread; and the Artificial Limb and Appliance Service in particular has received severe criticism with urgent recommendations for reform (Independent Working Party, 1986), which the government has accepted and has started to implement.

The requirements of each severely disabled person have to be individually matched (Keeble, 1979). Wheelchair users, for example, commonly require a ramp to the sill of an external door, wider doorways (simply removing a door may help), adequate turning space, and some form of lift to an upper floor. People with limited reach, who include many wheelchair users, need appropriate working surface heights with switches, taps and

Table 5.1 *Division of responsibility in the issue of equipment by public authorities: an example from one district in 1986*

Articles	Suppliers	
	Principal	Occasional
Special chairs and seating	Social services	Health authority
Special beds	Health authority	Social services
Commodes	Health authority	Social services
Bathroom adaptations	Social services	
Incontinence equipment	Health authority	
Wheelchairs		
self propelled	ALAC*	Social services or health
indoor electric	ALAC	authority
outdoor electric	No provision	
Special heating; fireguards	Social security	
Hoists and lifts		
movable	Health authority	Social services
fixed to ceiling or stairs	Social services	
Environmental controls		
simple	Social services	
complex	Regional health authority	
Communication aids	No provision	
Ramps, handrails, kitchen		
adaptations	Social services	
Building adaptations	Social services and housing (jointly)	

* ALAC: Artificial Limb and Appliance Centre

cupboards in accessible positions. For those who cannot grip, modified hand controls for taps and switches may be required; for those with only minimal hand movement, independence may be increased by 'environmental control' equipment which will open and lock doors, draw curtains and operate remote electrical apparatus. For personal care, special installations may be necessary in bathroom, bedroom and toilet, sometimes including a built-in (and if possible user-operated) electric hoist. Extra storage space may also be needed. If there is good external access, not just by a step-free entrance but also to a garage and/or pavement and roadway which leads to essential local facilities, clearly the scope for independence is even greater.

For some disabled people living alone, or who have to be alone for some of the time, there is an element of risk which occasionally and unpredictably may result in an urgent need for help; some form of reliable telephone link, alarm or surveillance system is therefore essential for their safety. Its exact nature will depend on the nature of the likely risk and the likely ability of the person at risk to operate any equipment. Communication technology now makes almost any arrangement practicable in any household, although it is not always obvious to which people the telephone alarm should be linked. At present the statutory services offer few formal arrangements; a small number of voluntary and commercial organisations now offer a service but families, friends and neighbours inevitably receive most of the responsibility (Consumers Association, 1986).

Shopping round for suitable equipment can be quite difficult. A market now clearly exists with commercial suppliers eager to satisfy it, and with the usual sales pressures in consequence. Ideally people should accept experienced advice before making expensive purchases, and if a request is submitted for public finance as for the personal issue of particular items, professional approval is virtually essential. To help the procedure – and professionals cannot always know everything that is available – 'disabled living centres' have been established in many places, modelled on the first such venture by the Disabled Living Foundation in London. They are showrooms and not shops; articles cannot be purchased there, but the staff give dispassionate advice to suit individual requirements so that appropriate issues or purchases are subsequently made. Some of the centres have been established under the auspices of voluntary organisations and some are run directly by the public authorities; their geographical distribution remains rather uneven.

Purpose-built housing

A newly built house or flat may sometimes appear the obvious alternative to residential care, but most people already have homes of their own in which most disabilities, even the severest of them, can be more or less adequately accommodated. In any case, not everyone can have a new home when or where they want it: many disabled people, and many of those with whom they share their households, prefer older property or do not want to move from the place they already occupy. On the other hand, not all existing property can be modified to requirement with the resources available, and this particularly applies to the requirements of wheelchair users. New housing may also be the best choice for a young disabled person wanting to leave the parental home, or for people who have been in residential care for a very long time; if a move is planned to a house or flat which is in the process of being built, individualised features can be included in the design.

Specific requirements for wheelchair housing have been laid down by central government (Goldsmith, 1975). Accommodation may, of course, be in separate houses, or in flats within a larger building; for this reason the term 'wheelchair unit' is used but, apart from the implications for the immediate environment, in either case the principles are the same. The majority of new units have been built by local authority housing departments but many important initiatives have been taken by organisations known as housing associations, which in their way parallel the voluntary residential homes. Their expenditure, however, is largely on capital projects for which they may receive public finance, 85 per cent of which is provided through the Housing Corporation. This national agency was established under the terms of the Housing Act 1964 to promote the housing associations, each of which must be non-profit-making and run by a committee of volunteers; in order to be eligible for a loan or grant it must register with the Corporation, which has to ensure that its funds are wisely managed and properly used (The Housing Corporation, 1985). Housing for physically disabled people only amounts to about five per cent of Corporation-sponsored schemes, but a few housing associations have specialised in this field. Private developers have hardly ventured into it except when specially commissioned, and the number of privately owned wheelchair units is not known.

If a person is moving to a house or flat which is at the design stage or is in the process of being built, individualised features can be readily incorporated. To achieve this, however, requires a certain amount of determination, good luck and usually finance, and it is not surprising that great reliance is placed on off-the-peg schemes which may be provided in the following ways.

1. Isolated wheelchair units in ordinary neighbourhoods. This is the simplest arrangement and has lately been favoured as a means towards 'integration' into the local community;

it certainly provides unobtrusive accommodation with the privacy which everyone
expects to enjoy. These households usually have no special arrangements for support
and care.

2. Similar units which are, however, grouped within the neighbourhood but still have no
   special arrangements for support and care. They do allow an opportunity for households to share resources as well as one another's problems, at the price of a certain
   amount of segregation.
3. Similar groupings with the services of one or more attendants who are usually called
   wardens. These people can usually only provide emergency cover for those who are at
   some risk; they cannot supply support and care on a regular basis, which has to come
   from another source. Housing schemes of this type are the ones most often referred to
   as 'sheltered'.
4. Units which are 'planned into' a mixed community of households with and without
   disabled members, with some sort of agreement that the community as a whole (or
   individual households within it) will provide emergency cover, social support and/or
   personal care on a neighbourly basis as a condition of tenancy. There are few schemes
   of this kind which must still be regarded as somewhat experimental (Davis, 1981).
5. Units which have a personal care service as an integral part of the tenancy. This is the
   system which was established in Sweden in the 1960s under the name of Fokus,
   attracting international interest. Even though the units may be scattered through a local
   housing development, the concept is not far removed from residential care itself;
   indeed several schemes have been registered as such. The similarity is even greater if
   the units are grouped as flats in a large building, but in theory they should allow more
   personal space, more opportunity for personal identity, and not only the opportunity
   but the stimulus for greater independence in daily living and personal care (Brattgard,
   1972; Dartington *et al.*, 1981).
6. Units which are attached to a residential home or (occasionally) a hospital, from which
   services are available on the basis of (2), (3), or (5) above. Some of these are part of an
   integral plan to provide a range of levels of personal service and supervision; some are
   seen as a natural development in a residential home which wants to help and if
   necessary encourage some of its residents towards independence, in which case the
   housing unit may be incorporated into an existing building; some are simply an
   arrangement of convenience, space being available on the site, and services potentially
   available with relatively little extra effort.
7. The disabled village. Here, although the layout is dispersed and the facilities may be
   generous, the segregation is complete. The only two examples in Britain which are
   concerned with physical disability are now 70 years old; the celebrated example in the
   Netherlands (more accurately described as an adapted part of a town – Klapwijk, 1981)
   has not been copied in Britain. The concept has, however, been more widely developed
   for mentally handicapped people.

Although individual housing departments and housing associations keep their own
registers of property and tenants, so far there has been no attempt at a unified register of
wheelchair or wheelchair-adapted housing. There are sometimes problems, therefore, not
only of potential tenants failing to find what they want but also of housing associations or
local authorities being unable to find tenants for their wheelchair units. Policies also have
to be established in respect of family tenancies if and when their disabled member moves
elsewhere or dies. In 1977 the Welsh borough of Torfaen surveyed its 90,000 population

and its ground-floor housing in public ownership: of over 400 'potential movers' of all ages, rather less than 50 would have wanted wheelchair units and of these, about half wanted more than two bedrooms so that they could live as part of a family; eight of the borough's 17 'paraplegic bungalows' were occupied by people who did not really need them (Hunt and Hayes, 1980).

For people with recently acquired disability or who have been in residential care for a very long time, whose only alternative option seems to be to live alone or who have chosen to live with an equally disabled partner, building up experience and establishing confidence become very important. For this reason the use of a wheelchair unit for a limited period has increasingly become a feature of good rehabilitation practice. The most usual arrangement is for accommodation within a residential establishment rather like (6) above, but in a few cases a unit or home has made a contractual arrangement with a local authority or a housing association so that a wheelchair unit may be rented permanently and made available to a succession of tenants, prior to their move into places of their own.

Many disabled people who have left residential care for a well-tailored environment have discovered that, left to themselves, they are far more capable of personal independence than they had imagined when readily available help was at hand from a care assistant for all their personal needs. For those who live alone or with a partner who can only offer limited assistance, the necessity of having to attend to oneself regularly acts as a stimulus to mental and physical activity, helping to prevent the apathy which is such a frequent aspect of life in residential care. Some, however, cannot manage without reliable outside help or surveillance; programmes of personal help are therefore likely to be an essential part of any severely disabled person's rehousing.

SOFTWARE: PERSONAL HELP

The statutory services

Just as people are at liberty to purchase their own homes if they have the resources, so they may also purchase the personal help they require. This is the strategy favoured by the Independent Living Movement (see p. 96), and it is true that an attendance allowance is payable from the social security budget with the same intention at least partly in view. At maximum, however, it will only cover about 12 to 15 hours of paid attention per week, and most people whose income is small (or has dropped because of disability) prefer or feel compelled to absorb the money into their ordinary household budget. Apart from the help their own families and friends can offer voluntarily, therefore, they become dependent on what is on offer by the health and social security departments: community nursing, home helps and 'direct meals', altogether often referred to as the 'statutory services'.

The National Health Service's nurses are available at all hours of the day or night without charge to the consumer, but during unsociable hours their numbers are very limited; although they are depended upon by many very severely disabled people, they have many other demands on their time. Emergencies, the care of acute illness, and the administration of necessary drugs and dressings all tend to take priority. Routines of help such as getting people up and putting them to bed tend to happen when other commitments allow, which can be very inconvenient for a person with a disability and a life to lead, and may at times be frankly unreliable. The nursing profession also offers a number of advisory services which differ very much from one district to another; health visitors based in the community have a role in this respect, and there is a small number of hospital-based nurses with different titles and responsibilities (advice on incontinence is one example) who work in the community too. A very large part of the uncomplicated work of personal care (dressing, undressing, bed-making, personal toilet) is usually delegated to unqualified nursing auxiliaries. District health authorities also issue special bedsheets, clothing and equipment to help deal with incontinence, and they can sometimes provide a free laundry service when incontinence is severe.

The home help service began with voluntary initiatives to help mothers of newborn children, but over the years it has enormously expanded and has become the firm responsibility of local authority social services. Its workers each have only a short list of clients, very often living within easy walking distance of their own homes, so that they can plan their time; many of them make firm friendships with the people they serve and can therefore help them in all sorts of informal ways. Emergency help can also be available to cover domestic crises. The service limitations are the social service department's budget, certain problems over the demarcation of duties, and competing priorities within the clientele. The service may have to be paid for, according to a means-tested scale of charges.

For many years the home helps' responsibilities were seen as those of domestic help, especially housework and shopping, usually once or twice a week to as many people as possible who might apply. Recent trends in some districts, however, have been towards personal care on quite an intensive basis if the situation justifies it, overlapping the responsibilities of the community nurses and often working closely with them. Nevertheless, the home helps still often stop short of, for example, assistance with personal toilet, and they still tend to provide a 'sociable hours' service except in emergencies, relying on families and other agencies to help out in the evenings, early mornings and at weekends. They are not generally employed to provide a 'sitting' service to relieve a family helper. Like so many local authority resources, levels of provision and management policies vary from one authority to another.

Two personal examples

A young man in his late twenties had multiple sclerosis which had affected his memory and his reliability besides making him wheelchair-dependent, unable to transfer without help. He lived in a bungalow, one of a small group specially built for disabled people by a long-established housing trust which was responsible for all the houses in the immediate neighbourhood. During relapses of his disease he had had to spend several quite prolonged periods in hospital in the course of a few years, and he had occasional periods of short stay (in a residential home or a hospital-based unit) to give his carers a break. He lived alone but his parents were not far away and his home help, who knew him when he was a boy, almost became one of the family. She shared a rota with his mother; she called in the morning to get him out of bed and clean him up, because more often than not there was some faecal incontinence; his mother called to give him his midday meal and help him to the toilet if necessary; the home help returned in the early evening to give him his supper and put him to bed, from which he watched television which he operated by remote control. That was from Mondays to Fridays; he used to go out a little, including a day a week at a day centre, and at weekends his family would take full responsibility for keeping him going. Eventually, however, his disease progressed to the extent that even this arrangement was no longer tenable; he had to be admitted to a Health Service unit for the younger disabled, and he died six months later.

A woman in her fifties also had multiple sclerosis which had progressed imperceptibly but steadily over a period of twenty years. Long since divorced and living alone, she had a deeply felt wish to be in her own place and over the years she had won the loyalty and friendship of the local statutory services. Her house was in a Victorian terrace and had quite simple adaptations, which included ramped access front and back and a level through run from front room, parlour and kitchen to the bathroom. Limited, in later years, to the partial use of one hand only, she could still eat on her own if meals were specially prepared for her: environmental controls allowed her to answer the door and operate switches, and she had an alarm system connected to one of the housing offices. Her need for help was now quite intensive, and she considered that she could not be on her own for more than two or three hours during the day although she was unattended for most of the night. She chose to spend two hours in bed in the middle part of each day, and she required turning in her bed halfway through each night; for these purposes and for getting up in the morning and going to bed in the evening, the regular outside input was therefore five times in each 24 hours. Nursing needs apart, the work she required was shared by the home help service, some privately arranged help and the informal visits of a small group of friends. A weekly visit to a geriatric day hospital allowed a bath. She actively participated in arranging her own programme of care, on occasions using advertisements in the local post office, and intended to keep the same regime going no matter what the odds.

If ordinary housing providers and statutory service can be as flexible as that, one might ask, perhaps there is no need for any other resource at all. But the input of the family was still important in the first of the two examples, and not everyone has the second person's determination and self-reliance. Others may be less fortunate in their social services departments, housing providers, community nurses, or personal home helps, or they may require more constant assistance, and in such circumstances yet other services may have to be developed. Now that several new initiatives have become well established and the general objective of 'care in the community' for the severest disabilities is socially, politically and ethically acceptable as well as demonstrably feasible, one is conscious of a ferment of ideas as research into family networks accumulates and a wide variety of new ideas is discussed, tried, put into practice and evaluated (Social Work Service Development Group Project, 1984). The impression is, too, that the public and voluntary sectors are equally involved in the exercise. Essentially two patterns of help are given, among which a few schemes have become sufficiently well established to require special mention.

Schemes to maintain, augment and relieve existing family support

All of these depend on paying people to fill in the gap left by the two statutory services – that is, to provide the kind of personal care that any close relation or friend would provide, to be available for social purposes such as 'sitting' or accompaniment on outings, to be willing to work unsociable hours, and above all to be dependable. As a group they are generally known as care attendant or family support schemes; most are considered to be in the voluntary sector but just like the voluntary residential homes, they all depend on funding from the public purse for most of their salaries and wages if not all of them

(Bristow, 1981; Inskip, 1981b; Lovelock, 1981). A few are not only paid for but organised by the public services, and a common source of finance is a joint agreement between local health and social services to contribute more or less equally to a budget. The usual practice is for no charge to be made to the consumer.

The Crossroads Care Attendant Scheme originated with the idea of keeping people with spinal injury out of hospital, the stimulus being a sequence of episodes in the television soap opera called 'Crossroads'. These had depicted a character who became paralysed after an accident, following him from the spinal injuries ward to his return home and dependence on his mother. Through contact with a person who really was in that situation the need for some sort of further help was demonstrated and publicised, and the television company offered to finance a pilot scheme. The money was first offered to a social services department which turned it down; instead, a district nurse tutor heard about it and invited one of her staff to take an interest. The project was not at first identified with any particular type of service, and the local team itself worked out the necessary components and the subsequent emphasis on support for the principal carer (Table 5.2). An article in a nursing journal led to further support from central government at the European Economic Community's Social Fund, and the whole project was formalised as a registered charity (Crane and Osborne, 1979).

Table 5.2 *Job description for a care attendant*

1	Bathing the disabled person in bed/chair/bathroom
2	Care of pressure areas, including turning in bed and helping to change sitting position
3	Toilet of hair, mouth, feet, nails, eyes, nose as required
4	Dealing with incontinence
5	Making beds/changing linen
6	Dressing/undressing the disabled person
7	Helping in/out of bed/chair, with hoist if necessary
8	Feeding if required
9	Overnight stay if necessary
10	To report immediately any change in the disabled person's condition or any other important complicating problem
11	Ask about needs and listen to directions and requests
12	Keep the disabled person's room clean and tidy
13	Cook and prepare meals if required
14	Essential laundering
15	Essential shopping if required

Source: Crane and Osborne, 1979

Interest soon became widespread: ten years after the first Crossroads scheme there were more than 70 in England and elsewhere, and the Leonard Cheshire Foundation had 14 Family Support Services which were managed on similar lines. Both organisations are still setting up new schemes; others have been purely local initiatives, a few of them directly organised by the public services themselves. Social service departments usually carry the main responsibility for financial support but joint-finance arrangements with the Health Service are becoming more common, and a few schemes have been supported by the Manpower Services Commission of the Department of Employment. All are operated on a district basis and most of the organisers make a point of ensuring that their service is flexible, being constantly adjusted according to current demand. As yet, however, there is no hard information about the effect of care attendants in preventing admission to residential care.

The disabilities that are supported reflect the pattern that has been described in Chapters 3 and 4, with the noticeable addition of people with arthritis and heart and chest disease; the age profile matches the prevalence of disability in the population as a whole (Figure 5.1). The commonest input is once a week during sociable hours but help can be daily, it

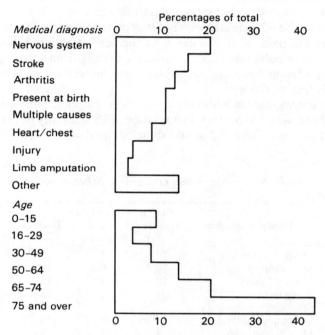

Figure 5.1 *Crossroads Care Attendant Schemes, 1985. Characteristics of the disabled people being supported.*

can be at any time in the 24 hours and the visits can be anything from 30 minutes to four hours. Some organisers develop firm long-term commitments to a few families: others prefer to give short-term help to tide over a crisis and then move on so that more families can benefit. Although the Crossroads schemes are intended to help families with physically disabled members of all ages, other care attendant schemes have different policies: for example, in one local scheme only a fifth of the people with disabilities were under 65, 100 care hours per week being utilised to cover a total population of about 50,000, whereas another service was restricted to people under 65 and considered that 350 care hours per week were just about enough for a population of about 220,000. Families caring for mentally handicapped people have been similarly supported too.

Creating household support where none exists

Apart from the programmes of support and care which are built into certain special housing developments, the only national initiative which is at all well known is the

One-to-One Scheme which has been operated by an agency known as Community Service Volunteers. It began in 1980 and consists of putting young people one, or two or three at a time into a direct personal relationship with one severely disabled person. Although in half the cases that person has been sharing a household with one or more other people so that the volunteers have a similar role to the care attendant scheme workers, the other half would otherwise have been living alone or would still have been in the residential care from which they have been discharged. In either case, the volunteers are given full board and lodging, sometimes in the same household and sometimes not. They work in shifts where there are more than one of them, they do not stay on the same project for longer than six months, and they are paid an allowance. Like the care attendant schemes the funding comes essentially from public sources – in this case usually from social services – and the social service department has to be responsible for the welfare of the volunteers. The whole package is free to the user.

This particular scheme can undoubtedly create a genuine alternative to residential care. By March 1985 there were 146 projects in operation, very unevenly but very widely spread across Great Britain, and Table 5.3 shows some of the data. Clearly, the emphasis had

Table 5.3   *The Community Service Volunteers One-to-One Scheme: national census, March 1985 (per cent of 146 projects)*

Age of client	(%)	Injury or disease	Living alone (%)	Not alone (%)	Total (%)	Project length (months)	(%)
Under 16	3	Multiple sclerosis	10	11	21	Under 6	18
16	22	Spinal injury	9.5	9.5	19	6	18
25	35	Cerebral palsy	10	8	18	12	13
35	21	Brain injury	1	2	3	18	20
45	9	Stroke	1	1	2	24	8
55	10	Other nervous system	15	10	25	30	6
65	3	Mental handicap	4	1	5	36	14
		Other	3.5	3.5	7	48	3
			54	46	100		

been on young people and the numbers were far too small to have made any impact on the thousands in residential units and homes, but the experience to that date had shown that the concept is viable and can be operated for dependent people of any age. Five years are, of course, not nearly enough to evaluate it fully, especially in view of the severe stable disabilities among some of the younger people that have been taken on, and difficulties have been encountered with recruitment and with some of the close personal relationships which are a necessary feature of the scheme. Some of the more ambitious plans for discharge from residential care have become dangerously dependent on this one agency, and there is a fairly urgent need for the same service on a much more secure, locally organised basis. Nevertheless, the scheme has already emerged as a most important way of giving severely disabled people opportunities to live in their own home which might otherwise have been very difficult to secure, and it certainly points the way to other programmes which might be set up on similar lines.

Day Centres and their equivalents

To be in a private household instead of residential care may be good for privacy and personal autonomy but it can also be very isolating, not at all the integration into the community which idealists might believe. For many this is not a problem; they are entirely happy where they are, enjoy their own company and/or good relationships within the household, have plenty to do and seek little more. Others want very much to get out and about, to work, attend a course of study, pursue an interest, visit family or friends, seek recreation or travel. A great deal of effort has been put into investigating and publicising disabled people's requirements for employment, education, mobility and access to all parts of the environment. Essentially, they have a right to the same opportunities as everyone else, but all too often they are unsuccessful in obtaining them.

Therefore many have to be satisfied with less: unemployment, difficulties with transport, poverty and/or poor motivation, or quite simply the lack of any alternative, may mean that they have to be taken somewhere to a more or less protected environment where their main contacts are inevitably with people who have similar disabilities to their own. The range of facilities, which for the purposes of this account can broadly be considered as 'day centres' (although that term usually has a much more limited meaning), can be classified into the following groups.

1. Very informal arrangements in any convenient meeting place, for example schools, church halls, community centres and sports centres. Input may be purely social or may include voluntary or paid expertise, as, for example, speech therapy at a stroke club, or training for a particular sport or recreation. Such activities are eligible for public sector grants, especially from social service departments, and some are organised by formally registered charities.
2. Day centres proper: equipped, staffed and often purpose-built in order to provide a variety of activities of an educational, social, creative or diversional nature. They are usually run by social service departments but in a few cases are run by some of the registered charities.
3. Sheltered employment. The principle of the day centre is narrowed and extended to the provision of employment, usually of a nature for which some kind of wage is payable. Some of them are able to operate semi-commercially as, for example, one of The Spastics Society's workshops which markets its wheelchairs as an independent business.
4. Attendance at a residential home or hospital unit. When this is arranged the day attenders may make use of whatever facilities are made available to them, and in the case of the more active hospital units this usually means physiotherapy or occupational therapy. Often, however, it is purely a social arrangement, providing maybe a few more contacts for the people with disabilities and also giving help and relief to their carers at home.
5. Rehabilitation departments and day hospitals. People who are considered to need physiotherapy, occupational therapy or speech therapy may of course be referred to their local hospital or to their local department of medical rehabilitation if there happens to be one. (On the other hand, domiciliary provision of therapy services has increasingly been developed because the therapists are often more easily mobile than their disabled patients.) Day hospitals, which have been widely developed in psychiatry and geriatrics, have not so far been provided for younger people with physical disabili-

ties, although in Birmingham the Health Service manages a daytime unit for people with head injuries.

All these services are liable to problems with transport because only a minority of their customers can get about on their own. Another common complaint is that the centres provide help at times which suit the sociable working hours of their staff but may not suit the working hours of disabled persons' carers at all well. A partner who has to leave in the morning at 7.30 and return at 6 in the evening may not be greatly helped if the only offers of day attendance for a very dependent person are well within the hours of 9 a.m. and 5 p.m. Often, too, there are people who feel they need physiotherapy as well as employment or social activities, and this is another instance of the national division into health and social services operating to the customers' disadvantage.

Whatever form it takes, the 'day centre' approach inevitably entails segregating people with disabilities from the wider community; however sophisticated the provision, for many the segregation is its greatest disadvantage. Yet even this issue can be tackled with imagination: in a well-equipped Midlands sports centre for disabled people, for example, which is managed by a voluntary agency, able-bodied people are also invited to make use of and share the facilities, and many of them are very pleased to do so.

'Fostering'

Taking the examples from services for people with mental handicap, a number of recent initiatives has allowed other people with disabilities to live in private households away from their own families. In most instances the local authority social services have assumed direct responsibility; aimed particularly at elderly people, the projects are likely to exclude severe disabilities but in at least one local scheme this has not been the case. The scheme has four components: short stay, permanent stay, day care, and visiting care in which the carer provides the service in the recipient's own home. Host families and carers are recruited by public advertisement and every effort is made to match them to the recipients. For residents (short-term or long-term) they are paid at about half the rate awarded by social security for residence in a private old people's home; for day care and visiting care a daily rate is paid. At present, it seems, suitable carers are easier to recruit than suitable people to be cared for, but that no doubt reflects public and professional unfamiliarity with the idea. The initiatives are too new for full evaluation, but if they were extensively developed they could be a major factor in altering the demand for residential care, even though the scope and limitations of helping people with the severest physical disabilities have yet to be explored.

CONSUMERISM: THE INDEPENDENT LIVING MOVEMENT

In Chapter 2 the example was mentioned of two severely disabled residents of a local authority home who organised their discharge into a small purpose-built block of flats. The venture was carried out in collaboration with the county council, officers of the social services department and a housing association, and the support was to be provided by other households in the block (see under (4), p. 88). A similar venture in the 1980s, backed by the management of a Cheshire Home, led a group of disabled people to write out their own prescription for independent living in general and support in private households in particular (Hampshire Centre for Independent Living, 1984). Linked with the general move towards community care, these and a few similar initiatives potentially had a powerful impact, and they identified themselves with the Independent Living Movement in the United States which had originated in similar predicaments and motivation (Lacey, 1984). The Hampshire group has prepared several statements of its aims and objectives (HCIL Papers, 1986), and one of them (Project 81 – 1979 to 1982) begins with two quotations from people actively associated with one of the best-known American centres for independent living.

> If you need someone to get you up every day, the best way is to hire that person yourself. That is important. If someone else is sending the attendants out, that is just another form of institution. You must schedule your own hours. It is hard for professional people to understand this, but it is so important for you to have that power to hire and fire – to be able to set your own hours and staff like that.

> People who have not experienced independent living might think that there is not all that much to it. But . . . it gets tiring sometimes: it is like a full time job just living, and so many things can go wrong. You have got to be able to think fast; to think of alternatives; all these kinds of things. It is a rough job, and people can see and some think, I'm not up to doing it. I don't think everybody who chooses not to do it is just lazy. I just think that their own capacity to deal with things is not strong enough.

The group also attempts to answer the criticism that they represent an élite.

> The most often heard criticism levelled at disabled people seeking equal status in society and advocating self-determination, is the dismissive: 'It's all right for the articulate few, but most disabled people cannot decide for themselves.' Before making such judgements it is important to determine on what basis one views one's fellow human beings and thereafter allow these principles to be the guide. We would suggest that means equal citizenship with equal opportunity. This response might be thought to beg the above accusation, but we would suggest it is a sounder moral foundation than the implied uninvited assumption of authority. In short, how can people learn to choose when they are for ever shielded from meaningful decisions by others making decisions for them? Further, we are seen as not being representative, but we would dispute this. We see ourselves as being those able to identify and articulate the problems involved. Most disabled people encounter these difficulties but are not always able or at liberty to express their opinions.

The group has clear practical ideas about living in private households. It is not in favour of dedicated or special buildings, which it believes lack flexibility; most buildings are capable of considerable adaptation, and that fact should allow disabled people the same choice of environments as their able-bodied counterparts and the same opportunities to move later if they wish. The long-term nature of severe disability requires care attendants with 'flexibility between tasks and time, while the well qualified specialists should attend to the short-term sick'. In the group's experience, severely disabled people are far more expert in terms of their own care than any specialist, which suggests that the care attendants can and should be lay people. When considering the care itself it is essential to move away from the orthodox or 'nursing' image, dividing the tasks into the three components already briefly mentioned in Chapter 1:

(a) *personal care*, which the group regards as straightforward, understood, and capable of being categorised and timed apart from the 'necessary flexibility that goes with life';
(b) *domestic care*, including shopping, housework, laundry, cooking and such items as changing light bulbs or mowing the lawn;
(c) *social care*, which is largely determined by the abilities, interests and circumstances of the individual and might, for example, include items as diverse as attendance at school or at a place of employment, putting paper in a typewriter, or accompaniment during leisure activities.

Table 5.4 summarises the independent living model. It has, however, been criticised, not only on the grounds that it is unlikely to be appropriate for all people with severe

Table 5.4 *The independent living model for disability*

Title and status of customer	Customer
Environment	Private household
Decision-making	
management	Customer
clinical/casework	Advisory only
Staff	Recruited and managed by customer
Occupying time	Customer's responsibility

physical disabilities, but also because the social and political background in Britain is significantly different from that in the United States where the model originated (Goldsmith, 1984). 'Integrated living' has been thought to describe the British objective more suitably, implying both integration into society generally, and a partnership of disabled people with the relevant statutory and voluntary organisations in particular. At least one joint initiative of this sort has been formally launched (Derbyshire Centre for Integrated Living, 1985); as regards personal care, however, its proposed strategy contains the statement that:

> conferences and working groups need to be planned, and constant contact with the planners of such services maintained, before traditional service-providers will accept that disabled people's experience can inform the provision of this vital service.

ENABLEMENT OR 'SOCIAL CARE', AND INFORMATION

Like innumerable other voluntary organisations, the Derbyshire group has therefore dedicated itself to activities other than personal care: they include counselling, the supply of information, and research and development with reference to housing, technical aids, transport, environmental access, employment, and 'outreach services'. The complexity of the various issues precludes detailed consideration here: it is essential, however, to emphasise their very great importance to all severely disabled people and their carers, including those who live in residential care. Many such resources are, in fact, provided within the public sector, notably in respect of education and leisure, but the voluntary organisations have not only taken very many of the new initiatives but have virtually been expected to do so.

In the Midlands, for example, one voluntary organisation has for many years provided guidance for severely disabled people who need educational or training opportunities, either for employment or leisure. A national group has concentrated on matching skills with opportunities in industry and commerce, persuading employers to accept severely disabled people if they are capable of doing the jobs that are required. Transport hire services are gradually being put together in a few localities, often with such titles as 'Dial a Ride': a national scheme allows a person's mobility allowance to obtain the use of a car at a manageable cost, and a few centres for training disabled drivers have been established. Successful surveys and campaigns for access to public buildings have been conducted in many areas. All these are just a few examples: the total list, if it could be put together, would be very long indeed.

There is general agreement that the readily accessible provision of reliable information is essential. A large number of information services for disabled people is now available throughout Britain, a majority of them loosely co-ordinated by a national voluntary agency known as Disablement Information and Advice Link (DIAL): often they work in close association with disabled living centres. Their services vary from informal arrangements for providing occasional advice, to ambitious schemes with outreach workers who have in effect assumed some of the social services' responsibilities. Some enlist disabled people as active participants while others are essentially service providers. Some are on financial shoestrings while others have either secured generous public subsidy or have raised considerable sums of money independently. Some give a service upon which people have come to depend while others are scarcely viable or reliable.

One of the most important kinds of information is a simple, clear explanation of the facts relating to each individual predicament or problem. Often the most suitable people to provide it are professionals, though consumers regularly complain that (for example) ordinary doctors and social workers do not talk to them in the ways that they would like. The fact is that anyone who works closely with a disabled person is liable to be asked exacting questions, and for professionals the practical difficulty can be the time it takes to answer them. Equally important as advisers and counsellors are those with personal, first-hand experiences of disability; known as 'peer group', they can be more valuable than any professional, but the potential which disabled people and their families have for helping one another in this way is still largely unexploited. The voluntary support charities, including most of those mentioned in Chapter 2, regard advice and counselling as one of their main functions, for which they may use professionals, peer groups or other volunteers.

THE QUESTION OF FINANCE

Reference has already been made to the essential aspects of financing and organising the necessary resources for personal care. The most affluent need have no insuperable problems obtaining equipment and housing, and deficiencies in the personal care services may compel them to adopt the independent living model and organise their own. Few very severely disabled people, however, have much personal capital or more than a very modest income: the majority are unemployed and are dependent on State benefits, of which the non-means-tested, non-taxable allowances awarded for severe disability amount to some £50 to £110 per week depending on employment status and age. As already outlined (p. 22, Table 2.2), even the highest sum is significantly less than the entitlement if a place in residential care is obtained, an anomaly in the regulations which is currently the subject of pressure upon the government from several national voluntary organisations. Additional means-tested benefits are also payable for certain special needs, although the framework within which they are paid is due to be substantially changed in 1988. A detailed guide to rights, benefits and services is published by the Disability Alliance and is regularly brought up to date, and Table 5.5 gives a very brief summary of the arrangements in 1986.

There have been some ingenious ways round the regulations in order to overcome the gap in financial eligibility between households and residential care. One recently adopted device has been for a local authority to fund an agency such as a Cheshire Home as though a residential place was being paid for, the agency then directing the money to private household support. Another, used by a charity devoted to care of the elderly, has been deliberately to continue some of the elements of housing and residential care. The charity seeks approval for a building scheme as housing, thereby securing government finance through the Housing Corporation; the completed project is then registered as a residential home so that supplementary benefit is payable to tenants at the rate appropriate to residential care, allowing the employment of staff to provide their personal and household support. Whether this hybrid is really housing or residential care is a matter for debate. In some cases the means-tested domestic help allowance can be awarded; in others the local health authorities or social service departments may make up the difference if they wish, but this is very much a matter of local discretion. The fact remains that many severely disabled people, especially those who are elderly, are compelled to accept residential care because this is the only way in which the government will pay for the whole of the help they require.

CONCLUSIONS

The considerable range of technology and equipment which is available to severely disabled people can contribute significantly to their capabilities and independence, but all too often crucial items are unobtainable through administrative inefficiency or lack of finance. Housing opportunities range from minor but essential adaptations to complete new purpose-built homes for wheelchair living, some of which, however, have been grouped and serviced in such a way as to replicate some of the features of residential care. Personal and household care can be provided by the statutory services at quite intensive levels, but people who need help or surveillance usually have to rely heavily on the informal support of their families and friends.

A wide variety of initiatives has helped to plug the gaps, care attendant schemes being an important example, but systems of finance rather than total availability of finance again limit what might be supplied. Providing household support where none exists remains one of the most persistent problems, although experience has been enough to show that solutions are perfectly possible. Enablement (social help) is a much more complex issue because individual requirements are so varied and the scope is potentially so great, but it is an essential component of support for disabled living.

Into the perplexities and preoccupations of the public services and voluntary organisa-tions, disabled people as customers have injected an important contribution. Their re-

Table 5.5 A summary of the principal social security allowances awarded because of disability in the United Kingdom in 1986

	Eligibility	Entry age	Withdrawal age	Medical assessment	Taxable	Beneficiaries (000's)	Cost (%) of social security spending
To severely disabled people							
Attendance allowance[1]	Need for personal help	2 and over	None	Yes	No	545	1.6
Mobility allowance	Very limited ability to walk	Between 5th and 66th birthday	75	Yes	No	400	1.0
Severe disablement allowance	Unable to work '75% disablement'[2] Not receiving invalidity benefit	From 16 to retirement age[3]	Retirement age (negotiable)	Yes	No	230	0.5
To disabled people previously in employment							
Invalidity benefit	Out of work for more than 28 weeks	From about 18 to retirement age[3]	Retirement age (negotiable)	Yes	No	800	5.6
To carers							
Invalid care allowance[4]	Caring for person receiving attendance allowance otherwise not employed for more than 12 hours/week	From 16 to retirement age[3]	Retirement age	No	Yes	10^4	0.01
To households							
Supplementary benefit[5]	Insufficient income. Certain special needs including clothes, laundry, heating, domestic help, blindness	n/a	n/a	No	(Means-tested)	(4800)	(17)

[1] Two rates payable, depending on need for attendance at night
[2] Based on industrial injuries scale
[3] 60 for women, 65 for men
[4] Previous employment ceased to be a requirement in 1986, which can be expected to increase the number of beneficiaries
[5] Scheduled for major changes in 1987–88

freshingly direct and practical knowledge of what is required provides a much-needed counterpart to professional and bureaucratic conventional wisdom. Altogether there can be said to be eight potential components of good community care: appropriate equipment, an adequate domestic environment, responsive and sympathetic statutory services, re-serve resources (money or people) for exceptional problems, adequate facilities for transport, readily available counselling and information, a comprehensive range of enablement facilities, and financial provision which should above all be flexible but also equitable. A very clearly stated set of guidelines for living options was published by the Prince of Wales' Advisory Group on Disability in 1985.

All these resources are equally necessary for people besides those with physical disabili-ties, yet the secondary-care services (including hospitals and residential homes) are separated quite sharply on the basis of a number of client groups; it is this fact that has led to corresponding categories for service planning. Individual people, however, may not fit neatly into one particular group, and the definition of each group is open to a certain amount of disagreement. The interfaces and overlaps between the various secondary-care services are therefore of the greatest importance.

6
Groups of people who share special needs

For the purposes of service delivery, professional practice, public administration and planning, people with physical disabilities are considered to form one of five groups which make special demands on health and social services, the others being children, the mentally handicapped, the mentally ill and the elderly. This categorisation has led to a rather widespread, simple belief that physically disabled adults below retirement age, or even more precisely those between the ages of 16 and 64 inclusive, somehow belong to a separate population with special needs of its own. The untruth of any such belief has been revealed by much of the information given in previous chapters, and four particular facts require emphasis.

First, and this applies especially to the severely disabled people about whom this book has been written, physical impairments are very often due to disease or injury of the brain; because the brain is such a complex structure, the variety of outcome is enormous and significant non-physical disabilities often co-exist with the others. Second, being in one category of special need does not preclude being in any of the others; people who are already mentally handicapped or mentally ill may acquire physical disabilities for example, and physically disabled people can grow old or become mentally ill or do both of these things.

A third fact is that the 16 to 64 age limits are arbitrary. Although the age of 16 does more or less coincide with several important biological and social events in a normal person's lifetime, the upper age limit of 65 is simply the age at which men qualify for a State pension in the United Kingdom. Occupational retirement has never been confined to that age and is increasingly likely to be chosen or enforced at other ages. The statutory pensionable age for women is five years younger, at 60; neither 60 nor 65 coincide with any biologically significant event in terms of the population as a whole. Disabilities acquired before the age of 65 will obviously not change just because people have reached that age and passed it.

Fourth, because any serious illness or accident by definition causes disability which is usually physical, the numbers of physically disabled people are constantly being increased and diminished by those who become ill or injured and those who recover. No particular length of time has ever been stipulated as a requirement before a person can be considered to have a disability, although periods measured in months of actual or anticipated impairment are in practice the commonly used criteria.

Almost all the boundaries defining the major groups of people with special needs are therefore indefinite, and there are several implications. The various ways in which the boundaries are interpreted influence the numbers considered to be in each group, and the consequent development and use of resources. Sometimes there are disagreements about the extent of each specialised service's responsibility: people whose circumstances put them into more than one category of need can find that far from receiving more help than they require, instead they encounter gaps in provision and evasion of responsibility.

Within the community services the problems of definition are not usually troublesome. The principal resources – general medical practice, community nursing, social work and the home-help service – exist to serve everyone in need. It is true that there is a growing trend towards specialism even in community care, but there are no physical institutional boundaries to prevent the specialists from working with others on behalf of the people who request their help. This does not mean that problems of collaboration and team work do not arise; it is just that they are very much greater across the administrative boundaries of separate hospitals, residential homes and even 'day centres'. Much of the practice which is inconvenienced by the divisions is medically dominated, and it is within the hospital service that the difficulties are best illustrated.

THE MEDICAL PROVISION OF SECONDARY CARE

Paediatrics

There are several important issues. The first is that two of the principal institutions concerned with disabled children, the educational service and the hospital paediatric service, expect to surrender their responsibilities once each child becomes an adult. Because a severely handicapped child may still be learning and physically developing at ordinary school-leaving age, and because all too often there is no equivalent service to pick up the responsibility, some local schools or paediatric departments may choose to retain their responsibilities well into a child's adult life. The fact remains that too many disabled children, who have received quite intensive input from medical, educational and social services, eventually pass on into a service vacuum (Hirst, 1984; Pillar, 1984; Thomas *et al*. 1985) – disappearing, in fact, into the care of their families, only to reappear by chance or as a further demand on the secondary care services when for one reason or another the family support cannot be maintained.

A second issue is that modern paediatric practice can influence the kinds of disability with which a few children grow up, with important implications for resources that may be required in future years. The best example is neural tube defect, with the rise and fall of enthusiasm for its treatment which was briefly described in Chapter 3. The result was a fairly sudden increase in the demand for appropriate services followed by an almost equally rapid decline as clinical practice changed again, new diagnostic techniques allowed the birth of affected children to be prevented, and unexpected and unexplained spontaneous changes in the natural history of the condition took place. Most of the surviving children who received surgery during the period of active intervention are now well into adult life.

Although there are no reliable figures, it is, however, believed that the number of very severely disabled children is increasing for other reasons. Many of them have multiple disabilities of movement, posture, vision, hearing, speech, intelligence, continence and physical development. An important cause may be the campaign to reduce perinatal mortality, especially the intensive care of underweight and premature newborn infants. One study, for example, showed that 18 per cent of children who survived birth weights below 1500 grams had one or more major handicaps at the age of two years, but most of these would have been impossible to detect until long after the crisis period of resuscitation had passed (Kitchen and colleagues, 1982).

A third issue is that changed approaches to rehabilitation, educational and community care services have allowed and indeed encouraged more disabled children to remain part of their families and to attend ordinary schools, providing another reason why residential institutions are having to cater for higher proportions of children with very severe disabilities than ever before. Inevitably there are changes in the tasks required of these institutions and the achievements they can expect, with corresponding implications for the input that will be needed if and when the children reach adult age.

A fourth issue is that following the Report of the Committee on Child Health Services (1976), British paediatricians have created the subspecialty of community paediatrics. Its concern is the health and welfare of all children, those who have disabilities among them, and among its policies has been the development of district handicap teams (Bax and Whitmore, 1985). These teams may well provide a model for adult services to copy, if only there were an equivalent medical commitment to adults with physical disabilities.

The mental handicap services

Independent institutions for the welfare of mentally handicapped people date back to the middle of the nineteenth century and beyond, and British local authorities were empowered to establish their own institutions from 1913 onwards. Overwhelmingly, the model of care was medical, and almost all the institutions passed to the National Health Service in 1948. The service dealt with all age groups; most of the institutions were geographically, administratively and professionally isolated even within the hospital service, let alone the wider world outside. Among the people accommodated were, at one extreme, those whose very severe mental handicap was inextricably linked with severe physical disability; at the other extreme were those with mild handicap whose abilities as a group graded into the lower limits of normal, and who were usually without physical impairments of any kind.

By custom, mental handicap is regarded as including only those disabilities which date from birth or before the development of a child's mind can be considered complete.* The overlap with the physical-handicap services therefore mainly concerns people with cerebral palsy, and the division of responsibility usually depends on which of the two aspects of disablity is dominant: when both are equally severe the mental-handicap service is usually called upon, if only because it has most of the resources. Indeed, at a census of mental-handicap hospital residents in 1970 it was shown that almost a quarter were seriously

---

* The Mental Health (Part 1) Act 1983 has confused the use of the words impairment, disability and handicap (see Chapter 1) by using the following definitions of its own.

Mental disorder: mental illness, arrested or incomplete development of mind, psychopathic disorder and any other disorder or disability of mind. Within the concept of mental disorder are:

(a) *mental impairment:* a state of arrested or incomplete development of mind (not amounting to severe mental impairment) which includes *significant* impairment of intelligence and social functioning and is associated with abnormally aggressive or seriously irresponsible conduct on the part of the person concerned;

(b) *severe mental impairment:* the same definition, substituting *severe* for significant.

physically impaired. Most of these institutions from time to time are also asked to accommodate people who have acquired brain injury later in life, but not all of them agree to do so.

From the 1960s onwards, the mental handicap services have been the source both of damning public enquiry (Martin, 1984) and of determined and successful initiatives for reform. The Mental Health Act 1959 paved the way for improvement; in 1971 the Education of Handicapped Children Act ensured that education would be available to all children no matter how severe their disabilities. In the same year a government white paper (*Better Services for the Mentally Handicapped*; DHSS, 1971) spelt out some of the detailed ways of improving residential care. Ten years later the government offered £1 million to match, on the basis of £1 for £1, any funds which charities might raise in order to move mentally handicapped children out of hospital. Progress in general, however, has remained patchy, varying from drastic and thoroughgoing closure of traditional hospital-based resources to improvements which are cosmetic rather than real.

In all these processes of change, issues have been raised which closely parallel those of caring for physical disability, and resources and practices have been established from which physical disability services might very well learn. So there are, for example, the relative merits of residential and community care, and of large rather than small residential institutions; the division of responsibilities between the health service, local authority services and the voluntary sector; the establishment of local mental handicap teams; and the relative worth of nursing and social work qualifications. The *Report of the Committee of Enquiry into Mental Handicap Nursing and Care* (1979) assembled a quantity of evidence, arguments and counterarguments, and whole sections of it could, word for word, apply just as well to the help that physically disabled people require. Developments such as community mental handicap units, adult training centres and group housing have appeared on the scene; money spent on improving the physical environment of hospitals has been vigorously criticised as diverting resources from these and other essential resources for community care.

Psychiatry

The hospitals and services for mentally ill people have much in common with those that serve mental handicap. Their history goes back even further (see Chapter 2), and many of them face equivalent difficulties of geographical, administrative and professional isolation. They are involved in the same movement towards community care, with similar controversies and commonly adopted approaches. The greatest difference is that although involvement with long-term mental disability is inevitable, the service is also very much associated with illnesses and disturbances which are recent or reversible or both, towards which most of the professional psychiatric attention is directed.

Until fairly recently the biggest single cause of long-term hospital residence was schizophrenia, which is now generally managed by combinations of drug treatment, intermittent admission and community care. The result is that the most dependent conditions are now due to organic disorders (those which are caused by disease or by recognisable injury of the structure of the brain) among which Alzheimer's disease presents the biggest numerical problem, principally in the form of senile dementia. Other cerebral disorders (the term used by Lishman, 1978) comprise a wide variety of conditions, among which psychiatrists are regularly expected to take responsibility for brain injury caused by chronic alcoholism or chronic epilepsy, and for occasional individuals with any of the disorders involving the brain which are referred to throughout this book (Newson-Smith, 1983).

Closure of all the large ex-nineteenth-century asylums was formally proposed in a Hospital Plan published by the government in 1962, but the first such closures were not achieved until 1986. As with mental handicap, movement in this direction has been very patchy and has met opposition; the organisational options for continued protection (when it is not provided informally within a person's own household) have included hostels, group homes, campus developments, supervised lodgings and fostering arrangements, and the use of commercial hotels, guest houses and boarding out (Olsen, 1979; Morris, 1981). The report on community care by the social services committee of the House of Commons (1985) was principally about people with mental handicap or mental illness; the authors found that despite the imaginative enthusiasm of many people in many districts, inertia, scepticism and deficiencies of provision remain widespread.

People with persistent mental illness may of course acquire physical impairments. Besides that, they have many requirements in common with disabled people generally; as with mental handicap, the patterns of response to their need for care are relevant to people with physical disability too. Mental illness may also complicate physical disability, some-times because of a person's reaction to his or her predicament, sometimes as a direct result of the same brain injury, and sometimes for quite independent reasons. The social stigma of mental illness usually appears to be much greater than that of physical disability; like their physically disabled counterparts, people who undoubtedly do have mental disabili-ties regularly prefer to be considered as disabled and not ill, and certainly not as mentally ill.

The sharp division of caring responsibility between the psychiatric service, the rest of the Health Service and the social services can therefore create considerable difficulties for some severely disabled people and their families and friends. Behaviour which is unbearable in an ordinary household may be no easier to live with in an ordinary hospital environment ('younger disabled units' included) or a residential home, yet the company of many other mentally ill patients and the environment of a large ex-asylum may be considered thor-oughly unsuitable alternatives. The staff of some mental hospitals even claim to have surrendered responsibility for organic cerebral disorders altogether; on the other hand, a few hospitals have attempted to give specialised attention to these conditions, although in Britain only one such initiative has been reported as achieving rehabilitative success (Eames and Wood, 1985).

Geriatric medicine

An important objective of many of the developments in relation to severe disability during the past 30 years – the Cheshire Homes, Section 17 of the Chronically Sick and Disabled Persons Act 1970, the Independent Living Movement, for example – has been to dissociate the needs and aspirations of younger disabled people from those who are beyond retire-ment age. The desire to do so has been reinforced by the decision in the 1940s and early 1950s to identify the chronic sick ward inheritance (see Chapter 2) with 'geriatrics' as a medical speciality. That decision was based on the facts that more than 80 per cent of the occupants of these wards were over the age of 65, and that their problems were very often due not only to illness and severe disability but to the psychological reactions and social isolation so commonly experienced by people as they approach the end of their natural lives.

Over the full extent of adult life however, from adolescence to extreme old age, there is an infinite complexity of predicaments due to disability with virtually no dividing line between young and old. In simple numerical terms Figure 6.1 demonstrates the problem;

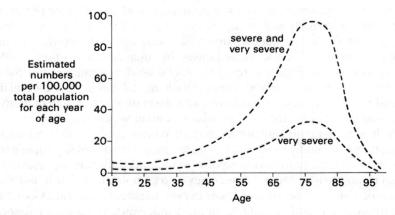

Figure 6.1 *People with severe and very severe disabilities by age*

Sources: population statistics and surveys of disability

the accelerating increase in the prevalence of disability with age has no hiatus of any kind which could justify division into two populations. The predicaments of people with recent spinal injury or stroke, for example, are not different because some are aged about 60 whereas others may be five or ten years older. During the last three decades when there has been such a large increase in the number of people in their seventies, eighties and nineties, and the health and life expectancy of people at all ages have demonstrably improved, the use of 65 as a reference age has become increasingly hard to justify except on the grounds of administrative or political convenience. In partial recognition of these and other arguments, the Chronically Sick and Disabled Persons Act tried to mitigate the effect of the age of 65 as a criterion for defining two different sorts of residential care, by referring rather obscurely to exceptions being permissible on the grounds of 'premature ageing' (Section 17). In a hospital memorandum under the number HM(70)52, the Department of Health tried to clarify the meaning in the following words:

> [The term 'premature ageing'] is not defined in the Act but it should be interpreted to conform with the Act's manifest intentions. Some younger patients reach a state in which their mental, social and physical capabilities have so deteriorated that it can be equated with the general deterioration often seen in the elderly sick. Such patients may find the greatest happiness of which they are capable in a geriatric ward, where the tempo of living and the type of support given is suitable for them. On the other hand a severely disabled person who still retains an active mind may find the atmosphere of a geriatric ward quite intolerable, and whatever his physical state he should not be considered prematurely aged. . . . The decision as to whether a patient is prematurely aged in this sense is predominantly a clinical one and is therefore the responsibility of the consultant in charge.

So the intentions were that without an 'active mind' it was quite in order for a severely disabled person to be accommodated in a geriatric ward, that senior hospital doctors were to adopt some sort of managerial role, and that this responsibility implied very considerable, even autocratic authority over people's lives.

The growing emphasis on community care for dependent old people may well have more to do with their rapidly increasing numbers than with any radical reappraisal of caring for physical and mental disabilities. Whatever the causes however, one result has been the creation of a strongly therapeutic role for geriatric medical staff among others, many of whom are now only too pleased to turn their backs on the problems of the younger disabled; they have more than enough to do without what they now see as this extra problem. The intentions of Section 17 of the Chronically Sick and Disabled Persons Act have therefore been distorted: instead of giving younger disabled people opportunities to break free from a restrictive form of residential care, it has given one important branch of the hospital service an opportunity to relinquish responsibility for them. Moreover, the reference age to which local geriatric services are now related is often much higher than 65. Severely disabled people in late middle life and early retirement are scarcely being helped by these trends.

In comparison with disabling conditions among young people, severe disabilities in later life generally have two important differences: the need to plan for years or decades of fixed disability is less likely, and living alone or in households with just one other person is very common. For these reasons older people tend to have less effort and money spent on them if a few months' rehabilitation has 'failed', and much more attention has to be given to support and care because of social isolation even though the attendant disabilities may not be particularly severe.

The two conditions which are very firmly attached to the image and day to day practice of geriatrics are Alzheimer's disease (as senile dementia) and stroke, even though senile dementia is also the most important cause of bed occupancy in mental hospitals. Individual old people are also liable to become severely disabled because of several different diseases or injuries. The large numbers of older people who are disabled by strokes have prompted many geriatric departments to accept responsibility for stroke victims whatever their age. Some hospitals have stroke rehabilitation units which are under the clinical management of geriatricians; a small personally conducted survey has shown that whereas some of them limit admissions to people over a certain age and take in other illnesses and disabilities too, others impose no age bar and confine their work to stroke, even taking the view that younger patients are essential if a unit is to succeed in its aims.

The general hospitals

Modern hospitals are under enormous pressures to admit, partly because their expertise is held in such high regard that people are anxious to make use of them if it seems at all desirable to do so. Equally, the expertise itself thrives on case-load; within reason, the more patients a hospital can admit and discharge the greater its competence, reputation and self-satisfaction. In an environment of this sort patients who do not soon become well enough to send home, or do not soon die, are liable to outstay their welcome. The hospitals also have more positive reasons for asking for some sort of transfer of responsibility; an ordinary hospital ward is likely to be too restless, noisy and cramped, and too preoccupied with medical technology, unpleasant illness and death, for living there to be acceptable for any length of time.

Pressures from the hospitals upon families, community services and residential care are often therefore wholly understandable, although different medical and surgical teams regularly exert these pressures in markedly different ways. Essentially it is a matter of competence in handing over responsibility; stories of misjudgement abound, especially in connection with sending people with complicated care problems back to their own homes. As far as residential homes and the traditional long-stay services are concerned, there are two important issues: the extent to which they should be expected to absorb requests for admission from the hospitals on demand, and the extent to which they may take over some of the hospitals' functions in respect of treatment, rehabilitation or terminal care.

The old chronic sick ward tradition was to take hospital transfers without question, although these wards' own very slow turnover made waiting lists almost inevitable. In retrospect at least, the outcome is generally considered to have been little short of deplorable; the patients were unselected, the nursing and care staff were not consulted and were usually insufficient, the regimes could be no more than custodial, and attempts at long-term resettlement or rehabilitation were never seriously considered. Some change in the tradition was essential if progress was to be made, and the solution was for the residential homes and slow-stream hospital units to take control of their own admissions along the various lines that were described in Chapter 4. But if a chronic sick ward or residential resource simply refuses to admit, or defers its help indefinitely by means of a very slow-moving waiting list, it does not of course follow that some other establishment can be persuaded to oblige instead or that the patient in question can be safely and acceptably sent home after all. Any mutually satisfactory policy is bound to be some sort of compromise, and some of the ways in which each case can be sorted out are described in Chapter 8.

As regards the extent to which the residential units should share the hospitals' interventionist role, it is almost a natural function for them to provide the very slow rehabilitation needed by some people with, say, stroke or spinal injury; if they can cope with unsociable behaviour they can become involved in head-injury rehabilitation too. They may also become specialists in particular matters such as the management of pressure sores or assessment for special equipment; they can even move into some of the shorter-term rehabilitation programmes required by much larger numbers of people, either taking them from the local hospital or more probably generating referrals from the community which the hospital might otherwise have had to absorb. Tasks such as these are particularly likely to suit residential units that are managed by the Health Service, and some exemplary developments are described in Chapter 7.

The hospice movement

Hospices are concerned with terminal care, and they were first conceived in the 1950s because of the disinterest and poor practice of even the best hospitals at the time in managing the final stages of malignant disease. To some extent, therefore, they parallel the Cheshire Homes, especially in their early idealism and in the perceived solution of offering a residential service within a small community, managed independently as a registered charity. Unlike the Cheshire Homes, however, they have not been united under a single umbrella; instead, they are linked together by an association, some are now managed directly by the National Health Service, and the model has been copied in countries outside Britain. Often there has been an overtly religious component, and there has certainly been the concept of a 'movement' united in the desire for reform.

Because of their primary involvement with cancer, their expertise has included the medical management of pain relief. The very nature of the responsibility means that committed long-term care is virtually never required; on the other hand, the hospices have discovered at least as much demand for their help in providing respite care, day care, and advice and support to people who prefer to remain in private households, so that these activities are now at least as prominent as the original objective of residential care. The interest extends beyond malignant diseases to some other conditions, among them some of the progressive nervous system diseases, and in this respect they can offer an alternative to homes and units for the physically disabled.

SIX INDIVIDUAL EXAMPLES

Very severe disability and growing up

A previously very healthy boy began to develop symptoms of progressive encephalitis at about the age of nine. Over the years his parents watched him disintegrate, gradually losing one faculty and then another until in his late teens he was incapable of movement or verbal communication, his growth stunted and his neck, trunk and limbs twisted into permanently abnormal postures. He had been well supported by the paediatric services and although he was now growing too old for them, the hospital paediatric department continued to provide some measure of support. Perhaps because his exceptionally severe disability had come on so gradually, his care at home was manageable by his mother and the ordinary community services which had lately been augmented by a new, semi-independent and highly flexible care attendant scheme especially for children with multiple handicaps, and regular visits from a social worker in a specialist physical-handicap team.

His mother finally became completely obsessed with his care, spending hours at a time giving him food, coping with his double incontinence and keeping him entertained. This she did with music: they were a musical family and he had already become a young musician when his illness began. She was convinced that he responded not just to a vague musical noise but to particular pieces which he had become to know well. She also had her own way of communicating with him by eye contact, which only she understood. The total input he required had become twelve hours a day or more, which she could not possibly have provided without the help of the care attendant scheme. Her husband, on the other hand, was fully occupied with his career, and the social worker tried to find facilities for respite care. A Health Service 'younger disabled unit' was approached and she was invited to come and inspect it, but she arrived as the hospital fire alarm was being tested and she considered that the noise and bustle generally would be quite unsuitable. A more satisfactory arrangement was eventually made with a terminal-care hospice but its help was not often sought; nearly all the care continued to be provided at home.

Physical and mental handicap

In the unit where I work we regularly admit a woman in her twenties with the physique of a ten-year-old, severely physically disabled by cerebral palsy and mentally handicapped too. She has to be strapped to her wheelchair, has almost no use in her limbs, and is incontinent of urine and faeces. She can say a few indistinct words but her ability to converse is extremely limited; she has been popular with some of the older residents because she responds to warmth and kindness and has an engaging manner and smile. Very occasionally she is noisy but most of the time she is a sort of quiet companion. The arrangement was made to provide respite for her parents and especially her mother, who has devoted a substantial part of a lifetime to her and is now about sixty years old.

Mother preferred the younger disabled unit to the local mental handicap hospital because it did not have the same stigma; she also felt that the company of more mentally able people would be preferable, and that perhaps care might be better in a unit that looked modern and was equipped for physical disability. That particular confidence was almost lost when one day a member of staff gave her daughter a hot mug of tea which she dropped when he was distracted by a call from another resident; the result was a scald on her thigh which took several weeks to heal. The mental handicap service is still involved because she attends a nearby adult training centre (managed by the local authority social service department) several days every week. Her mother's devotion is the only thing that keeps her at home, however, as the incident with the mug of tea illustrates. Protected care of one kind or another will be essential if daughter outlives mother, but the unit has made no undertaking to provide it.

Blindness with disturbed behaviour

A man in his thirties sought medical advice because of headaches and failing vision. The cause was found to be a tumour in the pituitary gland, deep-seated at the base of the brain and causing pressure on the nerves from his eyes. Surgery was advised and the tumour was removed, but not completely: in the ensuing years he had to have repeated operations and finally lost his vision completely, with quite extensive damage to the frontal lobes of his brain.

More than ten years after the onset he left his wife to become a resident in a home for the blind which was owned and managed by a national charity. The home was divided into three parts: one provided conventional residential care, one provided independent 'sheltered' flats whose tenants could make full use of the home's services, and the third part consisted of wholly independent housing. He was given a sheltered flat.

He never managed very well because his blindness was associated with inability to concentrate and learn. He lived in a kind of domestic mess which the staff tolerated to a degree, but he was able to find his way around the establishment and therefore made his presence felt elsewhere. His frontal-lobe damage added a degree of disinhibition to his behaviour which, while not dangerous or violent, the other residents (who were mainly elderly and, of course, also blind) found hard to tolerate.

After two years' residence he was referred for long-term care in a younger disabled unit but was turned down, on the grounds that he was quite able to walk and that his behaviour could be equally troublesome there. Instead, two months later he entered a mental hospital because of an episode during which he became uncontrollable. There he was easy enough to look after but it was soon evident that he was deteriorating; his tumour was found to have recurred yet again, he fell with increasing frequency until eventually he became too ill to get about, and he died just a year after admission.

Not really old

A man of 65 was put on to a programme of planned short stay in a geriatric ward at the suggestion of a social worker, but before the first fortnight was up his wife refused to have him home again and enlisted powerful support from friends to prevent it happening. He had had a right-sided stroke when he was only 52 which seriously impaired his speech but did not badly affect his mobility; according to his wife, he also underwent some kind of personality change which she found increasingly intolerable. There had been no attempt at follow-up by the hospital which had discharged him, and the family doctor was apparently unconcerned; the couple had no children and they found that their neighbours and friends drifted away, leaving them with a feeling of extreme isolation. The frustration of his disability and perhaps some disinhibition caused by the stroke led him at times to angry, unmanageable behaviour. Increasingly his wife took refuge in her work: no-one offered him any occupation.

At the age of 64, four months before his admission to the geriatric ward and twelve years after the first stroke, he had another one on the left side. This produced symptoms which frequently result from successive strokes on opposite sides: he became intractably incontinent of urine and completely unable to communicate because of uncontrollable grimacing and crying when he began to speak. He could still walk but he was clumsy and needed a good deal of help with many of the basic tasks of living. This was his condition when he was admitted and his wife completely rejected him; he remained in the geriatric ward because his incontinence was considered to preclude admission to a residential home (and there seemed no prospect that he could live in a home of his own), a pathetic, institutionalised figure, catheterised, unable to communicate except by the look in his eyes, and with absolutely nothing to do until his death two years and four months later.

Acute complications of continuing disability

A man in his fifties was a wheelchair user because of multiple sclerosis, and had recently been advised to use a permanent urinary catheter. His disease had begun fifteen years previously but the diagnosis had not been made until some years later. Shortly after a chest infection which caused him to be admitted to the local general hospital, a fortnight's admission to a younger disabled unit was suggested in order to give him and his wife a break. They lived in a small modern house with his bed downstairs, two wheelchairs, ramped access, help from the community nurses and a quantity of hi-fi equipment; his legs were spastic and completely paralysed, and he could not transfer from his chair without help. He was unemployed but she had a regular part-time job.

A year later he was admitted for a second period of respite, after which the regular breaks continued three or four times each year. The arrangement has continued to last for more than five years, but in that time he has had a number of quite severe illnesses including pressure sores, infections of his chest and infections of his urine. They have been the reason for many admissions to the general hospital under the care of different physicians, an operation for stones in his bladder, and two minor operations to correct the deformity of his legs. Although the younger disabled unit's team might well have taken responsibility for the overall management of his hospital-based care, they have been content to remain in the sidelines.

Cancer

A woman of 59 totally lost the use of her legs within the space of a few days, accompanied by some pain in her back. In hospital it was discovered that she had cancer of the bones of her spine, some of which had collapsed, and a small lump in her breast which she had not noticed. Otherwise she felt well. The lump was removed, radiotherapy and drug treatment relieved her pain, but her paralysis persisted. She had been widowed for a few years and her son and daughter had moved away; she lived in a pleasant, roomy house.

She accepted a place in a younger disabled unit but did not much like being there, and by mutual agreement the plan was that she should get back home. She and the remedial therapists worked enthusiastically together and after six months she was ready to go, with a self-operated electric gantry hoist to help her in and out of bed, some minor adaptations to the house and, of course, a wheelchair.

There was quite a sense of achievement, but sadly it was only to be short-lived. For a while she returned to the unit for a day or two each week, to maintain her confidence and to keep in touch with her new friends. But increasingly she became aware of widespread pain in her bones, and it was clear that the malignancy was advancing. This time it did not respond to treatment, and to expect her to live alone for much longer soon ceased to be reasonable. Somehow a decision emerged that a hospice should take over her care, and that was where she went to die. I saw her a few days before her death, two years after she had first become paralysed, and asked whether the rehabilitation had been worthwhile. She said it had not, but it may not have been a fair question to ask at that time.

CONCLUSIONS

Each specialist service for people with special needs has its own history, tradition and institutional framework, although parallel developments have taken place in all of them. People's individual needs, on the other hand, do not come in tidy compartments; it is therefore essential that the individual services should not be rigid in the implementation of their policies. It is equally important that they should consciously try to work together: they have relevant experiences to share, and relevant expertise to teach one another, besides an obligation to help one another out when the occasion demands. If resources are short, they may also make common cause in campaigning for more.

As things are, despite the variety of resources or more likely because of it, people with disabilities and their families can find that their freedom of action is very limited or disappears altogether. The largely independent way in which the separate specialties have developed, together with their domination by professionals and administrators who have limited responsibilities, combine to prevent the consumers obtaining information that would allow a reasoned choice, let alone the freedom to exercise it. The six individual examples described in this chapter illustrate the situation quite well, even though they are not described from the consumers' point of view: in the first two cases the parents were able to choose although the two disabled people could scarcely participate, in the third and fourth cases there were no options at all, just a series of declarations by third parties that they would or would not oblige; the last two disabled people could make choices of a kind although in each instance under a degree of coercion. The six cases also show some of the decision-making problems faced by professional advisers, an issue which is discussed further in Chapter 8.

Nevertheless, the aims of each service or institution do have to be defined, and it may well be harmful to agree to a commitment which, because of inadequate resources, has little chance of being fulfilled, or which could undermine the principal objective of the service in question. Even with goodwill and plenty of resources, therefore, it will never be easy to ensure that every personal predicament is adequately provided for at all times. Behind each local grouping of specialist services there has to be some kind of authority which can take careful note of the anomalies and deficiencies, has the power to bring the relevant services together to sort out each difficult issue when it arises, and preferably has a contingency fund on which it can draw if a real gap in resources has appeared.

At the level of planning and developing new resources, it is impossible to be firmly prescriptive about necessary resources without carefully defining, not only the aims and objectives of each service, but also the way in which responsibilities for responding to the whole spectrum of need are distributed in each district. The Health Service's younger disabled units provide an example: at two extremes, a unit which is willing and able to be involved with people who have severe mental disabilities, people in their sixties, medical and social emergencies and programmes of rehabilitation, will need far more resources than one which intends to confine itself strictly to 'pure' physical disability, people who are young in the popular sense, and non-urgent programmes of family support; the extent to which local residential homes and community services can be expected to influence demand for committed long-term care is another relevant factor. Most of these issues were not fully explored when the younger disabled units were created in the 1970s, and the next chapter examines some of the consequences.

7

A case study: the National Health Service's units for the younger disabled

In Chapter 2 I have described how a new generation of special Health Service units was conceived in the 1950s and 1960s and brought to reality, in the immediate aftermath of the Chronically Sick and Disabled Persons Act 1970, by an unusual piece of capital allocation from central government. The initiative was particularly encouraged by the enthusiasm of a few doctors, most of whom were in geriatric medicine; the avowed function of these 'units for the young chronic sick' as they were first called, like the few that already existed, was to be mainly committed to long-term care. In Chapter 4, the task they were fulfilling ten years later has been compared with the responsibilities of special residential homes for physically disabled people which are provided outside the National Health Service in England and Wales. The comparisons were based on the findings of the Royal College of Physicians' survey in 1984–85 (see Appendix 1), which included a more detailed enquiry among the Health Service units than elsewhere; this chapter is based on that further material.

To recapitulate the units' essential features: they are all on hospital sites, except for a few establishments opened before 1964, and their admission procedures are dominated by senior hospital doctors. Two-fifths of their residents are admitted from hospitals but two-thirds of them return to their own homes, in addition to the programmes of planned short stay which most units offer and some have developed to an extensive degree. As a group, the residents possess more severe physical disabilities than those who live in the special residential homes and, except for residents cared for by The Spastics Society, severer mental disabilities too; two-fifths of them have multiple sclerosis. The units' staffing levels and professional input are higher than elsewhere and consequently the units cost more. The service they claim to offer their local communities, and their use of volunteers in a variety of ways, at least bears comparison with similar initiatives by the residential homes.

The term 'younger disabled unit' seems to have crept in through progressively more widespread use, 'younger' instead of 'young' because two-thirds of the residents turned out to be in late middle age, and 'disabled' because 'chronically sick' was regarded as 'a most unfortunate term' (Pellatt, 1976); certainly it did not seem appropriate for the people for whom the staff were finding they mainly had to cater, people whose problems were predominantly not those of illness but of independence and self-care. Because of the growth of publicity about disability and 'the disabled', the extended meanings which were being given to these words seemed to provide an even more appropriate background of concepts.

There are several reasons for giving the units further special scrutiny, treating them in fact as a case study in a particular form of residential care. One reason was explained at the end of the last chapter; at least with hindsight, it appears that the units were conceived with inadequately defined aims. Another reason is that if only in respect of admission policy in management, there is wider variation among them in the residential homes which have been described in Chapter 4. Then again, they seem to fit very uneasily into the hospital environment and culture, both in managerial and operational terms and as places in which to live for any length of time. Unlike almost every other hospital-based resource they are not identified with any particular professional speciality. Yet there is enthusiasm within them too, and idealism even; people often speak well of them and appreciate what they do. It is hardly surprising that the people who work in them are frequently unsure of their role.

UNITS IN OPERATION BEFORE 1966

A few of the present younger disabled units have a long and a more or less unbroken history, in most cases dating back to charitable foundations of the last century, of providing care for incurables or the chronically sick. In the Midlands and North of England there are four, all of which are hospital-type establishments in their own grounds; according to information from three of them, more than half of their residents have lived there for more than ten years and, as in the Cheshire Homes, a quarter are over the age of 65. Two other units in Scotland and Northern Ireland have had more varied careers: the Scottish one is now linked with a modern geriatric department on the same site and was set up in its present form in 1968; the one in Northern Ireland is still on its own and able to provide a service for the whole province. The equivalents of these older foundations in the south-east of England have remained outside the National Health Service.

At least seven more units which were functioning in 1985 were opened between 1945 and 1966, three of them in large ex-private houses of the kind regularly used for residential homes in the voluntary sector. The other four were simply accommodated in ordinary hospital wards which, with one exception, were only minimally adapted. All owed their origins to local initiatives of one kind or another, and one pre-dated the National Health Service by three years. It appears that eight or more similar units which were in use during the same period were subsequently closed; another one made such compromises with geriatric practice that although the responsible authority regarded it as a younger disabled unit, its own staff did not.

STRATEGIES IMMEDIATELY AFTER 1970

New developments within the National Health Service which involve substantial capital spending are the responsibility, not of individual hospitals or districts, but of the regional health authorities which are each responsible for a population in the range 1.9 to 5.2 million. (In 1970 they were known as Regional Hospital Boards; Wales, Scotland and Northern Ireland have their own separate administrations.) Enquiries throughout the English regions in 1985 showed that most of the existing senior administrative medical staff knew little of the events of the early seventies; few of the contemporary records seemed to be available and few of these medical officers seemed to know, or to be willing to spend time finding out, how the relevant decisions were made. The information that follows is therefore mainly based on the evidence of the younger disabled units' present geographical distribution, with fragmentary support from available literature.

There were five different kinds of regional strategy:

1. To create units of less than 20 beds each, serving populations of about 250,000 and more than half of them in small peripheral hospitals. Only one region pursued this policy; the new buildings were cheap and their construction was prefabricated, offering accommodation which was little more generous than an ordinary hospital ward. Complete cover for the region's population was not provided and after the initial expenditure no new units were opened.
2. To create units of 20 to 25 beds each, serving populations of about 500,000. Four regions each opened at least three new units along these lines; together with several units in older and/or adapted buildings, some sort of cover for the whole regional population was envisaged. In one region nearly all the units were in peripheral hospitals but in the other three they were all in district general hospitals. One of the strategies was still slowly being implemented in 1985 but the other three had by then been suspended.
3. To create units of 20 to 25 beds but with the intention of serving populations of a million or more. By this strategy the whole of one small region could be said to have been covered; in 1985 a second authority was still planning to complete its coverage by opening a fourth unit. All the units were on general hospital sites.
4. To settle for compromise arrangements by which three regions were served by units of differing age, size location and catchment population, with less than complete coverage overall.
5. No discernible policy and very limited development: four English regions and Wales. In these parts of the country, coverage has continued to depend on past and district-based initiatives, with predictably patchy results. One region was instead served by a large independent hospital; another used to rely on a similar hospital which had passed to the National Health Service, but which had restricted its service to only one county from the late 1970s.

Scotland was slow to follow up Section 17 of the 1970 Act and did not issue a policy document until 1974; the first purpose-built unit was not opened until 1983. By then there had been time to digest the implications of the English experience; from the outset the new unit declared a policy of rehabilitation and short stay, not committed long-term care (Scott, 1985). Northern Ireland had its old home for incurables, but a neurologist there also instituted a hospital ward solely for the long-term care of multiple sclerosis, the only one of its kind in the United Kingdom.

None of the various strategies made reference to the contribution of social services, perhaps because of the reorganisation of local government which had only just taken place (see Chapter 2); there was also little reference to the voluntary organisations with relevant experience, and therefore no suggestion how the new units might work with these other agencies. The desirability of community care was hardly mentioned, but ten years later that had changed; some of the new regional strategies still foresaw a role for the younger disabled units but others were intent either on changing their function or closing them altogether. A memorandum from central government in 1983 cautiously encouraged this revisionist view.

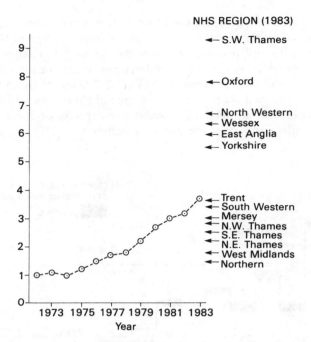

Figure 7.1 *Annual discharges and deaths per bed, NHS younger disabled units in England*

Source: DHSS

The government's statistics of discharges from, and deaths in, the English units for the younger disabled have been published since 1972 (Figure 7.1). They suggest that there was a gradual but widespread modification of practice, associated with a sixfold difference in 1987 between the region with the lowest number of discharges per bed and the one with the highest, and a fairly even scatter in between. The wide variation has been amply confirmed by information direct from the units themselves and has allowed them to be classified on this basis; the aim of the classification has been to discover the factors that are associated with a reduced commitment to long-term care.

A CLASSIFICATION OF THE UNITS ON THE BASIS OF THEIR ANNUAL RATES OF DISCHARGE

The data have been analysed on the basis of two pieces of information: first, the number of episodes of planned short stay in each year (for definition of planned short stay, see Chapter 4, p. 65) and second, the additional number of people returning to their own homes, each figure being related to the number of beds available. The figures for planned short stay have been based on the number of discharges, not on the number of people being helped; for example, sixteen discharges due to four people each being admitted four times a year have been counted in the same way as if they were due to eight people each being admitted twice a year. The additional discharges provide a crude index of therapeutic intervention such as medical treatment or conventional rehabilitation. It must be emphasised that the data apply only to the twelve months ending in November 1984 or February 1985; policies and practice within units can and do change, and the overall situation that the data portray is unlikely to have remained constant for long.

The basis of the classification is shown in Figure 7.2. Excluding two units with very high discharge rates, the planned short-stay figures ranged from none at all to just over ten annual discharges per bed; although there were no clear lines of demarcation, they have been divided into three groups according to whether those figures were less than 1,

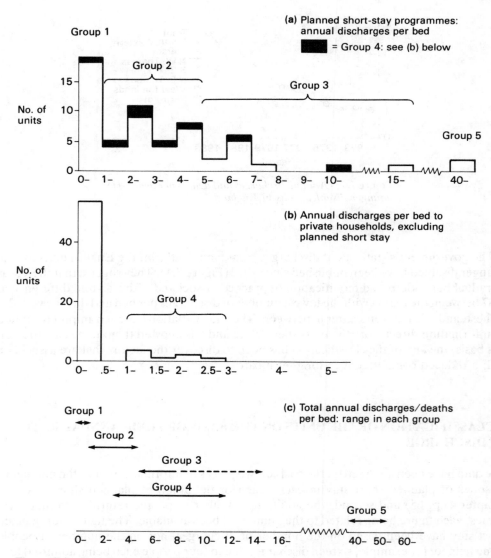

Figure 7.2   *Activity analysis. NHS units*
Source: RCP survey

between 1.1 and 5, or more than 5 per bed per year (groups 1–3, Figure 7.2a). Out of these three groups a fourth has been defined (group 4), comprising all those units which, besides their planned short-stay programmes, annually returned more than one person per bed to private households (Figure 7.2b). Finally, there were the two units with 40 or more planned short-stay discharges per bed per year; one was a five-day unit with no staff at weekends and the other aimed to provide an intensive planned short-stay programme and nothing else, and they have both been given the designation group 5. In the analysis which follows, the progression from group 1 to group 5 is for convenience referred to as a progressive increase in turnover.

The classification takes no account of day attendances (Table 7.1) which were, however, accepted by more than a third of the units, although by only a tenth of the units in group 1. Of the six units which offered the biggest programmes (ten people or more per weekday) all but one were in groups 4 and 5, so there was a rather ill-defined tendency for day attendances to be linked with increasing turnover. Large numbers of day attenders were evidently have been restricted to units with the space to accommodate them.

Table 7.1 *Numbers of units which accept day patients*

Number of day patients (census)	Group 1	Group 2	Group 3	Group 4	Group 5	All units
1–5	2	10	3	2	—	17
6–10	—	—	1	—	—	1
11–15	—	1	—	2	1	4
More than 15	—	—	—	1	1	2
Total in group	20	24	9	9	2	64

Source: RCP survey

BUILDINGS AND GEOGRAPHY

Table 7.2 shows how the groups were distributed in old and new buildings, on different kinds of site, among the regions of England and in Wales, Scotland and Northern Ireland. The units that were in old or adapted buildings, including all but one in Scotland, Wales and Northern Ireland, were confined to groups 1 and 2; that is, they were mainly committed to long-term care although about half of them also gave a modest short-stay service (group 2). Elsewhere, the more active units were scattered quite widely; of those that were apparently involved in rehabilitation (group 4), however, all were in new buildings on general hospital sites, and in England they were limited to three regions in the northern part of the country.

The distribution therefore suggests that busy short-stay programmes were probably due to individual intitiatives whereas external factors, including location within a general hospital, may well have influenced involvement with rehabilitation. This analysis necessarily ignores the units which did not respond to the enquiry, many of which were, however, known to be associated predominantly with long-term care; it may be relevant that the lowest response rate was from regions in which the units that did respond were confined to groups 1 and 2.

Table 7.2 *Distribution of five types of units among older and newer buildings and among the principal parts of the United Kingdom*

	Not responding to RCP survey	Group 1	Group 2	Group 3	Group 4	Group 5
Total number of beds	—	445	355	160	182	28
Average no. of beds/unit	—	25	15	20	20	14
Types of building						
Old institution	1	4				
Adapted arrangement	12	11	14	—	—	—
Purpose-built post 1968	7	5	11	8	8	2
Location						
General hospital	9	2	11	2	8	2
Peripheral hospital	6	10	13	6	—	—
Separate site	3	8	1	—	—	—
England – South						
SW Thames						1
SE Thames	2	3	2			
NE Thames	3	1	5			
NW Thames	1		3			
East Anglia	1			1		
Oxford	1	2		1		1
Wessex	1		1	1		
South Western	1	1	3	1		
England – Midlands and North						
West Midlands		2	1	1		
Trent	1	1	3		4	
Yorkshire		1	2	2	1	
North Western			3	1		
Mersey					2	
Northern	3	3	2			
Wales	2					
Scotland	3	5			1	
Northern Ireland		1	1			

Sources: DHSS, Scottish Office, district medical officers, RCP survey

The data go far to explain the government's statistics depicted in Figure 7.1. The region with the highest number of discharges and deaths per bed contained only one unit, and it was in group 5; the region with the second highest figure contained the other unit in group 5. The next four regions contained all but one of the units in group 3; in contrast, the four regions containing the group 4 units were scattered quite widely throughout the list. The evidence is therefore that the rising trend in the published figures mainly represents planned short-stay programmes, to which a few units have contributed to a disproportionate degree.

Almost all the units worked within defined catchment areas so that their bed-to-population ratios could be easily calculated (Table 7.3). A few had deliberately reduced their catchment areas within recent years; they included most of the old institutions which at one time had been expected to serve large parts of the country. In these cases, the objectives appeared to be reduction of demand for admission, reduction of beds with a

Table 7.3 *The relationship of YDUs' catchment populations to discharge rate and patients' age*

Beds per 100,000 total population	1	2	3	4	5	6	7	8	9	10	11 –	14 –	18 –	23
Number of units in:														
Group 1					3	2	2	2	2	2	1	2	1	
Group 2		4	5	5	4	3	1	1			1			
Group 3		2	3	3	1									
Group 4		2	4	1		1								
Group 5		1	1											
Total number of units	—	9	13	9	8	6	3	3	2	2	2	2	1	
Census: no. of units with more than 33% of patients aged 60 and over								2	2	2	1	2	1	
Waiting list or refused: average number of persons per unit	—	29	14	11	6	17	—	6	7	12	22	6	8	

Source: RCP survey

consequent relative increase in staffing levels, greater opportunities for contributing to local services, and reduction of expenditure. None of the higher turnover units provided more than 6 beds per 100,000 population and for most of them the figure was somewhere between two and four. Conversely, every unit providing nine beds or more per 100,000 was in group 1, with at least a third of its residents aged 60 or more. Put another way, the data suggest (though not conclusively) that above a limit of about 5 beds per 100,000 the more beds a younger disabled unit has in relation to its population, the more likely it is to accept older people and a commitment to long-term care.

ATTRIBUTES OF THE PEOPLE WHO ARE ACCOMMODATED

Further analysis of the data which have already been outlined in Chapter 4 (Figures 4.2, 4.3 and 4.4, pp. 63–64) has shown that the five groups of units were all dealing with the same kind of population in terms of physical disability, mental disability and medical diagnosis. Even in other respects only quite minor differences among the five groups of units emerge.

First, as regards residents who are not on short-stay programmes (therefore excluding group 5); the greater the units' turnover, the lower was the average age of these residents and the more likely were they to be admitted from private households rather than hospitals (Figure 7.3). Because the total number of admissions in the group 4 units was higher, however, these units actually took in far more people from hospitals than those that were in groups 1 to 3. The low discharge rate to private households from these other groups, especially group 2, matched that of the Cheshire Homes and was lower even than that of the local authority homes (Table 4.3, Chapter 4). Average length of stay, of course, diminished with increasing turnover, but there were residents who had stayed for ten years or more in all the groups except group 5 (Figure 7.4), and their number would have been greater but for the fact that many units had not yet been open for ten years.

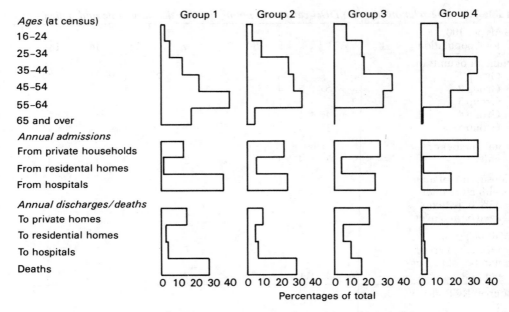

Figure 7.3   *Residents of NHS units who were not admitted for planned short stay*
Source: RCP survey

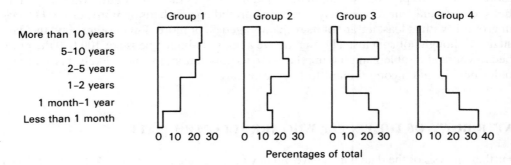

Figure 7.4   *Length of stay (all residents)*

In respect of their disabilities and medical diagnoses, according to the survey census the day/short stay patients were not very different from the longer-term residents (Figure 7.5): the staff considered that the physical disabilities were not so severe, but the mental disabilities differed far less and the profile of medical diagnoses was almost exactly the same. Comparing the same patients among the groups of units (Figure 7.6), only group 4 showed a big difference of medical diagnoses from the others; their patients included more people with stroke and brain injury and relatively fewer with multiple sclerosis. Figure 7.6 also shows that the differences between the groups applied both to the number of short-stay admissions offered annually to each person, and to the proportion of each catchment population that made use of the short-stay service.

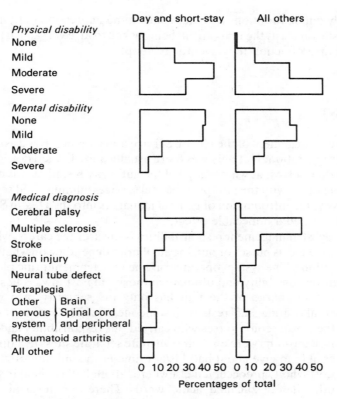

Figure 7.5 *All residents: all units*

Source: RCP survey

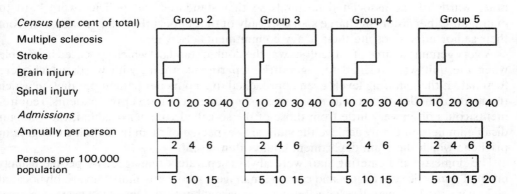

Figure 7.6 *Day attenders and short-term residents*

Source: RCP survey

The relatively minor variations together confirm the impression that, in terms of these very basic statistics at least, the units are all being asked to face very much the same task no matter what course of action they eventually adopt.

MANAGEMENT

In Chapter 4 the management of the Health Service units was described as chaotic, and this is scarcely an exaggeration. Not only was there usually quite limited delegation of authority to the units themselves; at whatever level the authority rested, it was divided between the various professions with the non-professional services administered separately. At the time of the survey, the introduction of general managers into the Health Service had been too recent to have had a noticeable effect.

One of the biggest management responsibilities is towards the carers, who in the Health Services are referred to as nurses or nursing auxiliaries depending on whether they possess nursing qualifications. The system operates on line management principles, which means that recruitment responsibility and ultimate authority almost always lies outside a small unit; if the nurse in charge of the unit has only the seniority of a ward sister, the responsibility for allocating staff rests with someone else. The survey revealed that only nine units had their own senior nurses who carried this responsibility and in four of these nine it was because the units were on their own quite separate sites. In a further five cases a senior nurse was able to give about half his/her time to the unit but otherwise the senior nurses were almost wholly preoccupied elsewhere, about half of them in geriatric departments and the other half in so-called 'acute' wards. There were no significant differences in these management arrangements among the five analytical groups, and there was a range of opinions about their effects.

Very many people told me how difficult they found explaining their units' commitments and ideals, such as they were, to their colleagues and seniors in the main hospital. Some of them, by hard dealing, force of personality or perhaps just the passage of time, had established a kind of *modus vivendi* by which their nurse managers had come to accept that the units were different and to some extent had withdrawn from all but the most necessary involvement. At worst the units were constantly being 'raided' for nurses to help in the other wards of the associated hospitals so that standards and policies were hard to maintain. Other sisters in charge spoke warmly of the support they consistently had from their senior nurses despite their heavy commitments elsewhere.

A very genuine source of difficulties was the double standard which appeared inevitable when the unit was attached to a geriatric department: there, with wards which were fortunate if their staffing levels even approached five hours per patient per day, in which the medical model of care was never seriously challenged and yet the patients' requirements could differ very little from those of the so-called younger disabled, the younger disabled units could only achieve the standards expected of them by claiming a degree of privilege which the main department could often resent.

The domestic and catering staff were always separately managed, by people usually entitled domestic supervisors and catering managers who were almost invariably located elsewhere and had overall responsibility to the parent hospital. One result was a demarcation of duties between care and domestic staff which could be more troublesome than in the residential homes; another result was that meals were always prepared elsewhere, except in those units which were on their own separate sites. The smell of cooking, such an integral part of ordinary domestic life, was therefore absent from most of the units, and many of them had to put up with plated meals services which took away even the social ritual of serving at table.

All the more active units (groups 3, 4 and 5), and about half of the others, had input of 30 or more hours from people variously known as administrator, secretary, clerical officer or in one or two instances housekeeper, hostess, house mother or activities organiser. None of these people carried budgetary responsibilities, however, and they usually had no say in the management of staff.

The professionals had their own arrangements. The remedial therapists were usually each managed within their own small hospital-based hierarchies. The social workers were in an even more detached position, accountable to local authority management which was located away from the unit, usually away from the hospital and in an entirely separate public authority. Hospital consultants are for practical purposes accountable to no one; this leads to the intricacies of what are known as medical politics with its endless committees, subcommittees, advisory groups and manipulative manoeuvres to secure more resources, but at least the consultants attached to younger disabled units were in a position to represent that unit at influential levels in a way in which the other senior staff were not.

The whole system depends on consensus between the senior people in each group: when that existed, a very positive spirit of joint endeavour could evidently be generated. In practice, however, it appeared that no-one in the younger disabled unit could be counted on both to take the necessary initiatives and to achieve the desired results. Since 1985–86, overall responsibility has been more directly given to each hospital's general manager, but if the hospital is a large one it needs to be further delegated downwards if the younger disabled units are to benefit. Meanwhile, the existing system of management is a stifling background for a place which is supposed to provide a home.

THE NURSES AND NURSING AUXILIARIES

In Chapter 4 it has already been mentioned that the input of nurses into the Health Service units varied from less than four to nearly eight hours per resident per day overall (figures which included day and night cover and from which absence due to sickness and leave must be subtracted); that complaints about the shortage of staff were associated with levels of five hours per day or less; and that the proportion of qualified nurses varied from 30 to 80 per cent. Figures 7.7 and 7.8 show that the staffing levels did not differ significantly among the five groups of units, which fits in with the fact that residents' dependency levels were much the same in all five. In more than half the units, however, the senior nurses were unsure what their night staffing levels were, this being yet another example of divided management. Units could also become unsatisfactorily dependent on nurses hired from private agencies to make up shortages due to absence or poor recruitment.

The nurses in charge were asked to answer an open-ended question about their views of the scope, responsibilities and problems of nursing in a younger disabled unit, and an attempt at a summary of their replies is set out in Table 7.4. The later comment of one well-informed person was that the list clearly demonstrated people in posts whose job descriptions and working relationships were inadequately defined, together with a need for a training programme which would include an overview of disability services in the

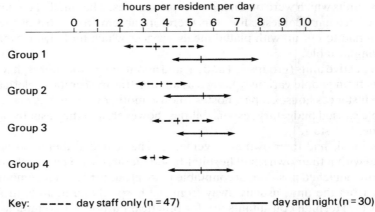

Figure 7.7 *Nurse staffing levels in four of the five groups: ranges and means*

Source: RCP survey

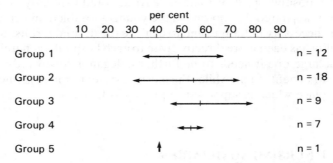

Figure 7.8 *Proportion of trained nurses among day staff: ranges and means*

Source: RCP survey

world outside. Complaints about higher management mentioned over-insistence on hospital procedures, restrictive fire regulations, and outside parties being taken round a unit without prior consultation. Another negative comment was a feeling of isolation, which had prompted one unit sister to write round to all the others asking if they had had the same experience; many replied that they had, especially those whose units had very few short-stay residents.

Arrangements for special training in fact varied a good deal, from none at all through very informal arrangements, conventional (usually geriatric) in-service training, occasional or regular group meetings and study days, to going out on visits and courses. In one region three hospital-based community nurses specialising in physical disability were employed, all in close association with their districts' younger disabled units. One devoted all her time to this task; another divided her time between it and the district's geriatric service; the third was the unit's own senior nurse who spent one or two days each week 'in the community'. Several other units had less formal arrangements which allowed their

Table 7.4 *The most prevalent opinions of senior nurses about the scope, responsibilities and problems of nursing in younger disabled units*

Positive comments	Neutral comments	Negative comments
Wide and challenging scope	Good basic nursing	Staff stress
Appreciating the psychology	Physical workload	Conflict with higher management
Dealing with relatives	Emotional involvement	Lack of support from colleagues
'Getting patients out'	Arranging recreation	Unrewarding patients
Community involvement	Death and bereavement	Staff shortage
Teaching and learning	Encouraging independence	Poor buildings
Rehabilitation	Behavioural disturbance	Recruitment
Teamwork	Patient mix	
Making a home		

Source: RCP survey

sisters in charge to go out to visit prospective patients or, when necessary, those who had been discharged.

Nurses were also understandably sensitive to people's appreciation, or lack of it, of the work they undertook; an example is a story in one unit of a resident who had been helped and encouraged to make her own Christmas cards, only to find that she had decided to send them all to her relatives who rarely visited, keeping none as an expression of appreciation to the staff. Only very few units had their nurses out of uniforms; one (in group 4) had asked its patients to vote on the subject and they are reported to have opted decisively in favour of the uniforms being retained. Perhaps of all the units, the one in which the staff seemed most at ease was in a so-called community hospital in a small town; the medical model of care was not challenged, the buildings were poor and the unit was in group 1, but it was part of the whole establishment and therefore had a sense of 'belonging'.

There were, in fact, no discernible differences between the five groups of units whether in terms of the senior nurses' comments, training arrangements or general morale (see Table 7.8 below). Links with 'acute' rather than geriatric services seemed to confer no particular benefits or disadvantages. While in a minority of units nursing morale was not too good, far more impressive was the determination to do a good job even if it had to be tempered by frustration.

MEDICAL STAFF

Because of the special status of doctors within the hospital service, and because of the confused and divided management responsibilities, medical consultants attached to younger disabled units have a potentially important task in helping to determine their policy. Table 7.5 shows some of the relevant facts. The consultants' specialties do not appear to have been of great significance, but the amount of time they devoted to their units did increase progressively from group 1 to group 5. In the higher turnover units, consultants were more likely to hold multidisciplinary case conferences as well as (or instead of) conventional ward rounds, and a little more likely to share or delegate decisions about admission. Two units were without attached consultants and they were both in group 1.

Table 7.5 *Data on the medical role in the Health Service units*

	Group 1	Group 2	Group 3	Group 4	Group 5
Consultants' specialties (number of units)					
neurology	3	5	2	4	—
rheumatology	4	5	5	2	1
geriatrics	8	8	2	1	—
medicine	3	6	—	1	—
YDU only	—	—	—	1	1
other	1	1	—	—	—
shared	7	4	—	3	—
no consultants	2	—	—	—	—
Average weekly no. of consultant sessions	1.1	1.3	1.9	2.5	4.0
Other medical input (number of units)					
general practitioner	14	14	8	6	—
junior hospital	4	11	1	2	1
Average weekly no. of non-consultant sessions	3.0	2.0	4.8	5.0	(3.0)
Consultants' involvement (per cent of units)					
case conferences	61	86	100	100	(100)
ward rounds	100	82	67	89	(50)
day-to-day cover	17	23	—	—	(50)
decisions about admission:					
always involved	100	95	89	78	(100)
sometimes involved	—	5	11	22	—
never involved	—	—	—	—	—
never shared	28	—	—	—	—
sometimes shared	39	41	11	33	—
always shared	33	59	89	66	(100)

Source: RCP survey

Table 7.6 outlines some of their responses to direct questions about the unit's policies and usefulness. Their views on policy matched the reported activity fairly well, except that a declared interest in rehabilitation did not always mean much in practice. Hardly any would set a time limit to rehabilitation but just over a third would under some circumstances return a person to a referring hospital, and this included most of the consultants attached to the units in group 4. Only about a third appeared to offer their residents security of tenure; only a sixth, on the other hand, would make a practice of asking for transfer at a particular age, while the remaining half had no particular policy in this respect.

More than half of the doctors also said that their units were initiating or had achieved significant changes of policy since they were first opened, very often because of a change of consultant. The commonest reform was to have intensified the planned short-stay programme, but in some units the aim was either less specific or obviously towards rehabilitation; expressions used included 'total turn-round', 'more active', 'to un-dump', 'towards turnover', or simply 'not long stay'. Some consultants believed that their units were very useful and effective, especially those in groups 3, 4 and 5; otherwise by far the majority

Table 7.6 *The medical consultants: some of their policies and their views of the units to which they were attached*

	Number of units				
	Group 1 (total = 20)	Group 2 (total = 25)	Group 3 (total = 9)	Group 4 (total = 8)	Group 5 (total = 2)
Principal aim, if there is one					
committed long-term care	8	3	1	1	—
planned short stay	—	5	4	—	1
rehabilitation	4	4	1	6	1
Whether excluded					
committed long-term care	—	—	1	1	—
planned short stay	3	—	—	—	—
rehabilitation	6	7	—	—	1
Might on occasions return a resident to the referring hospital ward	4	5	4	6	1
Would move a resident at age 60					
usually or always	1	1	1	—	—
sometimes	—	—	1	—	—
Would move a resident at age 65					
usually or always	5	9	2	5	—
sometimes	2	5	2	—	—
Evaluation of the unit					
very useful and effective	5	3	5	5	2
much needed service needing improvement*	10	22	4	4	—
of some value: no bad mistakes	2	2	—	—	—
misguided in several respects	2	2	2	1	—
badly misguided: should be closed	—	—	—	—	—

* This reply did not necessarily exclude one of the three following possible replies

Source: RCP survey

view was that the units constituted a much-needed service which required improvement, with no-one considering they were so badly misguided that they should be closed.

Rather more information about the consultants' contributions was obtained by visiting these units personally, although on nearly a fifth of occasions the consultant did not think it was important enough to be present. The two units in group 5 both depended very much on their consultants' leadership; to an outside observer they seemed to be doing very similar work but, in detail, the programmes were different and whereas one consultant insisted that it was not rehabilitation, the other made a point of explaining that it was. Of those fairly certainly involved with rehabilitation (group 4), for some the motivation was just to avoid long-term care whereas others were applying their rehabilitation skills as far as they were able; one consultant in particular was involved in research and advice on the prevention and management of pressure sores and on mattresses and wheelchair seating. Two consultants had orientated their units from the outset towards a rehabilitation policy, both units having been opened after 1980 by which time there had been a chance to begin evaluating the development of the past decade. Other units had moved towards rehabilitation which had not been an objective at first, and in three instances this was because the consultant had changed.

Commitment did not necessarily mean rehabilitation because some consultants actively fostered long-term care programmes instead, trying to continue the ideals of the original young chronic sick unit concept and often including respectable programmes of planned short stay. There were also the delegators: those who were there in the background but delegated to someone else the kind of work other consultants might have done – a clinical assistant perhaps, or a senior nurse. Several were involved with other parts of their local disability services – regular sessions at local authority homes for example, on the management committee of a Cheshire Home, or with a local disabled people's association.

Further important information about their function came from some of the nurses. Like all good doctors, they were appreciated because of the dependability of their help in times of crisis, but they were also valued because of their ability to get things done within the Health Service establishment – to 'stand up for' the nurses and the units generally when necessary, and to press for improvements to the buildings. Sadly, in a few cases the consultants were obviously not interested; one unit sister said 'I think if there was a doctor who was committed I would be overjoyed'. All these conversations confirmed that the consultants were chiefly necessary because of the hospital system: their committed interest and leadership were much more important than the exact nature of their specialist skills.

General practitioners were the principal form of day-to-day medical support and in two units in group 1 they also filled the consultant role. Usually they had obvious close working relationships with their consultants but occasionally the opposite was the case. Their input was much less obviously related to the activity of the units than was that of the consultants (Table 7.5), and indeed the basis on which they were paid seem to vary quite capriciously in relation to the work they were likely to have to do. Nearly a third of the units made use of hospital doctors instead, some of whom said that they found the 'slow pace' unrewarding, preferring to deal with a succession of patients in a short time rather than the small number over what were long periods to them. Depending on their ambitions and previous experience however, other junior doctors could find their attachment to the units valuable as an opportunity for experience of some not particularly common neurological disorders, and of the problems of severe disability generally.

REMEDIAL THERAPY, SOCIAL WORK AND PSYCHOLOGY

Average staffing levels in these professions tended to echo the input from the consultants in their progressive increase from group 1 to group 5 (Figure 7.9). Physiotherapists were

Table 7.7 *Percentage of units reporting little or no input from rehabilitation staff*

	Group 1 (total = 20)	Group 2 (total = 25)	Group 3 (total = 9)	Group 4 (total = 8)	Group 5 (total = 2)
Physiotherapist	7	9	—	—	—
PT aide	33	32	44	50	(50)
Occupational therapist	47	5	11	—	—
OT aide	13	23	11	25	—
Speech therapist	73	64	44	13	(50)
Social worker	27	23	—	—	—
Clinical psychologist	93	55	67	37	(100)

Source: RCP survey

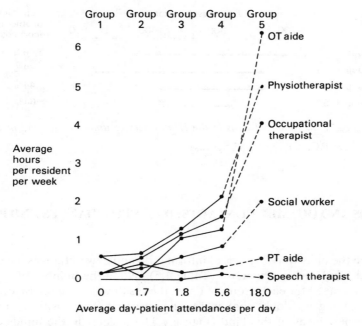

Figure 7.9   *Input from rehabilitation staff*

Source: RCP survey

the most consistent in this respect; the individual figures in the other professions, especially social work, varied considerably from one unit to another in each group. Table 7.7 displays the same information in another way, listing the percentage of units which reported little or no input from the various professions. Only ten units had fixed commitments from speech therapists, and only three from clinical psychologists. Social workers had fixed commitments with about a third of the units, and there was evidence that their help was particularly valuable in the programmes of planned short stay. The general impression was that most of these professionals had genuine interest in and enthusiasm for their work, though sometimes tempered by dissatisfaction with the way the system appeared to demand that the units should be run.

COSTS

The difficulty the administrative and other staff of the units had in reporting their costs has already been referred to in Chapter 4. Given that half the units could not report them at all, the conclusions must be cautious; Figure 7.10, however, shows that whereas there was apparently a wide range from £200 to more than £400 per week (1985 prices), the average cost did progressively increase with the units' increasing turnover. Such as they are, the figures are consistent with the similar progressive increase in allocated medical and remedial therapy time on the one hand, and the unrelated variations in nurse staffing on the other (Figures 7.7, 7.8 and 7.9).

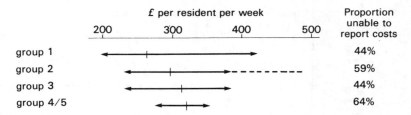

Figure 7.10 *Reported costs in the Health Service units: ranges and means*

Source: RCP survey (1985 figures)

INITIATIVES AND OUTSIDE CONTACTS: DAY ATTENDANCES AND PLANNED SHORT STAY

Ways in which the units were sources of information and new initiatives have been briefly discussed and tabulated in Chapter 4 (Table 4.5). When the number of such items was counted and averaged for each group of units, the result was an impressive, almost linear relationship leaving no doubt that increasing turnover was positively related to the generation of new ideas of this kind (Figure 7.11), at least in the minds of those who completed the questionnaire.

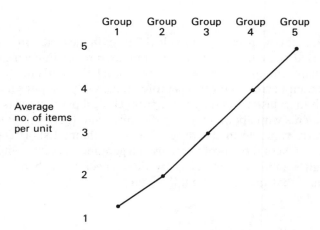

Figure 7.11 *The units as sources of information and new initiatives*

Source: RCP survey

Reference was also made in Chapter 4 to the use of voluntary help and to the frequency of contact with other services for disabled people. Among these Health Service units, diminishing emphasis on long stay did seem to decrease the input of voluntary help, but to increase outside contacts quite significantly (Figure 7.12). As might be expected, these contacts were particularly with local statutory services but they also included other younger

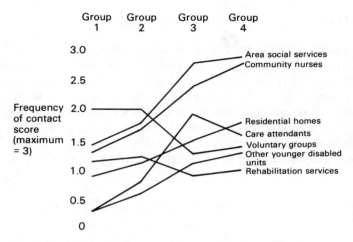

Figure 7.12 *Some data on units' external contacts*
Source: RCP survey

disabled units and residential homes. The data support the view that the group 1 units, where nearly all the effort goes into committed long-term care, were more isolated socially than the others.

Two very important components of outside contact are, of course, the provisions made for day attendances and programmes of planned short stay. Day attendances still contributed a service in some districts which was not available elsewhere. There was also plenty of evidence, talking to people with the different responsibilities in many different places, that the short-stay programmes were popular; not always, it must be admitted, with the short-stay residents themselves but certainly with their informal and formal carers who appreciated both the respite and the contact with other people who could understand a little of their task. The key to mutual satisfaction was good teamwork and many units insisted on prior visits by unit staff to the potential residents' homes, and/or by the would-be residents to the units, before final agreement to a programme could be reached.

The short-stay schedules themselves depended largely on the hospital teams' preferences or prejudices. Although the two group 5 units devised their arrangements in different ways with somewhat different aims, they both provided weekly as well as less frequent periods of stay, very active day attendance programmes and strong multidisciplinary professional teams. Impressive though these two services were, they were not total substitutes for more committed residential care; both units were obliged to make occasional use of other residential accommodation. At the other extreme, at least one unit rationed its short-term residents to one admission per year. The most usual arrangements were for fortnightly admissions once a quarter, or weekly admissions every six weeks or so; in one group 3 unit which favoured a quarterly programme, an informal survey of the short-term residents and their families discovered a high degree of satisfaction. Some units planned deliberately to phase their short-stay programmes gradually into committed long-term care as a disease like multiple sclerosis progresses; others struggled hard to avoid doing any such thing. Two units had resorted to a less defensible practice: abruptly changing or withdrawing a programme without consultation, either because the unit had decided to change its policy or because and ageing person had reached an arbitrary age limit.

STAFF MORALE

To a written question asking for an assessment of their unit's morale according to a seven-point scale, the replies from groups of senior staff are shown in Table 7.8. In just over a fifth of units the verdict was less than good; a simple scoring system showed no significant difference among the five groups with the possible exception of group 4. (Replying to the same question, the residential homes in the voluntary sector had all reported that their morale was at least good, with on average 58 per cent of the possible score; local authority homes were like the Health Service units, 16 per cent reporting morale that was less than good, with an aggregate 35 per cent of the possible score.)

Table 7.8   *The views of groups of senior staff on the morale of their units*

| | | | | Score (numbers of units) | | | | |
	Excellent (3)	Very good (2)	Good (1)	Nothing special (0)	Not good (−1)	Serious problems (−2)	Very poor (−3)	% of possible score
Group 1	1	8	5	2	4	—	—	33
Group 2	2	5	13	3	1	—	1	33
Group 3	1	3	3	—	1	1	—	33
Group 4	—	4	3	1	—	—	—	46
Group 5	—	—	2	—	—	—	—	33
TOTAL	4	20	26	6	6	1	1	35

Source: RCP survey

High morale, however, is not the same thing as achieving acceptable objectives or standards, even assuming that there is consensus about what these should be; within the quite large number of people associated with each unit, opinions are likely to have differed quite widely about both. Just one example will suffice: in a group 4 unit reporting that morale was very good and scoring well on the indices of initiatives and outside contacts, the attached social worker took a critical view. 'It is very hard to get the patients motivated,' he said, 'even though we try to explain that the unit is their home'. The fact that it was still a hospital meant that among other things that 'when people are admitted for short stay, all their drugs are taken away from them; if any person chooses not to wash, the chances are that someone will wash him'.

What did threaten morale was management uncertainty; in a unit reporting 'nothing special' one of the saddest things was to discover a threat of closure, partly because of a reorganisation of hospital resources in the district but also because care in the community was now the priority for planning. Not only did the staff feel threatened, but in a very real way their work was devalued.

SOME RESIDENTS' POINTS OF VIEW

Although in many units they were referred to as patients, perhaps indeed in most of them, the term 'resident' helps to emphasise that they were essentially in the same situation as anyone else in residential care. Several individual younger disabled unit residents have already been quoted in previous chapters, but some further accounts of a similar kind help to clarify their view of the various aspects of the units' work: committed long-term care, planned short stay, rehabilitation, crisis admission and terminal care.

Committed long-term care

Three women in late middle life were all admitted to their respective units in the mid-1970s when the units were still new. One of them had become a wheelchair user six years after she developed multiple sclerosis; six years later still, she suffered a severe but temporary complication. While she was in hospital her husband brought another partner into their home. She could have gone to stay with another member of her family but a few months later accepted a place in a group 2 younger disabled unit instead. Her initial reaction was that it was 'the biggest dump on God's earth', accommodating people with whom she would never ordinarily have mixed. But she learned to adapt and in fact used the unit as a base for all sorts of activities, amongst other things becoming involved in the work of two voluntary organisations. When I met her, nine years on, she regarded the unit as 'a bit special' and she felt she had definitely gained, especially valuing the freedom from risk. Her appreciation was partly because of previous experience of admission to a geriatric ward, and partly because during her long stay in the unit her upper limbs had slowly become weaker and were now almost useless. Only two-fifths of the people who were in the unit when she first moved in were still alive; there were two fairly recent arrivals but the rest were on short-stay programmes – 'like ships that pass in the night', sometimes (in her view) unsettling and demanding but also bringing new conversation. She had seen a film about independent living which she described as putting 'the fear of God' into some of the residents with its description of a life style which was 'just a dream to them now'. 'We have fun; we have got to have fun', she said.

A second woman had become disabled during childhood by two crippling diseases, and in later life one of her legs had been amputated. She lived with her parents until they died and then on her own for a while, but she was liable to falls and one of them severely damaged the cervical part of her spinal cord. She had to go into hospital as an emergency and was admitted to a group 4 unit soon afterwards. During the first couple of years there she made a very gradual recovery because the paralysis of her arms and legs was incomplete. She would very much have liked to return home but it seems that the available domiciliary services at the time were simply not up to giving her adequate support. After five years in the unit she finally sold her house and decided to spend the proceeds on a series of holidays in interesting places. She used to work in a medical setting and this helped her become as well-informed about the affairs of the unit as any member of staff. She believed that the mental disabilities which were characteristic of so many of her long-term resident companions made it essential that there should be short-term admissions as well, and she welcomed this aspect of the unit's function. In her opinion the new building had many defects of design including an insufficient number of single rooms, but she preferred to live in one of the dormitories herself because, as she put it, she had become used to it, liked the vantage point from her particular corner, and looked forward to welcoming old friends as they shared the dormitory in rotation on their various programmes of regular respite care.

A third woman had become paralysed on one side because of an unusual illness many years ago; although she could walk with a frame she also used an electrically powered wheelchair. Four years later she remarried, and her new husband had multiple sclerosis. For a while they lived in a bungalow specially designed for disabled people but his condition deteriorated and he was given a place in a group 2 younger disabled unit. Living alone, she too had a number of falls and soon accepted an invitation to join him rather than remain separated for what seemed likely to be for ever. The bungalow was given up and they had a pair of rooms to themselves; later they moved into a single room which had been intended for four beds but, because the unit had never been fully staffed, was made into their own bed-sitter. Predictably, her condition stayed the same but his did not, and for the last four years of his life he was profoundly disabled, unable to communicate and finally bedridden before he died. More than anything else she appreciated having been able to be with him throughout his long decline, which she believed would have been almost impossible in their bungalow during those last years, and she still appreciated having help at hand if she felt unwell for any reason or happened to fall, as well as the company the unit provided. But she said there was a troublesome lack of privacy and she believed that the residents were too easily cushioned against difficulty. She had worked out for herself that the best functions for a younger disabled unit were short stay, day care and the capacity to deal with emergencies, and she felt that the units should not be in hospital grounds. Now that she was widowed for the second time, and with gossip about possible closure of the unit which gave a feeling of insecurity, she said she would be willing to have another go at living in her own home and make use of the improvement in community services that had taken place in the ten years since she had become a resident.

A rather younger man had been living for several months in another group 2 unit when I met him. He had multiple sclerosis and had to use a wheelchair, and told me that he and his wife had been having endless 'trouble' and arguments at home. Their social worker first offered day care at a Cheshire Home but this did not appeal to him, so the next move was to try to fix up admission to the local younger disabled unit and one day they all went to visit it for an hour or two. Then some time later when the unit's sister telephoned to offer him a place he jumped at the chance, to use his own words. He was still pleased to be away from all the arguments but admitted that he missed his home very much, not to mention the job he used to hold. He liked the unit because the people were 'nice, sensible, you can talk to them' – unlike some of the 'bad cases' he had encountered during previous periods of short stay at a Cheshire Home. But he also said that life in the unit meant not doing anything constructive, although there were books to read and a volunteer art instructor came along twice a month. The residents had individual freedom to go shopping, and the shops and the public house were close. In his own words again, 'it is a way of life; it works; if you haven't been anywhere else you don't know'.

Rehabilitation

Three men in different units illustrate quite different aspects of rehabilitation. One was in his thirties and had had a fairly high spinal cord injury (C5/6) nearly nine years previously. After a year at a spinal injuries unit he went to live with his parents; he said they managed after a fashion but they were not 'getting any life', that tensions resulted, and that there were also problems with the unpunctuality of nurses. (He still needed manual removal of faeces and, lying on a sheepskin and an ordinary mattress, to be turned once each night.) He came to the group 3 unit initially for a short stay, after two episodes of which he was offered a place so that a new home could be found for him, where he might be looked after by Community Service Volunteers. That was two years ago; unfortunately the proposed home had not yet even been built but he was still counting on it. He said he would prefer the privacy, having his own telephone, and losing the company of fellow residents who in his view simply 'sat there doing nothing', and he added that he would not have stayed in the unit if he had not had a single room.

The second man was rather older and had suffered a fairly recent head injury, with an enormous visible defect in his skull and apparently a large part of the left side of his brain having been destroyed. At a case conference in a group 4 unit he had been described as sensitive to noise, ruling the roost in the day room and liable to try to attack people when he was annoyed; before his injury he was thought to have been rather rough in his chosen way of life. That is as may be: at the time I spoke to him Sister had wanted him to go to his room and he had been refusing. She had eventually got him there by telling him that there was a doctor who wanted to talk to him. In this situation I found him a pleasant enough character, frustrated by an uncontrollable speech defect which caused him frequently to lapse into nonsensical jargon, but able to write lucidly and clearly in the left-hand part of a piece of paper. He was previously left-handed, he told me, and had plenty of insight into his predicament, but just at that point his future was quite uncertain.

The third of them was the oldest; he had a degenerative disease of the nervous system which caused unsteady movements and partial paralysis, and his eyesight was poor too. He had been in a group 2 unit for a number of weeks but usually lived in a bungalow on his own. The staff hoped he would soon be going back there after some minor adjustments had been made. Meanwhile, for him the younger disabled unit was 'great, like a home from home; they'll let you lie in and go to bed when you like, and you've no worries; if you do wet the bed, just phone and they'll change it. Some good lads come in every six months and they are proper easy to get on with; the physios have done a marvellous job and the nurses are champion; we have a laugh, and we've been out to the pub'. Perhaps this was the easier sort of rehabilitation.

Planned short stay

A man with rheumatoid arthritis was spending a few weeks in a group 2 unit while his wife was having a surgical operation in the same hospital. Recently he had become an honorary officer in a newly-formed local disablement group; this and his involvement in a branch of local government, not to mention his own disability, had given him a good deal of insight into the opportunities and limitations of disabled living. He said that the unit had quite a good local reputation but after a month living in it he had become quite sure that many of the residents were capable of doing more for themselves and had simply got used to being waited on. As he put it succinctly: 'you need to push but you need the skill and experience to know how far to go'. But he certainly appreciated the help he had received during this short period and would welcome the idea that more people might be helped by more readily available periods of rehabilitation and short stay.

Three people in one of the two group 5 units briefly gave me their particular views of planned short stay. For several years a man with severe tetraplegia (C4) had been on a programme of one day a week and one night a week – that is, three days at the unit in all. He believed that this had preserved his marriage (which had taken place after he had become disabled) and had helped him to find ways of productively occupying himself, because the unit was expertly staffed and well equipped. An older woman with multiple sclerosis kept to a similar schedule; she lived with her daughter who had given up nursing in order to do the caring, apparently because she (the mother) had quite frequent drop attacks of some kind. She, too, liked the arrangement but had an uneasy conscience about what she saw as sacrifice on the part of her daughter. The third person was similarly disabled and was spending a fortnight in the unit while her husband was away on holiday. She said she usually came in twice a year but did not at all look forward to it; she also said that relations at home were strained and her husband had to do most of the caring since the community services were not as helpful as she thought they might have been.

Crises

Ideally the Health Service units should be able to respond to crises in severely disabled persons' lives. One such was presented by a woman in her late fifties with a paraplegic form of multiple sclerosis; she lived in a disabled person's bungalow and had been admitted a few weeks before I saw her, because of an influenzal illness. As a result she had lost some of her ability to transfer from bed to chair; the staff believed she was trying to find reasons for not being discharged, but she was anxious to tell me that she valued her independence and very much liked being at home. The unit was in an adapted ward, not purpose built, so her home was almost certainly a pleasanter environment, but she was clearly afraid of her very slowly increasing vulnerability. There was every intention that she should go home again but at that particular moment the difficulties had not fully been resolved.

An ex-nurse with a similar history of slowly progressive tetraplegia had battled over the years for her independence and had received a fair amount of support to this end. In the recent past it had, however, been necessary to amputate both her legs because of gangrene. She used to live alone in a specially built flat with a special bed and lifting equipment, an electric typewriter, a full environmental control system, friends who visited regularly and did a lot to help, and a cat. She was, however, rather dangerously dependent on the statutory services and there was no care attendant scheme in the neighbourhood. She was only too well aware of the relentless progress of her disability and dreaded the time when she could no longer use her upper limbs and no longer live in her own home. Matters came to a head when a brief admission to hospital resulted in a pressure sore; she was nevertheless sent back home but the pressure sore expanded almost explosively. A bed was available in a group 3 younger disabled unit nearby, where she went with her cat and a certain amount of grim resignation; she disliked the enforced community living and often felt critical of the care she received. The sore never showed much sign of healing and she did not want treatment which would still further limit her freedom. Her mother and numerous friends were regular visitors and she had to accept, though she never had a chance to confirm, that she could not have found better care anywhere else. She continued to live in the unit for twelve months until she died.

Terminal care

That last personal story is also an example of terminal care, and another one is provided by a woman in her early sixties who had motor neurone disease. She had previously lived alone in a first floor flat which was only accessible by stairs, but because of her increasing weakness she had been helped by a local councillor to find a warden-serviced flat at ground level which was close to one of her daughters. Then two things happened, within months: she found rapidly increasing difficulty in transferring from one chair to another, and her daughter left the neighbourhood. She now felt stranded and isolated and had made up her mind to accept care in a geriatric ward but was surprised and delighted when a group 3 younger disabled unit offered her a place instead. Her sons and daughters had understandable reasons for not being able to take her into any of their homes and she was terrified at the thought of going back to her flat. When she learned that her place at the unit was secure she was contented as she could be under the circumstances; her family visited regularly and often helped with her care, expressing their warm appreciation after her death just a year later.

RESIDENTS WITH DISTURBANCES OF CONSCIOUSNESS OR BEHAVIOUR

Many units accommodate people with permanently impaired consciousness, either on a committed long-term basis or as a form of terminal care; when oblivion is complete, the rather unpleasant term 'persistent vegetative state' is sometimes used. People like this very often have to receive their food by artificial means, either by nasogastric tube as in the case of one of the young men with head injury described in Chapter 3, or by a direct opening into the stomach (gastrostomy). Others are still capable of being fed by mouth, as in the case of a young woman whose progressive disease had caused her to become deaf, blind and bedfast. Unit policies vary with such people; many will not admit them, believing that they can be just as well cared for in an ordinary hospital or geriatric ward. Medical decisions, such as whether in any case to feed artificially in such circumstances, are also far from uniform.

Disturbed behaviour is another issue about which units' admission policies are not all the same. Attracted by the opportunities of helping people towards recovery and no doubt also responding to external pressures, units with a policy of admitting people with brain injury often find that they have very difficult problems of compatibility among the resident community. Such people are often noisy and freely produce verbal abuse; if and when their physical disabilities improve to the extent that they can walk about freely, they can and do occasionally attack defenceless paralysed residents without provocation. A general practitioner attached to one unit believed that to mix people in this way was wrong; a brief scene one afternoon in a group 4 unit was literally disquieting, with two or three very noisy residents in the day room and another lying on a corridor floor yelling for help.

Difficult relationships, of course, are not only caused by injury to the brain, and when they involve people whose disabilities are caused only by spinal injury this is clearly the case. Most usually there is a straightforward clash of interests between resident and staff, often coupled with a resident's persistent anger and resentment about the predicament in which he or she has been placed. From the staff's point of view the result can show itself in such ways as asking unnecessarily for help, refusing to co-operate with attempts at increasing the resident's independence, and social and emotional withdrawal. Accounts of what has gone wrong can, however, differ quite widely depending on whether they come from resident or staff.

One very common problem is the combination of apparent apathy and diminishing social awareness which is particularly frequent in advanced multiple sclerosis, and may indeed be the main reason why the unit's help has been sought. For example, the sister in charge of one of the group 5 units, where all the residents were on short stay programmes and spent most of their time in their own homes, commented on how many of the people with multiple sclerosis were like this in comparison with the others. On the other hand similar features can be produced by depression and also by long-term residence – the institutional neurosis described by Barton (1959) – and another sister said that it was only if one started going out with long-term residents that their loss of social skills became apparent, the hospital having long since taken over every detail of their thinking.

DID THE LONG-TERM RESIDENTS NEED TO BE WHERE THEY WERE?

Members of staff were asked a written question about residents who might have been better looked after elsewhere. Some of the personal stories certainly indicate that there were such people, as do the impressions briefly described in Chapter 4. Apart from those who were on planned short-stay programmes, on average more than six residents in each of the group 4 units were expected to return home but the equivalent figure was less than two in groups 1, 2 and 3. Senior staff also considered that there were other residents who could go out to a private household or a residential home and that at least half of them would benefit from such a change; the average was about two in each category except for group 3 in which it was thought that, on average, six residents per unit could live in private households and four in residential homes. From one unit to another, however, there was such a wide variation in these estimates that fairly uninformed guesses must have been made – reflecting, no doubt, the inherent difficulty of answering such a question honestly, and also different value judgements about the relative importance of a unit's turnover and of the residents' security, opportunities, and exposure to risk.

CONCLUSIONS

Born out of good intentions, the younger disabled units have suffered from many difficulties which reflect those of the National Health Service generally. The inherited old institutions were too few and too unevenly distributed to form the basis of a comprehensive service, and the living environments which their buildings provide have long since ceased to be acceptable for committed residential care. Prior to 1970, new initiatives were nearly all second-best developments making do with other existing buildings. Then there was a modest, rather sudden injection of new capital with built-in revenue consequences; the result was a rapid implementation of a concept dating from the early 1960s, which has had limited opportunities to develop further, and only in a couple of regions was the initiative even modestly maintained.

With a pattern of regional strategies which represented varying degrees of interest, and uncertainty rather than clarity of thought, the new units were first influenced mainly by current geriatric practice and the idealism of the Cheshire Homes. They were, however, soon outpaced by developments in social work, community care, and the growing number of disabled people's consumer groups. They were also conceived in isolation from mainstream medicine and rehabilitation, yet found themselves insufficiently detached from hospital administration. Unable to relate adequately to the world outside and incapable of establishing their identity within the hospitals to which they belonged, some of them were destined for disillusionment.

While many units stuck to the early principles through conviction, inertia, or inability to change, others sought refuge in pursuing opportunities to discharge their residents and reduce their commitment to long-term care. Essentially there were two patterns: to join forces with the community services in offering programmes of planned short stay, and to move into the field of medical rehabilitation. At least to the extent that they helped many more people, these newer policies soon became popular. Short-stay programmes varied considerably in the extent to which they were developed, no doubt reflecting the varied convictions of the staff. Other forms of increased turnover were adopted because there were staff available who were well trained and enthusiastic about rehabilitation, or a deficiency of rehabilitation services in the district, or simply disinterest in long-term care. To help the process some units also grasped the nettle of moving long-term residents elsewhere, to geriatric wards or to old people's homes.

The complex, dispersed management responsibilities of the Health Service units allowed the hospital consultants considerable potential for influencing their policies. Whether they did so or not depended much more on the time they could make available than on their specialties. Without this interest the prime responsibity could pass to a senior nurse, a therapist or an attached general practitioner, although the happiest units always managed to evolve some sort of multidisciplinary consensus. Whatever the units' policies might be, however, the nurses all faced similar problems of being understood by their hospital colleagues, and of staffing levels, emotional strain, inadequate conventional training and maintaining morale. The almost universal preparation of meals outside the units, and the accountability of domestic and maintenance staff to senior officers else-where, added to the difficulties of management.

In summary, the younger disabled units in reality have become very different from the paternalistic idealism that led to their existence: severely disabled people who 'still retain active minds', for whom the units were in the first place apparently intended, have always been more likely to secure adequate care in their own homes than those who are less able or inclined to take initiatives themselves. Improvements in community care in the 1970s and 1980s have increased that likelihood considerably, and the residential care need is for the less independent-minded and socially capable. A long-stay community made up of only the most severely physically, mentally and socially disabled is, however, likely to present a daunting task, which the residential homes resist by imposing strict admission criteria. Most of the Health Service units, to their credit, do more or less accept the responsibility, and in many cases it is in effect a form of terminal care. Both with staff and at least a few of the more thoughtful residents, however, a very strong view has emerged that mixing this commitment with other activities is not only the most satisfying option for the staff but also probably the only widely acceptable one for the future. In so doing, the units would be copying developments in the mental illness, mental handicap and geriatric services, but at present most of them lack the integration with disability services generally which such a concept requires.

8

Decision-making in the individual case

Underlying all the evidence set out so far, and almost as important as the facts about disabilities and their associated psychological and social tensions, is the way in which each disabled person is advised and decides upon or consents to a particular form of continuing care. Comparable situations are familiar in clinical medicine; individual decisions about medical investigation and treatment can have far-reaching consequences because of their built-in cost, the precedents that may be set, and the consequences for people's lives. Simply on economic and service provision grounds, let alone the more far-reaching issues of autonomy, independence and the quality of life, such decisions can hardly be made lightly. Brearley and his colleagues (1980) have reviewed many relevant factors, but their account is very much from the perspective of social work and has little to say about physical disability. In the medical and health care literature, remarkably little has been written. 'Cannot be expected to manage at home' and 'can no longer be cared for at home' are among several statements about disabled people which are regularly made and are easy to make, but they conceal an infinite variety of disabilities, personal circumstances, value judgements, professional competence and personal aspirations.

This chapter is an attempt to examine some of the relevant issues, principally in relation to committed residential care; it is based on ordinary personal experience in clinical practice, and not on formally conducted research. Because this experience has been very nearly confined to disabled people of early middle age and above, the account has a corresponding bias; in particular the needs of very young adults, especially school-leavers about whom there is so much current concern, are not given special consideration. It is argued, however, that the principles are applicable to people of all ages whose disabilities are severe enough for residential care to be considered, not only when it is just an option but also when it is an apparent necessity. The argument is directed principally towards professional people, especially social workers and doctors who so often assume (or are forced to receive) the decision-making responsibility, but its implications are clearly of the greatest importance to people with severe disabilities and their carers who wish to be anything other than passive recipients of other people's decisions.

THE CLIMATE OF OPINION

Individual decisions, of course, generate demand for particular resources and so help to influence what is provided, but provision also generates demand and therefore influences individual decisions. The available data from the United Kingdom (Figure 4.1, Chapter 4) suggest that in several regions significantly different levels of residential care for younger disabled people are considered suitable for support by the health and social services. Most of these special resources were established because of protests about the accommodation of young people in geriatric and psychiatric hospital wards, but the fact that they had come into existence almost certainly created a climate of opinion which persuaded some people into accepting committed residential care when they could have kept going in their own homes. In the geriatric context itself, Britain has until quite recently provided about one-third the amount of institutional care for elderly people in relation to its population, in comparison with countries such as the USA, Canada, the Netherlands, Sweden and Australia, with a corresponding relationship to the provision of community services and to demand.

The climate of opinion is, however, not just a national matter; each local community has one of its own, whether that community is a city or town, an urban or a rural district, a public service department, a hospital or even an individual hospital ward. Locally available resources and the local climate of opinion mutually influence each other and form the inevitable background to individual personal decisions and choice. It is one thing for people with severe disabilities to live in their own homes when institutional places are of poor quality and few, or if members of the community services and professions all share with determined enthusiasm the view that living at home is always to be encouraged and supported; it is quite another thing, even if a fair number of resources is available to a private household, when there are places to spare in institutions and everyone is convinced that the institutional way of life is preferable to the stresses and hazards of community care. Many professionals have experienced the ward or establishment where taking a protective line, giving priority to safety and security, results in decisions which would have been quite different in another establishment which believed in striving for attainment, the importance of individual responsibility and the justifiability of risk.

PARTICIPATION AND CHOICE

As already explained, the perspective of this chapter is that of a professional person looking into each set of personal circumstances from outside, but also involved in the personal decisions that have to be made. The involvement may range from very little to assuming the major responsibility, and provided it has been requested it is perfectly appropriate. As professionals we must never forget that our roles are to advise, act as advocates and if necessary persuade, not to organise people for our own convenience because our apparent authority and their defencelessness allow us to do so. There is a complication, however: frequently we are the custodians of the resources about which we have to give advice; we are still obliged to deploy those resources in ways which we believe are best for the whole community we serve. This is the background against which the individual customer's right to participate fully and to exercise choice has to take place.

It must be clearly understood that pressure from residential care is at least as likely to come from the informal carers, close family members especially, as from disabled people themselves. The usual professional experience is that it is the carers' choice and their rights to independence and freedom, or their evident lack of capabilities, which are the immediate issues to be considered rather than the wishes and capabilities of the dependent person.

Published studies such as those of Sandford (1975), Jones and Vetter (1984), Cantrell, Dawson and Glastonbury (1985) and Briggs and Oliver (1985) show the difficulties which carers experience and the significance of family ties. Problems such as disturbed nights, constant surveillance, hard physical work, unsociable behaviour and faecal incontinence are especially hard to manage, but just as important is the infinite variety of individual and family responses to stress which enables some people to tolerate and even enjoy managing some predicaments which others find untenable or even abhorrent. There is also the apprehension about problems which have never been encountered before, as with a new disability which has arisen during a stay in hospital; families can be understandably reluctant to take on totally unfamiliar responsibilities which they can see from the outset will be intensely demanding.

There are other factors, besides the preoccupations of carers and the climate of opinion, which undermine the principle that severely disabled people should be able to choose where and how they live their lives. A very important one is their frequent inability to be articulate enough to put their own case, for which there may be a variety of explanations; one reason is that they may be unskilled in doing any such thing, and another is that they may have very low expectations and be quite unaware what the available or possible options are. They may also find that they are expected or obliged to make far-reaching decisions at times of crisis, when the recent and rapid development of shattering events has left them bewildered, frightened and desperate. For some, their disabling conditions may have taken away their ability to communicate, either partially or, most tragically of all, completely. Quite a different factor is that a few individuals may choose an expensive and scarce resource when their needs are evidently less than those of others who might consequently have to go without.

For one reason or another, therefore, a number of different parties and interests are usually involved in each individual case. The professionals' share includes listening carefully to what each participant has to say, helping to sort out the relevant issues, and giving advice and encouragement when they are wanted. On the other hand, many people with disabilities also enter residential care because of a simple arrangement between themselves and their families with the proprietors or managers of privately owned homes. Most such people are elderly and relatively few younger people seem to have been involved, but this practice seriously challenges both the 'fair' allocation of resources and also the professionals' role. The conventional view remains that, given the potentially far-reaching implications of the decisions that have to be made, professional involvement is the more desirable practice. For better or worse, it is still the conventional practice, too, and decision-making along these lines may need to be repeated several times during the life of a severely disabled person, as needs change and new opportunities arise.

The particular issue of entering residential care may be raised when the person concerned is living in his or her own home or is already in hospital or residential care, and either at a time of crisis or when there is no need for urgent action. Each of the four consequent circumstances demands a somewhat different approach, but the process itself can be divided essentially into three parts: establishing the relevant facts, accommodating value judgements, and ensuring that the best decisions are made.

FOUR CIRCUMSTANCES IN WHICH IMPORTANT DECISIONS MAY HAVE TO BE MADE

Crises among disabled people in their own homes

If a previously able-bodied person has suddenly become disabled without warning as, for example, because of injury to the head or spine or because of a stroke, almost always the immediate requirement is medical care and admission to an appropriate hospital unit is the result. On these occasions, medical decision-making is paramount. The more debatable issues surround crises involving people who are living in their own homes and are already disabled; sudden and unexpected deterioration again calls for medical management (though not necessarily admission to hospital), but crises in the arrangements of care and support usually demand a different approach.

The relevant complications or extensions of pre-existing disability include incidental illnesses of any kind, especially pressure sores which can develop with explosive rapidity, and severe illnesses such as pneumonia or infection of the urinary tract. A particularly important crisis is the complete loss of ability to walk, and another can be the complete loss of ability to transfer from a chair; either of these may come about suddenly, for example during a relapse of multiple sclerosis, or as the final slide over a threshold of diminished capacity during a gradually progressive disease. Crises of mental health include acute confusional states and acute episodes of severe depression, events which may themselves be caused by progressive physical deterioration or the gradual increase of frustration and emotional strain.

Problems with care arrangements include a principal carer's sudden illness or even sudden death, or a family complication which means that the carer's services have to be diverted. Sometimes carers themselves reach a critical threshold, perhaps of physical health but more often of a mental or emotional nature or simply fatigue, caused by the responsibilities and tensions of caring which have not received sufficient support and relief. Personal relationships between disabled people and their carers can also deteriorate gradually but not become apparent to others until a crisis is reached. On occasions the caring partner develops a strong emotional relationship with another person; although this can be a support and reinforcement, often it leads to rejection of the disabled person and imperative demands for someone else to take on the commitment to care.

In all these instances urgent action is usually necessary and, if only to prevent a situation becoming even more intolerable, it may mean admission to a hospital or residential home. This particular solution, however, should never be adopted simply because it is the easiest response for professionals to make; the general rule is that whatever the response, it should take account of the uncertainty of the outcome of most crises in the first instance, and should therefore never be irreversible until the uncertainty has, beyond all question, disappeared. Irrevocable decisions made hastily can be bitterly regretted, and they include giving up one's independence and one's own home.

People recently admitted into hospital who present crisis problems of future care

These include some of the suddenly disabled people described in the last section who do not make an adequate recovery, together with those who have developed severe disabilities during their hospital stay. Also included are a few people with long-standing disabilities whose crises of care at home have been relieved by hospital admission. Some members of the group, often regrettably regarded as 'blocking' hospital beds, can be in a very unfortunate position indeed: deprived of the security of their homes, emotionally adrift, their future uncertain, too easily regarded by people outside the hospital as safely cared for, and so often in only partially sympathetic and certainly unsuitable surroundings.

In every case a careful decision-making procedure is essential. The part of the hospital in which the disabled person happens to be may or may not be an appropriate place in which he or she should stay while the process is carried out. If rehabilitation is an important part of the programme, clearly the best environment for that rehabilitation should be sought. In other cases, some sort of interim accommodation may have to be considered while the desired course of action is being set under way, either in a rehabilitation or a residential unit or perhaps back in the disabled person's own home. Choosing the right time for moves of this kind, though sometimes dictated by expediency and the availability of resources, is very much a matter for discussion, experienced judgement and mutual consent. As with crises presenting in private households, it is of the utmost importance that irrevocable decisions are not prematurely made.

A proportion of the group are people whose life expectancy can now be measured only in weeks or months, many of whom are being quite satisfactorily cared for where they are. Sometimes there is pressure to move them on for the convenience of the hospital, or to allow it to meet more pressing demands. Cases such as these regularly appear as statistics when surveys of long-stay patients in short-stay wards are carried out. Often it is best to accept that they should not be moved on, a policy which may also be appropriate for that small number of people who have the severest, multiple disabilities – frequently, it seems, oblivious to all but the most basic aspects of their circumstances and sometimes not even aware of those, whose requirements may be destined never to extend beyond bed-orientated nursing care.

Non-urgent difficulties in disabled people's own homes

This is the group about which there is probably the most controversy; it comprises the people who elect to go into residential care and are willing to join waiting lists to do so. From that definition it follows that their need for residential care is by no means absolute. If a disability is stable, a likely motive is gradual deterioration in the support network. Often there are pressures on a disabled person from others such as the principal carer, other family members, neighbours and friends, and many professionals, too. A potential resident may even be under pressure from a residential home who would like to add him or her to its number; this may be because of an attractive personality and perhaps not too severe a disability, and is especially likely to happen when a unit or home has newly opened.

A perhaps more important group comprises people with progressively severe disability, especially multiple sclerosis, but also other diseases of the nervous system such as muscular dystrophy, motor neurone disease and Huntington's chorea. The downward progression of any of these may be punctuated by a crisis, but the near certain knowledge of future deterioration is a powerful reason for considering residential care before it is strictly necessary. Here the arguments support opposite points of view: on the one hand, people may wish to enter residential care if the opportunity arises, to prevent a future crisis and to avoid disappointment when the need may be very much greater. Residential homes themselves may be anxious to admit residents before their diseases have begun to alter their personalities as well as increasing their disabilities. On the other hand, it may be very unwise to give up the pleasures, privacy and independence of one's own home long before one has to, and to allocate residential care resources which may well be more urgently needed by others, because of fear of a future which may be more uncertain than is realised.

Among the elective decisions in general, therefore, the scope for variations in opinion is great; these are the individual cases whose management can have the most substantial effect on the apparent demand for residential care and who provide the most 'controllable' element in that demand. For the same reason, reconciling their needs and priorities with those of the people who have reached crises in their lives is by no means always straightforward. Nevertheless it cannot be stressed too strongly that if resources are to be used fairly and if disabled people are to get the best deal available, a careful and competent procedure should always be put into operation with decisions of this kind. Sadly, as with the other groups, all too often this is not the case.

Disabled people in residential care for whom a non-urgent move is being considered

In this group the possible reasons for the proposed move include a resident's own wish, the wishes of the resident's family or friends, the view of staff and professionals that the resident could be encouraged to seek a better life elsewhere, or the opinion that a resident is no longer 'appropriate' by virtue of age, increased mental or physical infirmity or any other factor.

To take the last of these first: such an opinion can in fact represent a threat to all the residents of a unit or home, who may well come to the conclusion that if any of them fails to reach an acceptable standard in some way, the staff will resort to the ultimate sanction of eviction. The undesirability of the practice has led the Leonard Cheshire Foundation to emphasise that a Cheshire Home is a home for life, offering complete security from any such threat. In reality, however, there is usually fairly firm opposition; families are usually unwilling to receive someone back home for this kind of reason or are quite incapable of doing so, and hospitals which might once have been counted on to pick up responsibility now widely refuse to oblige. It is probably fair to say that there is now a general view that once in residential care, only very serious crises in a resident's physical or mental condition can justify a compulsory permanent move.

The issue of age is rather more difficult; a home or unit created specially for younger disabled people can justifiably take the view that at a certain age residents should expect to move on. It is an issue over which value judgements may sharply differ, and it arises, of course, from the unwise policy of creating such units and then offering committed residence to people whose life expectancy is likely to be considerable, while declaring no realistic policies for dealing with the consequences. Many would argue that to coerce a move just because of age is unthinkable, but others suggest that what matters most is the place to which transfer is being considered and the way in which the matter is dealt with. Going to a less satisfactory place would be hard to defend, but a move which led to an improvement in opportunities would be another matter. In principle and also in practice, a competent unhurried decision-making procedure, with a resident's full participation, may well lead to a very satisfactory result in the end.

If a resident asks to move, a properly conducted decision-making procedure is again essential. The same applies to requests from family or friends, though sometimes these pressures need to be viewed rather circumspectly because they can be quite at variance with a resident's own wishes. There is some controversy whether reluctant residents should be encouraged to be more independent and leave a residental unit if they can and, if it is agreed that they should, about the degree of encouragement and even pressure that should be applied to them. Some establishments explicitly state that it is not their purpose to stir up people who are happily settled as they are; others may almost regard it as their duty to do so. The officer in charge of one residential home suggested to me that it is the responsibility of a good unit gently to lay a path of opportunity in front of each resident, with discharge into the community, depending on the resident's circumstances, often in the background as a possible goal. This is perhaps the most humane and imaginative approach of all.

ESTABLISHING THE RELEVANT FACTS

The present need for physical help and/or surveillance

Physical help is required for those tasks which an individual is incapable of performing, and there are three aspects to be considered: the carers' need for physical exertion, their need for special skills, and the frequency with which the help has to be provided. *Physical exertion* is mainly involved with tasks such as lifting, pushing a wheelchair, helping a precariously ambulant person upstairs, and the drudgery associated with changing and laundering clothes and bed linen. *Special skills* can usually be learnt by any carer provided that proper instruction is given and a stable, unchanging disability ensures that the skills remain appropriate. The frequency with which help is needed, perhaps best defined in terms of the *independence time* (Cantrell and colleagues, 1985), determines both the amount of help which is required and also the demand likely to be placed upon the principal carer and the network of support generally.

Surveillance, as distinct from physical help, is needed for people who are considered to be at risk either because they are liable to unpredictable accidents such as falls, blackouts, extreme shortness of breath or convulsions, or because aspects of their behaviour are unreliable due to problems such as those of personality, memory, awareness or disinhibition, or because their sheer helplessness makes them worryingly vulnerable to extraneous risk. Here again the independence time is crucially important; frequently it is zero.

With both physical help and surveillance, it is essential to appraise the *anxiety and stress* which carers may experience because of unsociable or intolerable behaviour, or because of apprehensions about risk. Also, regardless of the independence time, key parts of the *daily timetable* have to be established beyond question: getting up, the principal meals, washing and bathing, dealing with bowels and bladder, going to bed, and the need for tasks during normal sleeping hours. The use of specially constructed records of care, an example of which is shown in Figure 8.1, may be a very useful means of displaying and monitoring the facts of a case.

NAME _____ DIAGNOSIS _____

UNIT/ADDRESS _____ DATE _____

TIME	ACTIVITY WHICH CANNOT BE PERFORMED WITHOUT HELP	No. OF HELPERS REQU'D.	PROPORTION OF HOUR TAKEN UP (Block out squares as appropriate) ¼ ½ ¾ 1				EQUIPMENT/ AIDS REQUIRED
0700							
0800							
0900							
1000							
1100							
1200							
1300							
1400							
1500							
1600							
1700							
1800							
1900							
2000							
2100							
2200							
2300							
2400							
0100							
0200							
0300							
0400							
0500							
0600							

TOTAL ACTIVITY TIME
FOR : DAY _____ HOURS
    NIGHT _____ HOURS

MAXIMUM INDEPENDENCE
TIME FOR: DAY _____ HOURS
    NIGHT _____ HOURS

SIGNATURES OF PERSONS MAKING ASSESSMENT: _____ _____

Figure 8.1 *24-hour dependency chart*
Modified from E. Cantrell, J. Dawson and G. Glastonbury, 1985

Changes with the passage of time

These changes have three aspects: the duration or history of the disability at the time of assessment, the outlook or prognosis, and fluctuations in a disabled person's capabilities. Self-evidently, the *history* profoundly affects the perception of both the disabled person and those who are providing the care: a short history, for example, is likely to be associated with acutely felt, profound and unstable emotions, whereas a long history will include an established routine but may also be associated with such features as a well-planned career on the one hand, or weariness, frustration, intolerance and despair on the other.

The *prognosis* is even more important, and here professional skills and experience are especially relevant: the three categories (fixed, unstable and progressive) described in Chapter 3 form a convenient framework for assessment. At the two extremes, for example, the implications of a lifetime of disability are very different from the probability of deterioration and death within less than a year. A particularly common mistake after the sudden onset of severe disability is for premature decisions to be made, before the full implications are understood and discounting many of the possibilities of recovery and rehabilitation. Prognosis, however, can never be completely certain, and particularly with the 'unstable' group a firm prediction can be impossible: under these circumstances it is essential to be aware of the best possible outcome despite the possibility or likelihood that it may not be achieved.

Fluctuations of capability are especially important to appreciate: most individuals experience 'good days and bad days' and many will put on a good performance for one person which they withhold from another. With severe disabilities these fluctuations can mean considerable variation in the help that is required. If professional assessment is limited to a period of a few hours or less, the occasion that has been chosen may not be adequately representative. Listening carefully to everything that others have to report, and repeating the assessments when necessary, are therefore essential parts of the fact-finding process. Periods of formal assessment in an appropriate hospital unit or residential home, in most cases lasting at least a week, may be essential too.

Personal angles

Each disabled person's own point of view is of the greatest importance and requires the most careful understanding. But because living with severe disability involves the help of other people, the opinions of all those who are making significant contributions have also to be taken into account. The informal unpaid care which is the usual component of disabled living in a private household is especially important in this respect: often it devolves upon just one person, the principal carer, whose views can be just as or even more important than those of the person who has the disability. In assessing all the relevant views it is convenient to think of two further aspects for each individual besides the nature of the caring task which has already been outlined: the reaction to the present situation, and desires and aspirations for the future.

In respect of the *present situation* it is essential to distinguish between the *underlying personal relationship* on the one hand, and the *responsibilities and tensions caused by the disability itself* on the other. If the underlying relationship is positive and strong the responsibilities and tensions usually call for appropriate support in the caring task, not substituting an entirely different form of care. One very important factor is the informal carers' own informal support, whether from an extended family, if there is one, or from neighbours or friends. This aspect of the caring relationship is frequently overlooked; its absence can be a powerful reason for involving the formal services and, on occasions, for requesting committed residential care. But it is particularly when relationships are cool or, much worse, antagonistic, because of deep-rooted differences of a personal nature, that alternative care programmes have to be seriously considered.

As far as *desires and aspirations* are concerned it is valuable practice to ask what (given that the nature and course of a given disability is unlikely to respond to further medical treatment) each individual would choose if expense were no object and resources were freely available. Many disabled people will respond with clear, practicable ideas which make decision-making easy; others may say that they do not know and are willing to accept any advice, but even if their ideas are not very coherent, their preferences can give important and helpful guidelines.

The potential for further treatment and rehabilitation

By the time residential care has become a serious option such measures are usually thought to offer no new opportunities, but this conclusion is not necessarily correct. Although further efforts might seem profitless from, say, the point of view of the person or persons who are asking for residential care to be considered, especially if such people are disillusioned by their experience or preoccupied with other problems of day-to-day casework or clinical practice, the potential may seem very different to the disabled person in question or to those who have been or will in future be closely involved in that persons care. In this context professional expertise and judgement are of the greatest importance, including a sound knowledge of all the relevant resources and the likelihood of their being useful; a willingness to try any option, whatever the odds, can often be a most welcome approach.

The use that has been made of special resources for supporting residence in a private household

These resources include *buildings and equipment* and *formal services*, which have been outlined in Chapter 5, and also the use of residential care to provide *respite for carers* as described in Chapters 4 and 7. Committed residential care should hardly ever be considered as an option without also considering the use that has been made of every possible facility of this kind; in most cases, if the resources that are readily obtainable have not been used to the full, the opportunities they present should always be pursued first.

The available resources for residential care

There is little point in settling for the sort of accommodation which does not exist, or if it exists is not likely to be available, so a realistic and up-to-date appraisal of the residential care options is essential if it is agreed that they have to be considered. This involves not just names and addresses but also an understanding of the admission policies and the accommodation and life styles that are offered, together with information about vacancies.

Except for establishments which have been newly opened or whose policies ensure an appreciable turnover of residents, the usual experience is that places cannot immediately be found when they seem to be required – scarcely surprising when small and finite numbers of places are regarded as providing security of tenure, so that most vacancies arise infrequently and unpredictably through death. The common strategy is to settle for inclusion on a waiting list but this has considerable drawbacks, one of which is a likely moratorium on further action of any kind. Waiting lists also encourage early applications in order to avert the risk of failure at a time of crisis; in other words, they generate demand for residential care which may well be entered prematurely as a result. There is much to be said for doing everything possible to avoid them, and one practical method is to be aware of as many different options as possible, advising that the first acceptable one to become available should be pursued.

ACCOMMODATING VALUE JUDGEMENTS

No matter how objective the assessment of a disabled person's situation, certain value judgements are inevitable when a course of action is being decided. Essentially they are in three categories: personal preference, ethical issues, and opinions about priority.

Personal preference is of course an integral part of each disabled person's right to exercise personal choice, but the preferences of carers are very important too. It really is a matter of preference whether to choose living in a busy environment or a quiet retreat, in solitude, a small household, a big community, or an institution large enough to allow anonymity. The same is true of personal responsibility for personal help, cooking and catering, household maintenance and household expenses; of sleeping in company or alone; and of being occupied or constantly idle. Sometimes carers and professionals feel sure that a disabled person's preferences are misguided and should if possible be re-directed, but their own views are in any case likely to have at least some influence on the people they are helping, simply because of the close personal contact. Anyone's preferences may, of course, change as new experiences accumulate, new ideas and opportunities appear, personal circumstances alter, or just with the passage of time.

Ethical issues include such matters as risk, personal obligation and freedom of choice, and ordinary personal experience is enough to show how much individual people may honestly and genuinely differ in their views. In the evaluation of risk, for example, some professionals, and some lay people, too, are horrified by what they see as unacceptable risk which others perceive as a price eminently worth paying in order that a desired object may be achieved. Another is the amount of work which informal carers should be expected to undertake, especially the extent to which reluctant marriage partners should be ex-pected to stay together when, if they were able-bodied, they might well have separated long ago. It is my practice never to recommend that a carer gives up work because of a disabled dependant unless he or she volunteers to do so; similarly I never suggest that a dependant should move to live with another family unless it is an arrangement which has been freely entered into. People with disabilities also have personal obligations, among which is not to place too great a demand on their families and friends, nor even on the people whose services to them are being paid. As already described, some people believe that it is unethical to challenge security of tenure in residential care, whereas others would consider that this can be an essential part of continued reassessment and offering opportunities for choice.

Opinions about priority also cannot depend wholly on objective fact. Given that most residential units have scope for decisions about admission and discharge, for example, some may give priority to responsiveness to demand whereas others will emphasise the comforts of the residents they already have. Many professionals and field workers give priority to demands from private households, whereas others prefer or feel obliged to concentrate on referrals from hospitals. Some people see shortage of resources as a reason to campaign for improvements, whereas others direct their energies to making the best use of the resources they have. Most institutions give priority to their own organisations but vary in the importance they attach to collaboration with others.

The point about all the value judgements is that they are not simply the product of the statistics of disability, nor are they dependent on professional skills. They depend on beliefs which are more fundamental than that; such beliefs can change or be changed, but while they are held they most certainly influence the demand for resources.

ENSURING THE BEST DECISIONS

The precise procedure will depend on the number of different viewpoints to be resolved, on the practical implications of the preferences that are expressed, and on the consequent resource requirement. If a severely disabled person has selected a care option to which nobody objects, which is easy to put into effect and which will not be held up by a shortage of resources, there is likely to be little difficulty in deciding what to do. In all other circumstances it is essential that there should be discussion among all the parties that are interested or may have to be involved, as equal partners whether consumers, professionals or anyone else. In difficult cases the discussions have to be careful, detailed and exhaustive, and may often require that considerable pressures are brought to bear on one party or another.

In seeking to attain these objectives, professionals will no doubt negotiate with one another in the usual way; it is, however, worth making the point that when the issues are at all complex, personal contact face-to-face or by telephone is usually better than relying on communication in writing. As far as contacts between professionals and consumers are concerned, ill-thought-out communications and meetings in unfavourable circumstances may do far more harm than good, and introducing consumers to large conferences of people whom they may not have met before can simply intimidate and provoke antagonism. My own preference is for relaxed discussions in quiet surroundings, on a one-to-one basis or with just a handful of people, on as many occasions and between as many different groups as are necessary, certainly before major decision-making meetings are held and very often so as to avoid the need for them altogether. Nevertheless, more formal multidisciplinary teamwork is now, or at least by now should be, an essential part of rehabilitation, discharge from hospital, and arranging the details of residential or community care.

Eventually, when all the issues have been brought together and a consensus is emerging, it is crucial to ensure that the chosen course of action is compatible with what can be provided. Broken promises are all too frequent in this field when, in order to reach a quick solution, vulnerable people are assured of resources that cannot be guaranteed. If a waiting list is inevitable, it is essential to appreciate fully what that implies. If community resources are not apparently available and the consensus is that they should be, a resolve to campaign and not accept the restrictions (which often turn out to be unnecessary) can be equally desirable. Very often there is reasonable doubt about the best course of action and then it may be advisable to pursue more than one goal simultaneously, leaving the final decision until the last possible moment or until the issues have resolved themselves further so that the best course of action has after all become apparent.

A very important task which, in Britain, is hardly being seriously tackled anywhere at the present time, is to review all the demands for committed residential care in a particular locality, and to reconcile them with available places. Figure 8.2 outlines a flow pattern of

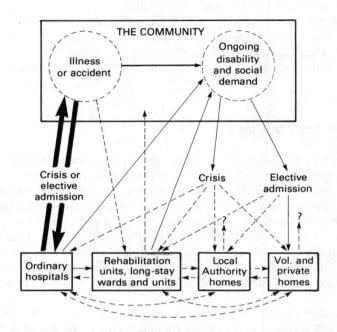

Figure 8.2   *Diagram of competing pressures for admission*

demand for admission to ordinary hospitals and the three residential care sectors, and the points it chiefly makes are as follows. Pressures for admission on account of acute illness or accident, or for elective medical treatment, hugely exceed demands because of continuing disability. A very small proportion of people admitted as emergencies to hospital subsequently acquire continuing disability but this is not readily predictable at the time of admission. Ordinary hospitals, however, feel obliged to keep up their turnover; if, meanwhile, the existing residential facilities are steadily being filled because of social crisis or by elective arrangements, tensions will occur between them and the hospitals. Sometimes these provoke unwise discharge from the hospitals back to private households so that the tensions are transferred back there. Conversely, failure to meet genuine social need can result in its being presented as a demand for medical care. In some measure the tensions and difficulties are inevitable, but without some attempt to relate the key decisions to one another the problems will be unnecessarily increased.

The necessary personal contacts, discussions and reviews of available options may take quite a time but at the end of it all, either a consensus has to emerge or someone – perhaps a professional – has to possess the skills and to be delegated the leadership to conduct a fair hearing and establish an acceptable outcome. In Chapter 4 it has been shown that hospital consultants, chairpersons of management committees and social workers are among those who most commonly take responsibility for decisions about admission to residential care. On the other hand arrangements can sometimes shift quite informally, as first one and then another member of a group seems to assume ultimate responsibility.

At its worst the leadership role becomes dictatorial, with all the other parties believing that they have to accept whatever judgement is made: doctors, and especially hospital doctors, have a particularly unfortunate record in this respect. Not to mention the risk that the disabled person will be allowed no say in the matter, there are other risks too: to avoid the emotional strain and hard work of doing the job properly, autocratic decision-makers can be quite disinterested in the personal consequences of their decisions, or they may give in too easily to pressures which are not necessarily the most appropriate. It can, undoubtedly, be much easier to settle for residential care, including the lack of action which usually follows acceptance on to a waiting list, rather than the considerable effort often needed to persist with care and support in a private household.

If and when a decision in favour of admission to committed residential care is reached, the staff (and, if it is the usual practice, the residents) of the chosen unit or home should always be involved and should understand the reasons for the decision. If they have not already done so in the course of the decision-making process, it can be a very useful practice for a few of them to visit the future resident beforehand, to break the ice and to find out something at first hand about his or her personal background. The disabled person should also have a chance to visit the home or unit and meet at least some of the residents and staff, having sufficient time to do the job properly; a quick visit for an hour or so is quite inadequate and a trial period of several weeks, which many residential homes require, is probably a sound arrangement. It must be recognised, however, that the purpose of this period is mainly so that the would-be resident may approve of the home and not, as too often, so that the home may approve of the would-be resident. This whole process is, of course, much more meaningful if the disabled person has an alternative place of residence if the first option proves unacceptable. Regrettably, however, there is usually no immediate alternative, a situation which may well be unavoidable but seriously undermines the principle of choice.

Finally, whatever course of action is adopted, once it is decided upon and put into operation it must be followed up by the professional people who have been involved. One particular person among them may well be chosen as a key worker with delegated responsibility for this task. It is certainly not good enough to plan and implement discharge from hospital or admission to committed residential care, and then withdraw completely; to be fully informed about the outcome is both educational for the professionals and essential for the well-being of the disabled person. What is more debatable is how long the follow-up exercise should be continued; common practice is to discontinue it quite soon, and whereas the logical extreme is to extend it indefinitely, simple practicalities may well set unavoidable time limits. This is another matter on which individual judgements have to be made.

THREE INDIVIDUAL EXAMPLES

The following accounts demonstrate three particular aspects of the issues that have been raised in this chapter: differing professional opinions, an almost unanswerable case for residential care, and family tensions which remain unresolved. Details of the decision-making procedures are not described; instead, the impact on each disabled person is outlined from the viewpoint of one professional person who happened to share some of the responsibilities.

A single woman in her sixties had been disabled by rheumatoid arthritis for many years but had lived on her own without too much difficulty. Because of increasing pain in her left hip she was admitted to hospital for the joint to be replaced, but the operation went wrong and she had to have the hip disarticulated and the artificial joint removed (Girdlestone's operation). Progress was further complicated by septic arthritis which made her very ill for several months and she ended much weaker than she had been before, with a fixed knee and consequent ramrod left leg which had no proper joint at the hip. A long-term geriatric bed was requested. The thought appalled her and instead, after about a year, she went to a rehabilitation unit for six months. At the end of that time she was considered unfit to go home and a geriatric bed was again requested.

Against her will and at the age of 69, she was transferred. In the ward she was thought to be potentially much more able than the long-stay residents, not least because of her mental competence and motivation to be at home again. A new physiotherapy team showed that she could after all be independent enough to manage the basic activities of daily living at home if her seating was at the correct height, and to move about her room with a special frame rather than the wheelchair which the rehabilitation unit had thought would be necessary at all times. Help was enlisted from community nurses to get her up in the morning and put her to bed at night, and to support them (and help monitor her progress) she was booked into hospital for three nights each week. Had the community services been better staffed this extra precaution would not have been necessary – but the system worked. She accepted it as the best compromise she could get.

A year or so later, however, the community services had improved as part of a deliberate joint policy of the health and social services. She no longer needed to come to hospital and the arrangement was terminated; there were no great difficulties afterwards although contact was maintained by one member of the hospital staff. Just over a year later I visited her in her ordinary (though quite spacious) Victorian terrace house; it had few adaptations, and she managed in her own way with a combination of chair, telephone, bed, the walking frame, and a 'chemical toilet' with a special lifting seat. Friends visited her regularly and helped with her meals: she enjoyed herself with books, magazines, radio and television and was entirely content, and her visitors were equally convinced that her home was the right place for her. That was three years after the shared-care arrangement had started, nearly five years after the professionals had first declared that residential care was her only option.

A man of 42 quite suddenly and spontaneously developed spastic paraplegia which was severe but not complete, accompanied by some weakness and loss of sensation in his hands and arms. A few years previously his elderly mother had come to the city from rural Ireland to live with him because his father had died. A medical consultant requested committed care in a newly opened younger disabled unit but it was not necessary; the disability did not worsen, and mother and son were able to manage in their modern flat perfectly well.

Five years later the old lady died quite unexpectedly and this time the family doctor asked for residential care. The request was refused, and before there was time to think of an alternative plan a sister came to the rescue, taking her paralysed brother to live with her and her family in their rather small house. They all got on well together and he was very well treated, but there were six of them and the accommodation was undesirably cramped. His disability, it seemed, had not changed at all. A social service team became closely involved, secured a ground floor flat which had been specially adapted by a housing association, encouraged him to be as independent as possible, and settled him in there – about seven years after he had first become paralysed.

For just under a year, all went well. It was very much a bachelor flat, sparsely furnished and decorated, but he contented himself with television, cigarettes and a bit of self-catering, and he was adequately supported by the statutory services. Then there was a catastrophe: he had a sudden haemorrhage from his stomach and was obliged to go into hospital where he stayed for about two months. By the time he got back home, for one reason or another he was very much less able: his legs would no longer straighten, his arms and hands were weaker, and he was in difficulties with constipation and abdominal pain. This time a younger disabled unit took him in.

After admission he scarcely responded to rehabilitation. There was not much doubt about the increase in his disability, and recurrent pain was a significant factor for a time. Most important of all however, he made it quite plain that he did not want to live on his own any more. His sister said she felt the family had done enough, and the professionals were inclined to agree with her. So he remained in the unit for a year, contented enough and in relatively good health, until a place was found for him in a residential home for younger disabled people. He was then aged 53; a year later, just a few weeks before this account was written, he had a sudden severe attack of breathlessness and died within a few days.

A couple in their thirties had always enjoyed a close, happy relationship even though the husband had developed multiple sclerosis only a few years after they were married. After the diagnosis had been confirmed they sought little in the way of medical help. They already had children and went on to add to the family during the next few years. They had few close relations otherwise, all their parents having died, but they received a certain amount of support from the members of a church community to which they both belonged.

Unfortunately, the multiple sclerosis progressed so that the husband first became unemployed, then housebound unless anyone took him out, and then an obligatory wheelchair user. Statutory support from one quarter was good; the occupational therapist of the social services department saw to it that their roomy Victorian house had adequate car parking space, ramped access, and accessible and usable toilet facilities. He had his bedroom downstairs and the rest of the family were upstairs. Offers of places at the local day centre, and of respite care at a Health Service unit were declined; the family unit was self-sufficient and they could make their own entertainments.

The worsening of his condition continued. There was trouble with incontinence; his speech became more indistinct; he was plagued by recurrent bouts of severe neuralgia; he became very depressed and his wife wondered whether his personality had begun to change. Inevitably, most of her time and attention was taken up with her children, and he began to feel out of it all, wondering if he would be better in residential care. She said she had never thought it would come to this, but if that was what he wanted he had better go. His family doctor considered that committed care was required; so did his social worker, and a formal request was submitted.

But the 'solution' was not going to be as easy as that, for several different reasons. The social worker thought he was too disabled for a local authority home. The nearest Health Service unit had declared a policy of discouraging (if not active disengagement from) committed residential care. Senior staff of the nearest Cheshire Home regarded the application with great sympathy, but in the end felt that another applicant had a greater need. Some professionals believed that, far from acceding to the request, real efforts should be made to relieve the pain and depression, support the overworked wife, and keep the family together.

Clearly the statutory services would have to do more and, as ever, while some of them were deficient many of them worked well: weekly attendance at a rehabilitation unit, fortnightly weekends spent in the local hospital unit, more nursing input, a better bed, invaluable support and friendship from a care attendant scheme, and a nursery school for the youngest children. The downward trend was arrested, at least for a while; the neuralgic pain suddenly ceased, the depression partially lifted, and the new contacts provided new friends. But the family unhappiness did not disappear and everyone remained somewhat uneasy. Next (and this was the first time it had happened), all the professionals met together in a partly successful attempt to resolve the differences in their own value judgements so that the couple could receive more consistent encouragement and help – although they themselves did not participate and this upset them. Increasing the weekends in the hospital unit from once a fortnight to once a week seemed to provide a satisfactory outcome.

Because multiple sclerosis is both unpredictable and progressive, even this was no more than a temporary arrangement, and at best there could only be contingency plans for what might happen in the future. There can be no 'correct' course of action in cases such as this, yet the way in which they are tackled can have far-reaching implications.

CONCLUSIONS

The demand by people with severe disabilities for each particular form of continuing care is based not only on the prevalence of the disabilities themselves, but also on expectations and the climate of opinion generally; these factors are, however, in turn influenced by what has already been provided. In other words there is a circular process whereby, at least within limits, supply and demand reinforce one another. In principle, disabled people should be able to choose what best suits them, but in practice very many constraints prevent freedom of choice and often prevent choice altogether. Some have persuasively and correctly stood up for their rights which all too frequently have been overlooked or discounted, but others may perhaps be required not to use limited resources extravagantly nor to abuse the services of their informal carers.

There are certain recognisable occasions when residential care may well become a reasonable option if not an apparent necessity. They include sudden deterioration of health, and also the breach of the threshold of a carer's tolerance in the course of a slowly worsening condition, examples being the onset of faecal incontinence, final arrival at complete wheelchair dependency, or yet another changed behaviour pattern on top of others which the carer has found hard to bear. On such occasions the available services should provide effective help as an urgent necessity if they are not to be resented and mistrusted in the future. Similar problems present themselves when a person with a new disability cannot return home from an ordinary hospital – because of social isolation, family resistance, lack of family resources or a general consensus of opinion.

Decisions can be more deliberate when there are no immediate pressures. In some ways therefore they are easier, although the art of timing them appropriately is not easy to learn.

One instance would be a premature decision to accept residential care which could lead to unnecessary restriction of a disabled person's freedom besides misuse of an expensive resource. A wrongly postponed decision, on the other hand, can also restrict personal opportunities besides risking an unnecessary crisis at some time in the future.

Whatever decision is being made, it should go without saying that professional advisers should seek all the relevant facts. To ensure competence, comprehensive check-lists can be very helpful; they should include the exact nature of the immediate problem or problems, the sequence of events which has led up to the current situation, a careful assessment of the disabled person's abilities and limitations, the requirements placed upon the principal carers, the advice and help that has already been given, the likely outlook, and the disabled person's wishes and aspirations. It is also essential that all the possible options are known, and their limitations and availability understood. Value judgements will sometimes be inevitable; they include personal preferences, ethical issues and opinions about priorities. Appropriate decisions, however, must also depend on full awareness of overall demand for the resources in question.

Correct procedures always include full opportunities for the people with disabilities and their carers to describe their difficulties, fears, achievements and aspirations. The manner in which this is done, and the circumstances in which it takes place, are both of the greatest importance; my personal practice is to ask the consumers, on the assumption that the disabilities are not going to diminish, what ideal arrangement they would choose for themselves, and to allow plenty of undisturbed time to discuss their answers. No decisions should be made without consulting all the interested parties; the procedure can be quite important and designated leadership may be necessary, who may be the disabled person, a family member, or a formally recognised key professional who can be relied upon to see individual programmes through. Finally, good professional practice demands following up the consequences of each decision to ensure that the correct things have happened, that the outcome has been as acceptable as could be expected, and that further action can be taken if these two objectives have not been reached.

9
Some issues for discussion and research

The theme of this book has been to consider the different ways in which care and enablement may be provided for people with severe physical disabilities, with particular reference to those of 'working age' for whom residential care may become an option or a necessity at one time or another during their lives. As explained in Chapter 1, they are people who depend on personal help for often the most basic of tasks, often very frequently and for months or years or even the whole of a lifetime, and some are so unreliable that they need an almost perpetual watching eye. The physical disabilities of a small minority are associated with unbearable behaviour, intermittent or incessant as it may be, which makes them hard to accommodate in the ordinary environment of a private household or residential care. To the extent that the book's emphasis has been on institutions, populations, the delivery of services to a community, and the significance of particular diseases and injuries, the perspective has been medical. An attempt has, however, been made to take a wider view than that with which medicine is traditionally associated, and to address a much wider readership than the medical profession itself.

DRAWING ATTENTION TO THE NEED FOR REFORM

The tradition in medicine is to rely on statistical evidence such as the prevalence of different diseases or disabilities. While this is an essential requirement when planning new resources, usually it fails to take account of many factors which are not easy to measure and it can easily lack emotional and political appeal. To present a series of case studies and anecdotes may therefore not only illustrate some of the statistics but may also provide valuable information in its own right. Annexes C and O of the Review of Artificial Limb and Appliance Services (Independent Working Party, 1986) consist of evidence of this kind, and it can be no coincidence that many other accounts of disabled living use anecdotal evidence too (see, for example, Townsend, 1979; Dartington and colleagues, 1981; Shearer, 1982; Briggs and Oliver, 1985). Some brief accounts of unsatisfactory practice, from three consecutive months of my ordinary professional work, illustrate just a few of the difficulties which disabled people experience with support and care.

A young man of eighteen returned from a local hospital to an unstable family, five months after a severe head injury; the medical treatment, nursing and remedial therapy were orthodox and adequate but the appraisal of his parents' difficulties and the advice given to them were not. Predictably, committed residential care soon appeared as a possible escape from the tensions; it fell to a couple of voluntary workers, whom the family had discovered almost by chance, to tackle what the statutory services should have dealt with in the first place. Two more young men were declared at a spinal injuries unit to be 'fully rehabilitated', but their destination was a younger disabled unit where they had to wait six months more for their own environmental control equipment and twelve months for wheelchairs which they could operate themselves, let alone the much longer time it would take them to rethink their future lives.

A married couple, who needed major adaptations to their house because of the husband's severe stroke, were told that the local authority's budget had been spent and the waiting list was three years long; as a result, his discharge from a hospital unit was delayed for almost a year. A severely disabled woman was offered an option on a flat by a voluntary housing association, her first after she had been in hospital for nearly two years, but she was also told that she had to weigh up all the implications and decide about it within ten days because the association could not afford to keep it unlet for longer than that.

The representative of another housing association seriously misled another potential tenant because of not knowing the difference between wheelchair and mobility housing. A woman with Huntington's chorea, living with her young unmarried son who had a full-time job, was gradually deteriorating and becoming less and less reliable; he justifiably wanted to keep his job and his independence but nobody seemed able to offer her committed residential care – assuming, that is, that she would have accepted it.

Another middle-aged woman with brain injury due to haemorrhage had spent five depressed years in a Health Service younger disabled unit, followed by a spell in a rehabilitation centre and then nine uneasy months with her husband before he died. The consequence was two and a half years in the psychogeriatric ward of a mental hospital before she was rescued to go into an old people's nursing home. A man of similar age with a severe brain-stem stroke, tetraplegic and mute but of apparently normal mental function otherwise, lived for nearly two years in a busy hospital ward without any contact with the local communication aids centre, only to be removed in the end to an old people's home for the convenience of his family.

The issues in this list of misadventures are certainly to do partly with the very severe disabilities and with failures of provision, but also with failures of information, poor understanding, closed lines of communication, inability of the different services to work together, and reluctance to accept responsibility. They are also to do with the concept of rehabilitation in the broadest sense, the importance of which was explained in Chapter 1; the concept should not be stretched so far that it includes all aspects of care, but it should certainly include the events which precede the establishment of a pattern of care and which should ensue if that pattern is for any reason disrupted. At the same time the conventional sectors of rehabilitation should not, as is still too often the case, have to argue their importance; the distribution of therapy teams across England is notoriously uneven, for example (Hamilton 1984), and it may be thought odd to campaign for an extended view of rehabilitation while ignoring the fact that even the basic components may not be adequately provided.

But although individual predicaments are what matter and are frequently the factors which sway public opinion, population data remain necessary to allow a sense of proportion, reveal trends in prevalence, help to determine priorities, and indicate the likely implications of particular policy decisions. The new British Government survey of disability should give valuable new information; meanwhile, we have to make do with figures from a variety of sources obtained in different ways, varying in reliability and neither necessarily compatible with one another nor necessarily applicable to every population. Many people believe that local registers of particular disabling conditions of, or people with severe disabilities in general, would be helpful for professional practice as well as for planning, yet it seems that in very few cases has this been proven. Among the difficulties of constructing any such register are deciding the precise objectives and the criteria for entry, establishing reliable methods of enquiry and of keeping the records up to date, ensuring the commitment and expense necessary for the undertaking to be worthwhile, and convincing sceptics of the use to which the register would ultimately be put.

THE IMPORTANCE OF HISTORY AND CONTEMPORARY PREOCCUPATIONS

It has been suggested that there were three phases in the responses of Western society towards disability (Finkelstein, 1981). The first was based in small, predominantly rural communities in which those who survived severe physical impairment would have lived as cripples among their families, with no reason at all to expect anything else. The second phase was associated with the industrial revolution when work became specialised, formalised and localised in large work places, and family units were broken up by the need for employment in the new industries and the corresponding social mobility. The third phase was brought about by the second: better education, more diversified services and new technology opened up opportunities that had not existed before. Another interpretation is that the second phase was due to the economic requirements of the new capitalism, while the third was made possible by an inevitable outcome of later capitalism: the development of a wide-ranging system of social welfare (Scull, 1984). It is certainly true, however, that better housing, easier and much more readily available transport, heating and lighting at the touch of a switch, technical innovations of every kind, and a greater understanding of the principles of rehabilitation have all created possibilities for disabled people's independence which even fairly recently could not have been imagined.

Visiting different residential institutions, for example, one becomes conscious of successive layers of contemporary preoccupation; different architectural features illustrate a historical sequence of social values and technical limitations as well as fashions in design. The older, larger establishments incorporate some of the features of old country estates. Other buildings reflect the long period of medical and nursing domination during which the model adopted was as far as possible that of the hospital ward. Whatever its management and function, residential care used to be pushed into corners: discarded property such as old private houses, the ubiquitous old workhouses, unwanted hospitals or parts of hospitals and even old hotels, not to mention new buildings on unwanted land such as the edge of a hospital site. Poor wheelchair access, even to quite modern buildings, shows how recently independent wheelchair mobility has become a major concern. Then, in the 1960s and 1970s, there was a new trend, as local authorities and housing associations built residential homes and disabled persons' housing as integral parts of new housing developments. The most recent architectural movement has been from communal towards individual living, no doubt matching the diminishing size of households in society at large.

As for present-day preoccupations in Britain, in this historical context there are four which may be singled out. The first is the powerful and effective articulation of a consumer view of disability, by people who are themselves disabled. The second is the growth of non-medical professional approaches to disability, associated with separation of the health care professions and social work into two unrelated departments of public administration. The third is the very rapid development of a private sector in residential care, almost entirely financed by revised rules for social security payment which were introduced almost surreptitiously and without public debate. Finally, there is the vigorous emphasis on community care and the ferment of ideas and innovations with which it is associated.

THE IMPLICATIONS OF VERY SEVERE DISABILITY

Now that far more attention is directed towards the place of people with disabilities within society, the issues of personal care have ceased to be the private matters or the exclusive responsibility of the professions that once they were. Even now, however, members of the public are usually unfamiliar with the consequences of severely disabled living unless as individuals they have had personal contact with severe disabilities themselves. Certainly in my experience, visitors to a younger disabled unit often express astonishment at the severity of the disabilities which it accommodates; I can also remember my own reaction on first starting work there, having to appreciate that reality takes on different proportions in the face of such considerable dependency and disadvantage. Care staff who have been without previous relevant experience, and this includes many nurses with only conventional or even geriatric training, often have to make just the same adjustment. There can be legitimate protests, as for example by some of those whose work is with mental handicap (Heaton-Ward, 1977), that the trend towards integration and community support could cause the special needs of the most severely handicapped to be conveniently overlooked.

At the risk of undue repetition, it cannot be stressed strongly enough that even within the quite restricted group of those who are most severely disabled, there are wide variations in the anatomy, age of onset and course of the disabilities which the full range of diseases and injuries can produce. At the extremes there are differences which can make individual disabled people scarcely compatible in one another's company – between those whose brains are intact and those whose brains are substantially injured; between those who have been disabled ever since they can remember and those for whom it is a development quite late in their lives; and between those who can look forward to the rest of a lifetime of the same disability (or even improvement if suitable rehabilitation is successful) in contrast to those who can only expect to deteriorate. Together with the personalities, social circumstances and motivations which, in any case, make every individual unique, the infinite variety of factors makes it impossible to generalise safely about need. But if there is one urgent requirement which can be said to stand out above the others, it is the need for informed, sympathetic and constructive understanding of the implications of injury or disease of the brain.

It has often been urged that there should be residential homes or hospital units which become expert in that particular understanding, and if there were they would have to cater for at least five specific requirements. These would include methods of caring for people with awkward behaviour patterns which complicate their physical disabilities; research programmes to enlarge our knowledge of what can be expected of different patterns of brain damage; methods of re-educating people with damaged brains; continuous programmes of partnership with those who have the disabilities, and with their carers; and programmes of educating professionals and the public about the whole range of relevant issues.

Much of this is within the field of neuropsychology but, although the detailed expertise may be specialised, the principles are the same as those of managing mental and physical disabilities in general. Would it therefore be right to try to segregate the expertise and, if so, would it simply be to avoid mixing incompatible people or to create the best possible environment for the various tasks? Given the complex range of disabilities which brain disease and brain injury can produce, on what criteria would segregation take place? Would there not also be a danger of encapsulating yet another minority group for committed care, perhaps as the responsibility of staff who are allowed few insights into the opportunities and aspirations of other people with disabilities, and as a group of customers far down the list of priorities for attention within the caring services as a whole? That would be segregation with a vengeance, for the care staff no less than the people for whom they were caring.

DISABLED PEOPLE AS CONSUMERS

In Chapter 1 reference was made to the concept of people with disabilities as customers or consumers of services, rather than patients or clients, and in Chapter 5 the same concept was linked with the importation into Britain of ideas from the Independent Living Movement in the United States. The two approaches are not quite the same, and the linkage was partly for convenience in referring to that group of disabled people who not only seek their own independence but are also campaigning in a more general way for changes of attitudes and new priorities for disabled living. As also mentioned in Chapter 5, 'integrated living' has been preferred by some activists as more appropriate to their aims in Britain.

Individual people with even the severest physical disabilities have been able to play a full part in society, valued in their own right for their own personal skills and insights in the same way as any able-bodied person. Some have preferred to be integral members of whatever enterprise they are involved with, distancing themselves as far as possible from the social implications of disability. Others are aware that their experiences of disabled living allow them the privilege and the responsibility of offering something for the greater good, in ways that able-bodied people cannot match; for some, this has meant working for voluntary or statutory organisations which exist to serve people in similar circumstances. Most service providers welcome this kind of input; they are only too well aware of the sometimes awesome responsibilities they carry for other people's lives, and are both pleased to have the guidance and relieved to share the responsibility.

There are also the activists who have adopted what amounts to a political stance which, to an outsider, certainly has the beneficial effect of shaking the complacency of conventional views. The main concern in evaluating this approach is, however, to identify the constituency which the activists claim to represent. Certainly it is part of everyday rehabilitation experience that situations arise which do not seem to fit the Independent Living Movement's scheme of things: while this may often be because the service providers have quite the wrong perspective, on many occasions there is more than a suspicion that issues have presented themselves which the activists simply have not taken into consideration. There is no question of challenging their understanding of the experience of disability, but they may have relatively little experience of the pressures that can be brought to bear on the service providers. In other words, for good reasons they may have chosen consciously or unconsciously to exclude certain groups of people from their terms of reference, but that of course does not diminish the service providers' responsibilities. Perhaps what the Movement is really doing is speaking for the group referred to in Section 17 of the Chronically Sick and Disabled Persons Act: people under the age of 65 who are not suffering from the effects of 'premature ageing'. Their arguments (quoted in Chapter 5, p. 97) may be accepted, but the people they are leaving out may include a good many about whom this book has been written.

If that is so, those for whom the activists' campaigns are appropriate have to be recognised as a proportion within the total population of people with disabilities, and the size of that proportion is at present not known. They are the people for whom the increasingly acceptable policy is for the resource allocators to give spending power instead of resources in kind, leaving all other decisions to the consumer and the market (Bray and Wright, 1980; Walker, 1981). Despite the evident appeal of this 'subsidised consumer model', it is essential to recognise that it does not abolish professional decisions about resource allocation; instead, they are shifted heavily in the direction of the assessment of individuals for eligibility of benefit. (As it happens, the personnel currently involved in these assessments in Britain – doctors and social security employees – are usually quite separate from those involved in the allocation of resources such as equipment, personal services and residential care.) And because some severely disabled people are incompetent to use any financial allocation in their own best interests, or seek to evade the responsibility, or fail in its use through no fault of their own, it is likely that a safety net of traditional public service will always in some measure be required.

WOMEN, CARING AND NURSING

The care of dependent people is women's work, and the numerical facts are overwhelming. Surveys of the carers of elderly dependent people, for example, have repeatedly shown that three-quarters of them are women (Equal Opportunities Commission, 1980; Finch and Groves, 1983; Jones and Vetter, 1984); the proportion of women in general nursing, the home help service, the remedial therapy professions and among the domestic and care staff of residential homes is much higher still. There is an astonishing contrast between the usual attendance at, significantly, a meeting of hospital physicians or surgeons which is overwhelmingly male, and a meeting of professionals who work with disabled people which is overwhelmingly female. The issue relates to the entire economic status of women and to the question of payment for household tasks in particular: whether, for example, women should be paid for their own household management, for bringing up their own children, or (literally or figuratively) taking in one another's washing. Most domestic caring responsibilities until very recently have been in the household tasks category; not so much unpaid as simply not justifying recognition within the formal economy.

Yet, to an outside observer, it can seem curious and unjust that the formally employed work force, engaged in its infinite variety of activities, expects and receives payment more or less as a matter of course, whereas the informal carers of severely disabled people can be expected to work long, hard hours, often without respite and still in many cases without adequate recompense. It can seem equally odd that just the same arduous work is not only paid for without question once a person is admitted to residential care, even though it is still more likely to be done by women, but may well also qualify for the usual rights that go with formal employment. The introduction, from 1970 onwards, of several State benefits to compensate for disability has been an important advance, but in respect of very severe disability it has, in most people's opinion, not gone far enough; it took until 1986 for the European Court of Justice to declare that carers deserved recompense as of right. Despite the availability of (also formally employed) community services to bridge the gap, the transition from informal to formal care can seem quite arbitrary and abrupt.

A related issue is the relationship between personal care and professional nursing. Nurses have had to fight long and hard for their status and the right to a proper income, and part of that fight has consisted of striving to achieve and maintain high standards of practice (Abel-Smith, 1960). The fact remains that, according to a recent survey conducted by the National Association of Carers, there is not a single item of personal care performed by nurses for disabled people that is not also performed by at least some informal and otherwise untrained carers. Care attendants are expected to carry out basic nursing tasks (Table 5.2); the care staff of residential homes, most of whom are without any formal qualifications let alone a qualification in nursing, regularly undertake work that would be the responsibility of trained nurses in hospitals. Yet, with very severe disability, because one person may need so much help with personal care, if residential care is required it is often assumed not only that trained nurses are essential but also that people with severe disabilities of this order should be grouped together so that trained nurses may undertake the whole administration of their welfare. In the British National Health Service this almost inevitably means that senior hospital doctors are expected to be involved too.

The whole subject needs much clearer thinking, better leadership and if necessary some well-conducted research; it is indeed quite common to discover instances of what can only be called restrictive practices, as paid carers are forbidden (or occasionally refuse) to carry out tasks they are well able to perform. The specialist knowledge, experience and expertise of nurses and doctors are required when people are ill, especially when a patient's condition is unstable or changing or the treatment is elaborate. Severely disabled people hardly ever enter residential care for that reason, and the idea that people must be sick if they are also very dependent hardly stands up to examination: that is why this book contains little mention of chronic sickness as such. Even procedures such as catheter care, manual removal of faeces and giving routine injections (maintenance insulin is the chief example) are all tasks which, while certainly part of the regular work of nurses, can be delegated to close relatives and other untrained people. In general it can be said that when disabilities are constant and carers have close, regular responsibilities for the people they care for, they do not need nursing qualifications. Equally, health service administration and the 'medical model' (see Chapter 4) have been thought necessary more for reasons of convention and administrative convenience than because of any fundamental need (Wade and colleagues, 1983).

The issue is also important because nurses are paid more than unqualified carers, even if their salaries are not high; they are also in short supply, and in the main believe themselves that their training is wasted if they are 'only' pairs of hands. The use of trained nurses undoubtedly increases the cost of an individual's care, which depends on pay scales as well as the number of paid hours that are considered necessary, the extent to which the hours are efficiently used, and whether people are paid at all. There is indeed a conflict of interests among groups of people who are each pursuing legitimate aims: disabled people and their carers, whose needs are individual and may therefore be dissimilar, even at times opposed; service providers and professionals, who want good conditions of employment and as many resources as they can get for the work they are doing, and whose pride in their work leads them to defend the expertise and resources they already have; and managers and governments who have to decide priorities, control expenditure and want value for money.

ASPECTS OF RESIDENTIAL CARE IN BRITAIN

It is often argued that the diversity of provision by different agencies is a benefit, because they all adopt different approaches from which consumers may choose and others may learn. But in Britain the relevant agencies are not in genuine competition, and on the other hand it is rare for those with an interest in physical handicap in a particular district to work very closely together. At worst there can be open hostility, especially between the health and social services when it may not be confined to services for physical disability; the only nationally recognised formal relationship between these two agencies is to do with planning, although it is fair to say that informal operational arrangements are steadily increasing in number. Within the Health Service itself there are other barriers which surround the two big services for mental illness and mental handicap, each of them all too often segregated for reasons of history, local geography and professional isolationism.

An inevitable result of the fragmentation is the lack of a clear understanding of needs, demands, and where the priorities should lie. An assortment of residential homes and units for younger physically disabled people has been added to the relatively massive resources for the institutional care of people who are elderly, mentally handicapped or mentally ill, and their relative proportion does not match the age-related prevalence of physical disability in the population as a whole (Figures 2.3 and 6.1). As a result, despite growing opportunities for community care, those who are responsible for accepting admissions to the units and homes are usually conscious all the time of considerable pressures to admit, and some of them complain that the pressures make them 'vulnerable' – obliged to take on responsibilities that others can in some ways avoid. For whatever reason, however, most of them have no choice but to be selective, although their philosophies and policies of care are not always easy to distinguish from rationalisations of inability or reluctance to help.

Each Cheshire Home, for example, has usually insisted that residents should be able to contribute something to its residential community, and the result has been a strong disinclination to accept people with mental disabilities. To be fair, the Cheshire Homes were never intended to provide a comprehensive residential service for younger disabled people, but often because of the lack of any alternative they have been expected, by local health and social services, to do just that; the result can be a genuine and unresolvable clash of interests. The social service departments seem almost to have drifted into their residential responsibilities: having set upper limits to the levels of disability which they thought they could manage, at least in any numbers, they then found that they had provided residential care for many people who could have managed without it in the first place. For the Health Service units there has been no clear philosophy either, and it is hardly an exaggeration to describe many of them as just muddling on, trying to provide a decent living environment for exceptionally disabled people but often in quite remote isolation from the rest of the hospital culture and from the world of disability elsewhere.

Although nearly all of the private homes are intended for care of the elderly, a small number of younger disabled people has been admitted to them. The development has raised a host of questions including the appropriateness of the profit motive within a caring service, the desirability of residential care which can be entered without professional advocacy and approval, the open-endedness of the State budget which has been made available (despite rate limits on the individual fees that will be reimbursed), and yet again the desirability of segregating people below the age of 65 from those who are older. Many proprietors are finding that the higher fees chargeable for residents under 65 are a positive incentive to take these younger people in; many such people (or their carers or professional advisers) are apparently grateful for the access to this new resource. At the same time, new registration requirements have caused upsets among the longer-established voluntary homes, challenging their established practices but not always for good reason.

These private sector trends have increased public concern about standards of residential care. Reference has been made several times to the medical and alternative models (Table 4.6), and codes of good practice to the alternative model were briefly mentioned in Chapter 2. The Leonard Cheshire Foundation's contribution (Inskip, 1981a) is the only one which deals specifically with physically disabled people: *Home Life* (1984) was directed at the new private homes and is therefore concerned with elderly people, but it contains much that is relevant to all forms of residential care. These documents, and Clough's account (1982), place emphasis on such matters as individual rights, the dynamics of a residential community, the importance of common courtesies, the problems of personal relationships, and the social significance of properly conducted meal times. *Home Life*, however, explicitly assumes that nursing homes also exist as a separate category to which its advice need not necessarily apply, an unfortunate assumption in view of the widespread uncertainty and misgiving about dividing responsibility for residential care in this way.

The most serious objection to the medical model is that essentially it has nothing to offer once the needs of assessment, treatment, rehabilitation and bodily care have been met. No British document based upon it has properly tackled the issues of disabled living: of the relevant codes of good practice, the Royal College of Nursing's booklet on improving the continuing care of old people in hospitals (1975) questions neither admission policies nor the medical model itself. The National Association of Health Authorities' guide to the inspection of nursing homes (1985) is a cold, regulatory document which is disgracefully insensitive if it is the only judgement applied to places where disabled people have to live for any length of time. If a person's requirements have deteriorated so far that they have become limited to physical care without any need for the fulfilment of personal aspirations, a hospital-based regime can no doubt do the job tolerably well. It is surely the case that for all other people receiving committed residential care, medical and nursing skills are chiefly helpful when there is intercurrent illness or an unexpected development in a person's disabling disease; even remedial therapy skills have little relevance to the organisation of a whole, albeit severely restricted, way of life. Nevertheless, it would be wrong to assume that the medical model cannot be made at least partly responsive to need: Table 9.1 compares brief summaries of two of the published checklists of good practice and shows that, although the two models of care differ in what they regard as most important, there is a shared concern about doing the job well.

DISABLED LIVING IN PRIVATE HOUSEHOLDS

The majority of people with severe disabilities do nevertheless occupy private households, and it has to be said that on a long-term basis this is usually by far the more attractive

Table 9.1 *Summary outline of two published checklists for good practice in committed long-term care*

Geriatric care in hospital (1975)	No. of items	Residential care (1984)	No. of items
Checklist for senior staff and educators		Social care	
General aims and objectives	9	Admission procedures	10
The patients' day and personal needs	18	Terms and conditions of residence	3
Environment	25	General administration	14
Staff	19	Security of tenure	1
		Privacy and personal autonomy	13
Good practice for ward staff		Financial affairs	15
Identity and dignity	8	Health care	11
High dependency care	3	Dying and death	7
Mobility	6		
Security	2	Physical features	
Independence	4	Location, size, accommodation and	
Pattern of the day	3	space	8
Social needs	11	Patients' own rooms; bathrooms and	
Appearance	4	laundry	12
Promotion of continence	3	Diet and food preparation	8
Communication	4		
Terminal care	3	Individual client groups	
		Physically disabled people	6
		Other groups	39
		Staff	32

option. Although some of those who live in residential homes and units believe that in consequence they have real opportunities for a fuller life, for others the freedom from constraint and the preservation of a place in the wider society, which are what being in one's own place is all about, are of the utmost importance. Not only do people not want to give these up if they already possess them; even if they move out after many years of residential care they can enjoy the freedom, privacy and status in just the same way. I have personal recollections, for example, of the way in which one woman was able to re-establish a long-neglected relationship with her family; of the alertness that regularly returns to people's faces and manner once they are away from the restrictions of a hospital unit; and of the genuine surprise of one rather apprehensive person who, after half a lifetime in a residential home, rediscovered the pleasures of domestic life with a new partner.

For the service providers too, community care has some immense advantages. In most cases existing buildings are used, and so is the existing social fabric, which indeed is often strengthened because the need to bring in help not only increases a household's range of social contacts but does something towards creating a community sense of social responsibility. There is also the important functional reason that community care is flexible: not only is unpaid informal support an essential part of it, and quite reasonably so if the individual carers' hours and duties are not excessive, but paid help is task-orientated and can be augmented or lessened as needs change. All this is in marked contrast to the inflexibility of traditional residential care, with its finite limit to the number of people who can be accommodated, its more or less fixed input of care hours which often means too many at some time and too little at others, the limits to the contribution from unpaid helpers which it usually allows, its residents' security of tenure which results in unresponsiveness to new demand, and the restricted outlook which its isolation from the wider community so often can impose. Community care may or may not be cheaper, but that is not the main reason why it is to be preferred.

But if care in private households is to be acceptable, it has to be well organised and reliable; people must have confidence in it, and it must be seen not necessarily to imply isolation and loneliness or an intolerable load for carers. Until these things happen, the comfort, safety and security of residential care will remain attractive alternatives. For planners, therefore, faced with the fact that far more expenditure currently goes into hospitals and residential homes than into community services, the current priority must be to spend more on community care. The problems are not so much of finding the money but of how to organise the resources and make the finance flexibly and responsively available. Organisation of the issue of equipment in particular cries out for reform of the current disparate, almost random arrangements (Wynn-Parry 1986), ideally into something as well managed and professionally well advised as the pharmaceutical and opticians' services.

There are other grounds for caution too. 'Institutionalisation' can be discovered in some private households in which disabled people are subjected to quite severe, often well-meaning constraints, and in such cases residential care may well offer wider opportunities, at least for a time. Grouped housing developments have, on occasions, been so designed and provided with staff that they may be little different from residential homes, so that moving into them from residential care could better be described as 'transinstitutionalisation' than as a move towards independence and integration into the community. Moreover, however good the living environment, grouped housing runs the risk of replicating the evolution of a residential home: because of the sudden availability of a number of new properties, occupants are likely to move in who strictly do not need the facility, and as the group of households grows older, the occupants' dependency can be expected collectively to increase. The inherent flexibility of any community service – a day centre or a care attendant scheme for example – can be undermined if it is committed on a long-term basis to a few individuals without critical and regular review, instead of ensuring that it can always be deployed where there is greatest need. This 'flexible' policy can be quite taxing and requires good management and good diplomacy as well as a clear understanding of the overall priorities of the community being served.

The new enthusiasm for community care has almost certainly come to stay, but it is fair to add that its 25 or so years are a short time in comparison with the total documented history of caring for severe disability in Britain. Inevitably it will be a while yet before all the developments can be fully evaluated and understood; good research procedures are essential but the information will take time to collect, just because of the lifelong persistence of so many disabling conditions. Existing policies may well have to be changed, or new policies may have to be established, long before the process can be regarded as satisfactorily complete. Some future problems are predictable, for example the care of people whose lives in private households are entirely dependent on the devotion of parents whom they can reasonably expect to outlive. Meanwhile, because of the lack of certain knowledge but also because of the individuality of each disabled person, the greater the variety of provision the better – only by having a wide range of options is there a real chance that each disabled person will receive the care which is most suited to his or her requirements.

PHYSICAL DISABILITY: OVERLAPS AND PARALLELS

Some people with severe physical disabilities may have other special needs too: they may be children, or elderly, or mentally handicapped, or acutely mentally or terminally ill. People do not fall into neat categories just because the services they use have been set up in a certain way. No matter exactly what those special needs are, they and their carers usually have to call upon the same community services: it is only when they are grouped together in hospitals, residential homes or 'day centres' that special resources and special expertise may have to be created. This may happen deliberately to promote expertise as in paediatric medicine, the hospice movement or among medical and surgical specialities; or for social convenience as in many cases of disturbed behaviour due to mental illness or mental handicap; or for social advantage as in the case of many of the residential homes for younger physically disabled people. In some instances it may not be clear whether the speciality or the social factors are more important, as in much of psychiatry and geriatric medicine.

Because many of the basic requirements of dependency due to disability are the same, overlaps and parallels between the specialist health services are inevitable. As already mentioned, on the other hand, large quasi-independent organisations have developed, and the people who work in them have become preoccupied with their own commitments, resources and internal affairs. Their size encourages the process of isolation, with some very undesirable results: buck-passing and policy disagreements at the service interfaces, failure to share expertise, and a tendency to 're-invent the wheel' by working out policies from first principles which could just as easily have been copied from or shared with others. The process is strongly reinforced when the boundaries of administrative and professional responsibilities coincide.

It can therefore be no coincidence that the three groups of severely disabled people who seem to be least well served are up against just such boundaries of medical responsibility. The small but important group of school-leavers upon whom a great deal of therapeutic, educational and counselling effort is likely to have been expended, pass into an adult world in which few of the statutory services will show the same organised or informed concern. Then there are the much larger numbers of people who cannot be described as young but are not yet old: the separation of geriatrics within the hospital service has created uncertainty and ambivalence about them, and indeed the issues of disability and ageing are often hopelessly confused even within the geriatric specialty itself. Third, the failure to provide resources for people with impaired brain function has been described as a national disgrace, and must surely arise from the barriers between the psychiatric hospitals and the other public services, quite apart from the difficulty everyone experiences in accommodating to changed personalities and abnormal behaviour. In fact, many individuals qualify for inclusion in both of these last two categories, and clarity of thought is not helped by the obscure wording of Section 17 of the Chronically Sick and Disabled Persons Act which may or may not, according to interpretation, imply segregation of young from old on the principal grounds of mental deterioration.

Communications are, of course, always helped if there are easy opportunities for face-to-face contact. Deliberately encouraging the development of separate services in close proximity, on the same site whenever that is to the advantage of the community which is being served, would therefore be sound policy. This, after all, is one of the main justifications for the concept of the district general hospital, and it is one reason why the Health Service was encouraged to develop its younger disabled units on general hospital sites. Well-meaning attempts at dealing with neglected groups by setting up 'a nice little unit somewhere' or 'a few beds', run the risk of simply adding to the boundary problems and should not necessarily be welcomed. One attractive idea is that of a small community hospital shared by all the disability-orientated specialities; another is that a residential home or a day centre might be developed as a community resource and shared by health and social services.

THE YOUNGER DISABLED UNITS: OBJECT LESSON OR OPPORTUNITY?

Apart from the old Homes for Incurables which the National Health Service acquired in 1948, these special units appear (at least in retrospect) to have been products of a political compromise, in which members of the medical profession have more or less willingly and more or less consciously been implicated. It is always a temptation for professionals to seek residence in hospital as a solution to difficult problems of physical or mental dependency in a private household, especially when, as in Britain, that residence is free at the point of demand. Similarly, transfer to another residential institution can be an all-too-easy solution when returning a newly disabled person from hospital to a private household seems likely to be fraught with difficulty. These are major reasons why the Health Service has remained responsible for so many long-stay patients, even though there is no formal legislative provision for them outside the specialities of mental handicap and psychiatry.

The 'young chronic sick units' were simply to provide segregated accommodation of the same kind: in that sense they were not a radical departure. Although they have come to represent a degree of medical dominance over the lives of people with disabilities, which disabled people as consumers have rightly decried, it is perhaps less readily appreciated that the physicians concerned with their development believed that they were only responding to the pressures upon them and acted in the best way they knew. Countless hospital doctors would indeed be only too pleased if the community or social services would relieve them of their empires of committed residential care which they are ill-equipped, by training, to comprehend.

Be that as it may, the sudden appearance of the new units in the 1970s did at least provide the Health Service with a focus of attention on some aspects of disabled living, and the units' staff appear generally to have approached their commitment, whatever it was, with at least a degree of idealism. Essentially, the model was hospital geriatrics, which had developed as far as defining certain standards of physical and institutional care, had established a claim that committed hospital consultants were essential to the proper running of hospital care, and was largely committed to programmes of assessment, fairly straightforward rehabilitation, a day hospital service and long-term residential care. The changes within geriatric medicine itself which, during the 1970s, began to concentrate far more on a comprehensive approach to the diseases of old age, and the widespread general movement towards care in the community, were yet to come.

The units soon found themselves with unresolvable contradictions. They were indeed 'nice little units somewhere': conceived in isolation, there was no service to which they could obviously relate, and their parent specialty was one from which many of them wished to distance themselves. Health Service administrative mechanisms ensured not only that the units were provided more or less complete, usually with no planned incremental build-up of accommodation and staff; it also turned out that hardly any of them were destined for expansion afterwards. As places in which it was expected that people should make their homes they were impossibly restricted by the professionally dominated, unwieldy National Health Service bureaucracy, just as described by Miller and Gwynne (1972). Stories of conflict with orthodox procedures abounded, and hospital nursing and medical practices seemed inescapable – uniforms, hierarchies, ward rounds, drug rounds; even the immediate availability of remedial therapy was a kind of clinical distortion of the recreation that ordinary people naturally seek. Hospital rules dictated that residents were deprived of all but pocket money, unless they had private income; if they did not live in a single room (and 80 per cent of them could not), their property was likely to be limited to what could be fitted into a locker and immediately round a bed. Location on a hospital site was the final indignity, conferring on each resident the status of patient, permanently under doctors' orders.

But not everything was bad, and some of the opportunities the units provided were very important. Planned short stay – respite care, shared care, holiday relief or by whatever term it is known – was a service which a few of them discovered they could operate well. The reasons were among the very ones which tended to undermine the practice of good long-term care: the free service at the point of demand, with its personal financial implications, and the immediate availability of professionals to monitor each person's progress and (in many cases) changing needs. Only a minority of units, however, managed to put on intensive programmes, and it is clear that these were the result of deliberate policy rather than a passive response to demand. It is also of interest that the staff were generally pleased with the service they gave, believing (with some evidence) that any committed residents they were caring for benefited too, whereas similar programmes have been condemned as 'disruptive' in residential homes (*Home Life*, 1984). There are, however, still relatively few critical reports of planned short stay, especially in relation to younger people with physical disabilities, and at least a certain amount of new research is needed, not to establish their value as such but to evaluate different programmes and methods of provision. Oswin's study (1984) of respite care for mentally handicapped children is an example, and family fostering schemes probably have to be recognised as an important alternative to short stay in residential care.

Some Health Service units also declared their intention of deliberately encouraging rehabilitation. This is another rather contentious issue: rehabilitation, too, has been regarded as disruptive of committed care, besides being liable to under-achievement if the two activities are mixed. Perhaps this is to overlook the fact that rehabilitation has no definable limits; people on short-stay programmes may need it, for example, and some residents thought destined for committed care may have unrealised potential. Certainly if the process is likely to take many months or even several years, as after severe head injury or high-level spinal injury, a partly rehabilitative, partly residential environment can be very appropriate: precisely, in fact, what the Health Service units can offer. Good rehabilitation sometimes depends on tackling a problem as soon as it presents, so a logical further development has been willingness and ability to admit residents at short notice instead of allowing waiting lists to build up, and to accept people on an emergency basis if necessary.

One more function envisaged from the outset for some units was to accept day attendances. Since that time, however, other kinds of day centre have been established: as with committed residential care, if the needs are for diversional or creative activity and social contact, the best of these other facilities do the job better. An influx of a large number of day attenders into residents' principal living space can seem an unwarranted intrusion, but the evidence suggests that those units in which day attendances, planned short stay and rehabilitation have been combined, to the near-exclusion of committed care, have provided a more valuable service than the others. A long way from the original, largely residential concept and fairly close to the work of any good rehabilitation department, these are tasks which the National Health Service is well fitted to undertake.

HOW MUCH RESIDENTIAL CARE FOR YOUNGER DISABLED PEOPLE DO WE NEED?

Short stay, rehabilitation, emergency admission, and the committed and terminal care of the most severely disabled, especially those with disease or injury of the brain: these are the functions a residential unit can carry out, with day attendances as a sixth component of the list. Available evidence suggests that together they form a resource which families and good community services are likely to appreciate. An important question is the scale of any such resource, to which the answer must depend on the age range and the precise disabilities that are to be served.

If the age group is 16 to 64 and the disabilities are those described throughout this book, evidence from the 'group 5' units described in Chapter 7 suggests that the maximum provision for respite care need be no more than 2 places per 100,000 total population. The necessary provision of rehabilitation is more difficult to quantify, particularly because of the variable extent to which ordinary hospitals do the work: one regional medical rehabilitation unit however gives a very active service and also offers 2 places per 100,000. Emergency admissions are made possible by turnover, not by the total number of places; terminal care is short-term and needs a relatively tiny resource. Hospital-based day places should be restricted to those who really do need hospital-based services; again the numbers are uncertain but are unlikely to be large.

The number of places needed for committed residential care is just as difficult to be certain about; given the average provision of 30 per 100,000 total population for physically disabled people aged 16 to 64 in Britain as a whole, and assuming for the sake of argument that at least a third of the residents could just as well be living in private households, it would not be unreasonable to plan for some 20 per 100,000 total population. If it is further assumed that not all of them need to be in homes or units especially for that age group (and indeed there would be many 'boundary' problems if there were), about 75 per cent of that figure – 15 places per 100,000 – would be an acceptable, perhaps even generous working target. As it happens, this is about the proportion which, in fact, is specially designated for younger physically disabled people in Britain, although the geographical distribution is uneven. As for the Health Service units' share of the 15, the best available study is that of Fearn (1982) who concluded that at least in one district it need be no more than three. All the figures given in these last two paragraphs are summarised in Table 9.2; if the age range is to be extended upwards, the figures need to be increased in line with the population prevalence of disability.

It is the Health Service units that have revealed the community support potential of residential care much more clearly than the residential homes, and the final question is whether the six component parts should be accommodated under one roof and one management. Certainly this is not essential, but my impression is that many health care professionals would or actually do welcome a commitment which includes them all, exacting though such a mixture can well be. At least some of the residents seem to share the same view, but the staff do have an obligation to make any such mixed service acceptable to the majority of people who use it. One of its greatest advantages is avoidance of the inconsistencies and rigidities which are almost inevitable if the component parts separate out. The figures in Table 9.2 do, however, suggest that a certain amount of separate, traditional committed care is still likely to be required, say about 12 beds per 100,000 for this group of people under the age of 65. It is my submission that such residential care should scrupulously avoid the medical model.

Table 9.2 *Residential care for younger adults with severe physical disabilities: very tentative recommendations for provision*

	Age group		
	15–54	55–64	65–70
	Places per 100,000 total population		
Planned short stay	1	1	1–2
Longer-term rehabilitation	1	1	1–2
Emergency and terminal	(dependent on turnover)		
Committed care: Health Service	1	2	3
all other	6	6	uncertain

INDIVIDUAL DECISIONS AND THEIR IMPACT ON SERVICE PROVISION

Whatever the numerical calculations, the resources that are actually chosen to support severely disabled living depend heavily on personal and social factors. Many families want to care for their own members come what may; some people with disabilities are for one reason or another entirely without informal support whether from their families or elsewhere, and a few have families who are hostile or positively unhelpful. Some of the ways in which a society provides care are determined by factors with origins in much wider issues; the need for residential care is, for example, likely to be much greater in a society which encourages individual social and geographical mobility, or in which mass urban development has reduced living options and disrupted the social fabric generally. Remote rural communities present yet another pattern of options and needs.

So, although there are likely to be margins beyond which provision of paid help is by any standard unnecessary, or beyond which certain kinds of help, residential care among them, are by any standard essential, no-one has yet defined what those margins are; they are likely to vary considerably from one community to another and they may well be indefinable. Within the margins there is scope for personal decisions, and in Chapter 8 it has been explained how these are influenced by professional competence, the existing provision of resources and the prevailing climate of opinion. Personal value judgements undoubtedly contribute however, on the part of professional advisers no less than that of the consumers.

Mention of value judgements was made in Chapter 8, including personal preference; ethical issues, which include evaluation of risk, personal obligation, and what constitutes freedom of choice; and opinions about priority. The trend, during the past two decades, has been to regard freedom of choice as more important than freedom from risk; this is an important example of a changing climate of opinion but many people are still in residential care because of decisions made when the prevalent view was different. A very important issue is the extent to which individual decisions can be made in isolation from pressures generally: a case which, on its merits, may seem unanswerable can seem a very poor one if it is related to the predicaments of other people in greater need. The medical services in particular are constantly dealing with urgent demand and so, to a lesser extent, are the social services, and if there is no attempt to relate these pressures to one another or to the steadier demand for non-urgent help, some very inconsistent decisions may emerge.

It is against this background that a disabled person's liberty to choose has to be given serious reappraisal. At its worst, medical, paramedical or social work consensus can inhibit choice completely: on the other hand professional enthusiasm can over-stimulate essentially unambitious individuals towards goals which they neither particularly desire nor are particularly suited to attain. Then there are the people who are dominated by their families and informal carers and can hardly get a word in, and perhaps most unfortunate of all are those whose inability to communicate means that certainly their deeper thoughts and often even their simplest aspirations remain inaccessible for ever. Those people with disabilities who are able to make well-informed, dispassionate choice and have plenty of time to make it in, may at least in that respect be very privileged.

Individual decisions and the provision of resources have a kind of circular inter-relationship, each helping to determine the extent of the other; innovative decisions become precedents, helping to determine future policy and practice. The importance of the decision-making process can hardly be overestimated.

EDUCATION AND TRAINING ABOUT SEVERELY DISABLED LIVING

Throughout this book, the importance of knowledge and understanding of the realities of severe physical disability has been repeatedly stressed. The inappropriateness of services and their inadequacies about which complaints are so regularly made, it is argued, to a large extent arise because of inadequate grasp of the issues that matter. Examples include Section 17 of the Chronically Sick and Disabled Persons Act and its interpretation (Chapter 2); failure to cater for people with acquired brain injury (Chapter 3); poor understanding between different agencies which provide residential care (Chapter 4); unresponsive provision of community resources (Chapter 5); confused thinking about the distinctions between the major dependency groups (Chapter 6); and the perplexities of nurses who work in many of the Health Services residential units (Chapter 7).

Yet in Britain, relevant formalised courses of instruction are few, as are relevant certificates, diplomas and degrees. Almost the only option is the Open University's course entitled 'The Handicapped Person in the Community'; available as a one-off course of special training or as a half-course component of a BA degree, it takes a consumers' and sociological view of disability and by definition excludes consideration of residential care. The courses of training for all the professions who work with disabled people inevitably contain relevant material but particular attention to severe physical disability is usually lacking; this applies especially to undergraduate and postgraduate training in medicine. Even some of the optional courses, certificates and diplomas which do relate to disabled living are similarly deficient, such as those offered by the Central Council for Training in

Social Work, and the Diploma in Rehabilitation of the Royal College of Physicians. Within nursing, a syllabus for two courses in physical handicap has been available since 1975 but ten years later only one such course had actually been implemented, and that was outside the National Health Service.

Whatever the profession or group to which training is offered, there is a basic core of knowledge about severely disabled living which needs to be imparted. Outlining a complete curriculum would be outside the scope of this discussion, although many of the components have been included or touched upon in each chapter of this book. As an example, however, Appendix 2 gives a summary outline of the essential items of which the medical profession should be aware.

CONVERTING IDEAS INTO ACTION

In Britain, available resources for the care and enablement of severe physical disabilities are not well co-ordinated and are frequently unavailable when they are most needed. Their funding does not always encourage the most satisfactory set of options, and they have not always adapted well to changing patterns of disability in the population. The real, hard issues of severely disabled living are by no means as well understood by the decision-makers or the resource-providers as they should be, and courses of appropriate training are few. Developments in one service have frequently left others backward and isolated, having to cope with challenging and even intransient problems yet without the broader-based approach which is necessary to the enlightened provision of care. There may be some scope for business enterprise unassisted by public spending, but the expense of severe disability and the limited income of most severely disabled people are likely to ensure that it will remain small.

Of course not everything is bad, as the previous chapters have shown. Yet almost nowhere is there a complete set of well-organised resources, and almost everywhere there is concern that improvement is necessary. Indeed indignation is such that it has become almost customary for every account of disability and disabled living to end with a more or less impassioned statement of the requirements for reform. There is, in fact, a wide consensus about what needs to be done, exemplified by a number of planning documents produced by the public authorities such as Kent County Council/Kent Area Health Authority (1981), Lambeth Social Services (1982), Holland, Crawford and Peberdy (1985), South West Thames Regional Health Authority (1985), and Martin, Pfingst and Goldring (1987). It is however not enough to wait for major new developments or to call for more evidence; individual consumers want prompt, efficient responses based on the resources that already exist, and professional people want to know what course of action they should adopt. The issues raised in this chapter all require further debate; the next and final chapter is devoted to some firm recommendations.

10
A strategy, and a last personal example

Because the facilities and services which disabled people have to use are in such disarray, and because of the high degree of dependency on others which severe disability entails, many different agencies may have to be involved in meeting individual needs. The complexity of the task is increased by the uniqueness of each disabled person's requirements, and difficulties are made worse by the fact that very few departments of the health and social services, the two principal agencies of public support, have made physical disability among adults of working age a first priority for concern. Marginalised not only by their disabilities but also by this downgrading of their status as patients or clients, consumers far too often encounter a lack of coherent commitment from the services whose help they seek. While there have been some dramatic improvements, especially since the Chronically Sick and Disabled Persons Act 1970, reforms are still necessary. Some of them demand new money and new systems of organisation, but a great deal can be achieved within the systems and resources that already exist.

GUIDELINES FOR IMPROVEMENT

Awareness of the consumers and their needs

Much of the essential information has been outlined in Chapters 3 and 6. It is helpful to define an individual disability in three distinct ways: whether it began at or near the time of birth or in later life; whether it is stable (and therefore of sudden onset), or unstable or gradually progressive; and the extent to which there is a non-physical component because of disease or injury of the brain. Especially because of brain involvement, people with severe physical disabilities are not an entirely distinct group; many, for example, share difficulties with those who are thought of as mentally handicapped or mentally ill, and there is no firm boundary between the young and the old.

Bearing these facts in mind, the numbers between the ages of 16 and 65 are quite small: somewhat more than 1 per 1000 of the total population of whom only five per cent (say 16 in a community of a quarter of a million) are between 16 and 25. Among a total of some 300 in a population of that size, only about a quarter are less than 45 years old; another quarter are between the ages of 45 and 55, and no less than half are between 55 and 65. The prevalence curve goes on rising with age, so that the biggest total numbers are between the ages of 75 and 80.

No assessment of disability is complete without an understanding of its effect on the aspirations and the career of each disabled person, and upon the day-to-day lives, responsibilities, aspirations and career of each principal carer. Indeed the complete network of support and care has to be taken into account, including the means by which the carers themselves find support in their task.

Consulting the consumers

People with disabilities and their carers regularly complain that their own understanding is regularly ignored by professional people. Consulting a disabled person or client, or in many cases simply listening to them, is an essential part of good professional practice. It consists of going beyond the questions and assessments which (for example) medical education conventionally requires, learning from what disabled people and their carers tell us spontaneously about their experiences and knowledge, asking what they think is a correct course of action and what their preferences are if there is more than one, and asking about their aspirations generally. Working in this way as people's advocates and partners, not just for them as experts and advisers, can be one of the most rewarding aspects of the professional role.

Some consumers may, however, wish to contribute in a different way, by self-selection or being selected as formal representatives to councils, authorities or committees, or by forming autonomous groups (coalitions, centres for integrated living, for example) of their own. These initiatives have been discussed in Chapter 5; their input is almost always to be welcomed and encouraged, although at the time of writing they involve only a very small minority. The arts of delegate status and committee membership, and of preparing, presenting and pursuing a case, come naturally to only a few people and often have to be arduously learned. Often it is wise or necessary for professionals and service-providers to stimulate hesitant or apprehensive potential activists to consider participation along these lines. At this more formal level too, partnership should be the principle.

Optimism, not despair

Many people, perhaps especially doctors and nurses, are discouraged from working with disabled people for a variety of reasons. Their education and career structures allow physical disability no place, and their prejudices and lack of experience may lead them only to imagine inadequate resources, a lack of scope for conventional treatment, and the 'burden of care'. While severely disabled living undoubtedly places harsh demands on everyone concerned, it has its positive aspects too: the satisfaction of problem-solving and challenges overcome, the stimulus and interest of personal responses and relationships, the opportunities to learn and innovate in a still inadequately charted and expanding field of knowledge. To encourage and foster a spirit of enquiring optimism is one of the most important leadership tasks; it is equally important to publicise what is being done, by whatever means are available. Practical devices include case conferences at which principles and policies are discussed besides the immediate matters in hand, working groups such as planning teams whose members stimulate one another by the wide range of knowledge and experience that they bring, and the encouragement of innovation whenever the opportunities are there.

Collaboration

The multiplicity of agencies, managements and services makes collaboration essential. To varying degrees it is being implemented all the time, as for example when community nurses and home helps work together, or adjoining public authorities jointly sponsor and finance a new project. The principle of the multidisciplinary team within rehabilitation is generally well understood and put into practice. It is, however, still too easy to find disturbing examples of failure to co-operate or consult when a little imagination, a telephone call or just good manners would have prevented a great deal of difficulty. Still worse, deep-rooted animosities among the various services can arise for a whole variety of reasons. One elementary precaution is to remember that face-to-face contact is almost always preferable to relying on formal procedures and written communications. Formal collaboration at managerial level is discussed later in this chapter.

Defining the limits of responsibility

The complexities of organisation are made worse if no apparent limit is set to them, and the risks of over-commitment and broken promises correspondingly increase. Besides specifying just which consumers are to be served, a disability service is usually best limited to a defined population even if the limits are not always interpreted rigidly. Community services are accustomed to such limitations for obvious reasons, but many secondary care services (general hospitals and voluntary residential homes, for example) can escape the necessity, fundamentally because they feel able to deflect unwanted referrals for committed long-term care. Hospitals and public-sector homes which do have to accept such referrals almost all respond by limiting the geographical areas which they serve.

This, however, is a negative view of a catchment-area policy. The positive counterpart is the opportunity to identify a group of residential homes and/or hospital units with a particular community, allowing the links between the primary and secondary care services to be strengthened as another necessary form of collaboration. There must, however, be one very important precondition: no decision to limit a service should be made until there has been discussion with the services across the proposed boundaries, so that there is agreement and not conflict about where exactly the boundaries should lie.

Awareness of what is available, and what should be provided

Knowledge of the essentials for supporting severely disabled living, besides the resources that families and informal networks provide, should be possessed by everyone involved if only to ensure that services which may be available are not overlooked through ignorance. The necessary framework, essentially a summary of Chapter 5 and part of Chapter 7, is set out in Table 10.1. While deliberately avoiding any estimate of quantities, the table also gives service-users a checklist against which their local provision may be judged.

Table 10.1 *A checklist for the support of severely disabled living in each district*

1. *All resources should be available without undue delay*: well-managed, well-publicised points of access are essential. Crises of care demand immediate availability.
2. *Care in private households* (primary care)
   (a) *'Hardware'* (i) *Equipment* for issue, loan, hire or purchase, with a range of choice and sound advice on which to choose: preferably issued from one public-sector source in each district, together with trade retail outlets
            (ii) *Accommodation*
              • a housing adaptation service
              • a home-finding service based on a register of purpose-built or already-adapted properties
   (b) *'Software'* (i) *Personal and household care*, based on social services (home help) and health service (community nursing) teams, together with other schemes to augment or replace informal support (care attendants etc.)
            (ii) *Enablement or social care*, including
              • access to educational, training and leisure services, and to one or more appropriate 'day centres'
              • advice and help on employment and leisure
              • an adequate transport service
            (iii) *Relief for carers* based on care attendant and fostering schemes.
   To help carers who are also in employment, software services should be available to cover normal working hours including travel to and from work, and should therefore also be available outside these hours.

3. *Residential care* (secondary care) Five components: planned short stay (respite care etc., complementing the software services above), rehabilitation, committed long-term care, terminal care of severely disabled people, and a capacity to deal with emergencies. The exact location and combination of these resources is a matter for local arrangement.

4. *Specialist advice* One place, or a very small number of places, where consumers may go
   (a) for information about available resources for disabled living
   (b) for personal advice and counselling about disabled living.

5. *Access to very specialised services* (which may be outside the district: tertiary care)
   (a) for unusual physical disabilities: bio-engineering and related services
   (b) for severe and/or unusual brain injuries: behaviour modification and (re-)education, which may be residential.

6. *Programmes of education and training in all aspects of disabled living*, with ample opportunities for staff (untrained and professional), volunteers and consumers to participate.

It is, in fact, almost impossible to specify how much of each service or resource should be provided. The limits of community care have yet to be fully explored, and the limits of demand for it are likely to be very elastic. The demand for a particular kind of residential care also depends on many factors, although in this case a little more certainty is possible (Table 9.2, Chapter 9). A thorough understanding of the prevalence of the severely disabling diseases and injuries, if it could be established, is likely to prove the most reliable way of estimating demand.

Item 4 in Table 10.1 is a specialist advice service, one component of which should be a comprehensive, reliable and up-to-date bank of relevant information.

Item 6, education and training, is essential if service providers are to give of their best, and many educational programmes will have to be innovative. Both items are absolute requirements for the dissemination of the knowledge and awareness that every district should acquire.

Organising access to the resources that exist

However adequate the resources, their effectiveness is diminished if access to them is hindered or disorganised and if their response to requests for help is half-hearted or delayed. Great attention, therefore, has to be paid to this aspect of a local disability service, to ensure the promptness and appropriateness of help which the consumers rightly require. Ideally there should be one point of access, certainly for each individual component of the service and preferably for several components if not the whole of it, when it may also be the location of the specialist advice resource. The reputation of any service depends as much on the way in which it responds as on the nature of the response itself. The point of access is its reception area and shop window, and requires corresponding efficiency and consumer appeal.

Crises and the implications of uniqueness

Severely disabled people need many resources and services, and each set of personal circumstances is unique; it follows that everyone with a severe disability requires an individualised, complex package of care. Such packages may be more or less expensive but they are almost always complicated to organise. When personal circumstances are stable or evolve only slowly and the care has become routine, the anxieties and organisational problems can be tackled gradually, as they appear.

   On the other hand, crises are a regular if infrequent feature of disabled living, for reasons that have been discussed in Chapter 8. Complex individual needs can therefore arise at very short notice, creating urgent needs for complicated organisation. Large institutions such as general hospitals solve similar problems by having many different resources under one roof and one management, justified by a huge caseload. But the number of younger physically disabled people is by comparison very small, and their crisis needs are not necessarily best dealt with by admission to a place like a hospital. Crises are therefore very often badly handled, with a great deal of consequent frustration as, for example, when housing adaptations take too long to complete, systems of personal care cannot be set up, or hospital beds are inappropriately 'blocked'.

   One managerial solution is never fully to commit the relevant resources, always ensuring that there is a reserve of such components as unoccupied residential places, stand-by staff, and a contingency fund. By themselves, however, such measures are not enough: the problem is unlikely to be solved without formally recognised arrangements for overall managerial responsibility.

Residential care revisited

Table 10.1 demonstrates residential care as an integral part of each local disability service, not a separate institution into which people are put away. Among its five components, planned short stay will only succeed if there is a commitment to the principle, and if time is spent ensuring that each programme fits well into the requirements of particular individuals and families and their other forms of enablement and care. This requires that staff should be expected to give time to develop the necessary relationships based on mutual trust, understanding and co-operation.

Programmes of rehabilitation present problems of deciding objectives and selecting the customers. Very short-term rehabilitation, over a period of a few weeks only, is usually a relatively easy task and can be carried out within the framework of the general medical services or a planned short stay programme. Rehabilitation over longer periods implies that disabilities are more severe and goals more ambitious; it follows that declared objectives may not always be achieved so that there must always be a well thought out, implementable plan of action if they are not. In practice this means dependable access to different options for continuing care, including good community services, appropriate housing, and committed places in residential care. Even with this dependable access, some programmes may take many months or even years, and without it the more ambitious goals can, sadly, not be worth attempting.

But the task usually identified with residential homes is committed long-term care – to which, it has to be said, living in a private household must almost always be considered preferable. The reasons for this view have been outlined in Chapter 9: people's personal identities, aspirations and careers should be considered at least as important as their freedom from risk; community care has a degree of flexibility and responsiveness that can scarcely be achieved if the main emphasis is on secondary care; giving priority to community services is likely to encourage social interest in, and understanding of, severe disability generally.

There are, however, three groups of people for whom this view may be challenged: those who, despite having received a well-matched programme of community care (and this qualification is very important) nevertheless prefer the option of residential care at least for a while; those whose informal carers are for one reason or another justified in asking to be relieved, again at least for a while; and those whose home circumstances, whether physical or social, are manifestly undesirable in the disabled person's view as well as in the opinion of the professionals. When judgements are required on any of these issues, it is essential that they are only made after careful consideration of all the relevant facts and in consultation with all the relevant parties.

The medical model of committed care is inappropriate. Living in a community demands an understanding of interpersonal relationships and group dynamics, and of the importance of privacy, possessions, freedom of action, and a well-organised but individually responsive regime. Attractively prepared meals, space to move about, places to meet people and opportunities to do things are at least as important as correct medical, nursing or therapeutic techniques. For someone whose options are severely reduced, to be able to look forward to something is more important than the abolition of all risk.

If an establishment is largely or wholly devoted to committed long-term care, it will rarely be able to respond to urgent calls for help. This kind of response is therefore most likely to be associated with units or homes which have appreciable programmes of planned short stay and rehabilitation. The problems created by emergencies frequently resolve themselves quite quickly so an emergency admission policy itself guarantees some turnover which is self-perpetuating, although not reliably so. The demand will depend on exactly what emergencies are considered to justify admission – whether purely social crises such as the illness or departure of a carer, or certain specific medical crises such as pressure sores, or more general medical reasons such as any complicating illness in a severely disabled person. Clearly there is overlap with the relatively enormous resources of the general hospital service, and a disability service's total commitment to emergency admission will probably never be very great. The extent to which it is involved in practice is likely to be related to the availability of professionals who are trained and experienced in dealing with the crises that are likely to present themselves.

Allocating resources fairly

The services under discussion are not provided through a free-enterprise system; responsibility has to be taken for consumers who on their own initiative cannot obtain what they need, and there is no open competition. Available resources also generally fail to match demand; people who go without may do so by default, which can include being on a waiting list, or there can be a system of allocating resources to those who need them most. If this second option is accepted, it follows that some applicants must be denied what they have asked for; while the suggestion may appear insensitive, it can often be better that consumers should know that (and know why) a service is not available to them, so that they may argue their case or seek or be offered an alternative, than that a large number of unselected people should have the frustration of awaiting a service for an indefinite period with no guarantee that it will appear in time for their needs.

This is yet another reason for collaboration: priorities cannot be reliably met if related services in the same area make no attempt to relate their decisions to one another. For key resources in limited supply, each district therefore requires some sort of resource-allocation panel which meets frequently and regularly to review and resolve supply and demand.

Mobility and transport

People with severe physical disabilities cannot travel easily, with three obvious consequences. The first is that to provide transport is an essential part of any service they are offered away from their own homes; to establish a day centre or a residential unit without it is an evasion of responsibility. The second consequence is that professionals, who generally have no mobility problems, should expect in the normal course of their duties to visit people's homes and other establishments than their own, in accordance yet again with the principles of collaboration and partnership. Third, confinement to one place can be one of the most frustrating aspects of physical disability, and is a particular reason why the availability of day centres and transport is so important.

Advocacy and campaigning: an altered professional role

Reference has frequently been made to the need for professional people to modify the approaches which are conditioned by their conventional training. It is not for a member of one profession to specify in any detail where the responsibilities of other professions should lie; this is the reason why I shall emphasise the medical role, not because medical responsibilities to disabled people are of paramount significance.

In some ways doctors need to be more involved. Important as it is for them to give priority to treatment which may lead to recovery, they can also do a great deal for people who will do well simply to keep going as they are, or who can only expect deterioration. It is bad enough for people with disabilities and their carers to be told that they are unlikely to get better; it is far worse to be told that nothing more can be done to help them. Usually this is simply not true; giving and organising help, listening, counselling, being on hand should there be crises, acting as advocates through the maze of difficulties that all severely disabled people have to face – the list is potentially a long one. For this reason, defining the doctors' commitment as 'disability medicine' in preference to 'rehabilitation' is to be welcomed, not to suggest that disabled people always need doctors but as an indication of the medical obligation.

In other ways the medical profession should be less involved; less willing to be authoritarian or to impose its own views on the management of relevant resources as of right. Many doctors need to improve the art of working in a multi-disciplinary team, and of trusting judgements to others while not relinquishing their proper responsibilities for their patients' health and welfare. Within a team a doctor may or may not be expected to adopt a leadership role; the way in which this is decided, and the way leadership is exercised whoever assumes it, can require some skill. Doctors also have to accept that their own judgements (as discussed in Chapter 8) may have to be reassessed in the light of the knowledge and experience of others, not least their own patients.

In their advocacy role, doctors should also be willing and prepared to press, and if necessary to campaign for, resources which apparently do not exist, and to challenge policies and practices which are evidently not in their patients' best interests. Bureaucracies are not totally inflexible and people within them are often eager to innovate if they receive encouragement and can see why it is necessary. New approaches can result, which become precedents, and this is one way in which well-run local services can develop their response to need. Finally, in respect of decisions whether or not to enter residential care, doctors should be at pains to help their patients consider all the available options and opinions before making irrevocable decisions.

The other professions' responsibilities are not very different; they include the need to be better and more widely informed, to play a full part in a team, to give their patients or clients some hope or encouragement or at least some worthwhile counselling, and to act as their advocates in the face of difficulty. In a good multi-disciplinary team the individual roles are not sharply defined; considerable overlap is the rule, and it is right that it should be so.

GETTING THE MANAGEMENT RIGHT: A DISTRICT DISABILITY COUNCIL

While there is wide agreement about the framework of a district's services and while a great deal can be achieved by co-operation, making use of existing resources and adjusting personal practice, limits are inevitably set not only by total resource provision but also by the need for coherent management and administration. Indeed, it is hard to believe that the necessary cohesion can ever be achieved without some person or some group identifiably in charge, yet at the time of writing there is no consensus about how this may be attained.

There are, however, a few currently operating models that suggest what could be done. In essence, they consist of appointing or electing groups of professionals, consumers, and representatives of the voluntary services to some sort of planning group, council or committee, but the vexed question usually remains of how much executive authority the groups should be permitted. Ideally, every locality should be covered by groups of this kind, whose responsibilities should at least extend to participating in relevant decisions about future development but could also include the deployment and allocation of certain critically important resources. While most resources and services would remain the responsibility of the agencies or authorities to which they belonged, some of them could be delegated for direct administration by the group which would hold a budget for them. Properly established, such a group might be termed a district disability council.

Each council's terms of reference would obviously have to be carefully set out. It would be essential to cover the population of severely disabled people of adult 'working' age, but there may be a wish to extend consideration to at least some cases of mental as well as physical disability within that age group; to disabled children; and to severely disabled people above retirement age. Depending on these decisions, the number of potential customers could be as little as a hundred or two, or as great as 1500 or more. Decisions to become involved with less severe disabilities would raise that figure still further. The actual numbers are less important than the need to be aware of the implications of the alternative policy decisions, which are likely to be influenced by the effectiveness or otherwise of existing services.

An effective service, however, needs a certain minimum population in order to acquire sufficient expertise and, in respect of the more expensive resources, in order to be economically efficient. Depending on the exact terms of reference, therefore, and also because the local public services often have geographical boundaries which are not co-terminous, the arrangements for most district disability councils would have to incorporate some anomalies from the public services' conventional point of view. In one area, for example, a council might be based on one social service and one education department but two health authorities and/or housing departments; in another it might be accountable to a single health authority and only part of a social services or education department. Local public authorities are unlikely to come together on that sort of basis without leadership from central government and, therefore, if the entire population is to be covered, some sort of government ruling is likely to be essential (see below).

To be at all effective, at the very least the councils would each need a secretarial service. On the assumption that they would be given a range of service responsibilities, however large or small, each one would also need to employ a person who would carry executive authority. Such a person would be expected to respond to a wide variety of interests and pressures, including not only the public authorities and the professions but also the consumers. He or she should also relate well to parallel interests such as local services for other dependent and disabled groups, and in general should take an effective place in the matrix of local services. In that the primary responsibility would be to make use of existing resources, the role might be described as that of co-ordinator, yet this term is not strong enough to imply the authority which the person should be given and should be expected to exercise. In the currently fashionable jargon, therefore, he or she might therefore be designated as district disability manager.

Figure 10.1 gives a general outline of the structure that is envisaged. It is, of course, essential that individual roles should be mutually understood, that authority should be adequately assumed or delegated as appropriate, that communications within the structure and with relevant people outside it are good, and that the resolve to leave no problem of severe disability unanswered should be mutually agreed. Within this framework the district disability council would have several important specific tasks to perform. Even if the framework is not adopted, the tasks remain, and the local services still have to deal with them in the best way they can.

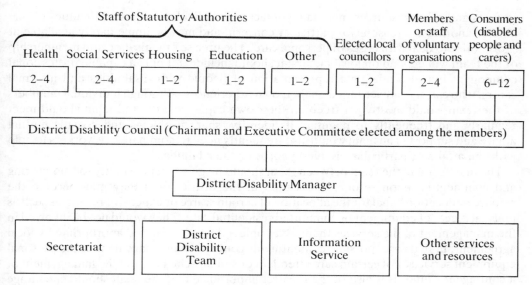

Figure 10.1   *Model for a District Disability Council*

THE RESPONSIBILITIES OF A DISTRICT DISABILITY COUNCIL AND ITS MANAGER

Obtaining and disseminating information

Arguably the first task of all is to arrange that deficiencies of service are recognised, documented and regularly analysed. At the time of writing, among those which are most frequently encountered are the lack of help available to people with severe brain injury, including stroke; to people with progressive brain disease; to disabled school-leavers; to those who are housebound and frustrated, at any age but especially perhaps those who are still young; and to those who require regular if not constant personal help. A formally established deficiency register would be of considerable value. More conventional registers of disabled persons have proved difficult both to establish and to maintain in the past, and if they are to be set up they should be orientated towards particular problems or groups as revealed by the deficiency register, and kept regularly and reliably up to date. The second aspect of the exercise requires considerable co-operation among many different groups of people, and considerable sophistication of method.

The other aspect of data collection is to provide an information bank as outlined earlier in this chapter. The precise method of its organisation is less important than that its services should be competent, widely publicised and widely used. In this way, all the available resources can be perceived in context; such information is essential if they are all to be allocated effectively and fairly.

The District Disability Team

The council and manager should be responsible for the selection of a district disability team, which among many possible activities may provide counselling, facilitate access to services and other resources, maintain contact with individuals whose difficulties of one kind or another are reasons for particular concern, and may be immediately available at short notice to deal with crises of personal care. The precise organisation and membership of the team will depend on local factors; it should include not only a capable professional component but also adequate representation of people with disabilities and informal carers, who can give advice based on their own experiences. Although individual members of the team would mostly act freely in their own capacities, the full team should meet regularly and frequently to maintain its identity, share problems and provide mutual advice and support. The team would also frequently need to nominate key workers to help with the affairs of particular disabled people or their families.

The manager and the team between them should be given responsibility for monitoring and commenting upon resource allocation in the district, and they may become the resource-allocation panel for the allocation of certain scarce or expensive resources such as unusual pieces of equipment or committed residential care. They would not be involved in the management of the services themselves unless it was considered appropriate by local agreement; in that case, possible commitments could be the management of the personal equipment service or of certain care attendant or similar schemes, and the management of a contingency fund. It is also of the greatest importance that the team should encourage and implement programmes of education and training, by whatever means are thought likely to be best.

Social care in the widest sense

The district disability council will certainly wish to be involved with local issues of enablement of social care. These are large subjects and in the main are beyond the scope of this book; they have, in any case, received wide publicity elsewhere. They are the concern of all people with disabilities and most of them are outside the ordinary limits of professional responsibility. Here, it is sufficient to mention that they include transport facilities, wheelchair access to buildings and neighbourhoods, and opportunities for recreation, occupation, education and employment. Since many of them can be very deficient indeed they often require, or have been the subjects of, local or national campaigns or programmes of publicity. They are issues of which all the members of a disability team must be aware, and in which professional interest and support are often desirable and appreciated.

CENTRAL AND REGIONAL GOVERNMENT

There are four issues which require central or regional government leadership, and a fifth which would be helped by it.

Making disability councils a statutory requirement

Given the need for public service co-operation, and given the resistance to it which is fairly predictable, there can be no doubt that strong government leadership is desirable even if new legislation is unnecessary or impracticable. Exhortation is rarely sufficient: it should be a statutory requirement that district disability councils are formed and that their constitution, defined responsibilities and scope for action should satisfy a required minimum. The aim should be to ensure that every part of the country is adequately covered by a district disability service; whatever the details of each local arrangement, there should be no gaps. The appointment of a district disability manager, or some similar person or group of persons with cross-boundary authority, should similarly be a statutory requirement. If the district disability services became responsible for access to all forms of residential care, there could then be one form of registration of voluntary and private residential homes (at least for physically disabled people), with eligibility for social security payments dependent on a person's disability and not on the registration status of a particular home.

Equitable funding for community and residential care

This consideration leads on to the inequities and anomalies of public funding for the support of severe disability generally, and the requirements that as far as possible they should be minimised. It has been argued for years that payments to disabled people should be based on the severity of their disabilities and not on the historical development of particular services, and in principle this objective is sound. In practice, however, there can be considerable problems in the assessment of each individual's eligibility, in keeping the assessment up to date as the individual's abilities change, in setting the rate to be paid, and in dealing with contested decisions. Providing a new system of allowances has, in the past, resulted in many more claimants than were anticipated, and the government's awareness of this problem is the reason for the new survey of disability which is to be published in 1988. While accepting the understandable need both for caution and for the avoidance of cumbersome procedures, the principle must be that eligibility for public funds should not unnecessarily bias the choice of a particular form of care whether in a private household, a residential home or a hospital.

Development of tertiary resources

Some severely disabled people have such unusual special needs that a district service, however well run, cannot be expected either to have enough experience or the appropriate resources to deal with them. For this reason another tier of disability services needs to be created so that there shall be certain centres of expertise, available to help populations of at least one million. Essentially each centre would have two principal commitments: the provision of special equipment for highly individual needs (special seating and communication aids, for example), and a resource for the re-education of people with the more exacting forms of brain injury. Special equipment also includes limb and other prostheses, which in Britain are currently provided by an entirely independent service; it has been suggested that this service might be incorporated into a pattern of regional disability centres.

Establishing requirements for audit

All these developments need some form of external evaluation and regular review, to ensure that adequate goals and standards are being set and achieved. Central government should therefore ensure that this 'watchdog' function is firmly delegated to appropriate local groups, of which the district disability councils would be an obvious example. Relevant statutory bodies already exist in Britain, however; the community health councils which are local, and the Health Advisory Service which is national. There are also numerous consumer groups, both national and local, funded either by public money or privately, or a combination of both. The report of the Royal College of Physicians (1986a), which was mentioned in Chapter 1, has cited a number of specific issues which such groups would be expected to monitor and, if necessary, publicly criticise.

Incentives for education and training

Central government could also help by recognising the need for education and training. Although such matters are usually the responsibility of professional bodies and local authorities, there are two reasons for government involvement. The first is that there is a core of knowledge which should be the common requirement of a number of professions, and central encouragement of a joint approach could be of considerable value. The second reason is quite simply that when resources are scarce, education and training are often not seen to be high priorities; it has been argued in this book that the reverse is the case, and government incentives to the allocation of finance would undoubtedly be helpful. Perhaps the best approach would be the development of a nationally recognised qualification in the care of physical disability, which people with a wide variety of backgrounds would be eligible to attain.

POSTSCRIPT

Chapter 1 began with a personal story, of someone whose disability had lasted only a few years and who had still even to consider making a move from a hospital environment to more independent living. It is appropriate to end this chapter with another account, of a person whose disability lasted 27 years and whose example significantly influenced the Health Service's approach to the care of severely disabled people in the district where she lived. Her life story above all reflects her own passionate commitment to what she believed to be right, but it also reveals her changing needs as the nature of her disability and her personal relationship changed, and the slow transformation of the statutory services' responses over more than a quarter century of changing attitudes to disabled people, from 1959 to 1986.

Mrs M was 29 when she took her second child to the local clinic for polio vaccination. While she was in the waiting room she began to feel unwell, and within three days she was in the respiratory unit of the regional infectious diseases hospital nearly 30 miles away. She was totally tetraplegic and was in an 'iron lung' for seven months before being given a tracheostomy and positive pressure ventilation, which, with one interval, she used for the rest of her life. Fortunately, during that first few months she slowly regained enough use of the muscles of her upper limbs to be able to read, write and eat without help. Because her paralysis was due to poliomyelitis she was not permanently troubled by incontinence or vulnerability to pressure sores, and she was eventually able to manage without her ventilator for as long as seven hours at a time.

Two and a quarter years later she went to the newly opened Mary Marlborough Lodge in Oxford where she immediately developed severe pneumonia which led to a further period in an iron lung, surgical removal of a lobe of the right lung and a transient left-sided stroke. Eventually, nearly three years after the first illness, she spent three weeks with her family in the rehabilitation flat at the Lodge. It had been agreed that they should all live in a house that had been specially adapted (the family had already moved once to be near the respiratory unit) but a suitable property did not become available for yet another two and a quarter years, and she had to stay in another hospital for the whole of that time.

When she finally did get back home, well into the sixth year of her disability, her marriage was already in trouble. The next five and a half years were difficult, punctuated by frequent readmissions to hospital for as much as three months at a time, and she was never continuously at home for longer than three months. By present-day standards the equipment was not very adequate either: a portable hydraulic hoist and a non-motorised wheelchair besides, of course, the ventilator. She was, however, enormously helped by a very experienced voluntary worker who introduced her to various courses of study, including what subsequently became her lifelong interest. Then an orthopaedic surgeon admitted her to a recovery ward, partly to attempt treatment for excessive lumbar lordosis, and she never went home again.

Instead, after a year or so she was admitted to a newly built geriatric hospital on the understanding that when a Health Service unit for younger disabled people was also built on that site, she would go to live there instead. Unfortunately, that took another four and a half years, during which she became a foundation student of the Open University. She also began to receive regular postural treatment for her chest from an expert physiotherapist and the long sequence of respiratory crises was arrested at last. Understandably, however, she felt incarcerated and at times very lonely in the geriatric ward, although by the time she came to the younger disabled unit she was leading a somewhat more active life, equipped with a powered wheelchair, studying and occasionally going out to visit friends.

The new unit was an improvement on the ward and it enabled her to go out rather more, but early idealism that it might be like being in her own home was soon shattered by re-emergence of the familiar hospital restrictions and routines. For a time she tried to keep a shop but the administration never supported the venture and it had to be abandoned. She regarded the grouping of sixteen or so severely disabled people who were all much of an age (mostly betwen 35 and 50) as unnatural, and the idea of a residents' committee never appealed to her either as a useful or a practical proposition. After a couple of years she was equipped with an adult-sized swivel walker with which she could 'walk' down the corridor; perhaps the high point of this phase of her life was when she used the walker to go and receive her degree at an Open University ceremony when she was nearly 50.

But her long-standing disability began to produce an added range of problems. Trouble from her chest had diminished, partly because of the physiotherapy and partly because of an aseptic suction technique through the tracheostomy using disposable catheters, but she became obese and developed mild diabetes which fortunately responded to dietary management. She also developed bilateral cataracts which had to be removed. Troublesome, fairly persistent intestinal distension also became a problem, but the worst thing was pain; the bones of the lower part of her body became severely decalcified and she developed soft-tissue pain as well, especially in the wasted muscles and ligaments around her spine.

Before the pain really asserted itself, however, she had managed to persuade her social worker that she really wanted to live in her own home. Again, there was a long delay before a housing association offered her a flat, but she required a ceiling mounted hoist and the building was not very suitable for adaptation. It so happened that a member of the unit's staff had learned through personal contact that the local housing department was building a number of new 'wheelchair' bungalows. (No information about such schemes, then or now, has ever been formally released to Health Service staff in that particular district.) One of the bungalows was duly secured for Mrs M but the suggestion that she might move into it to live on her own produced immediate scepticism. One of her close helpers in the hospital said it was hard to understand why she wanted to leave the unit where she was secure and had most of the things she required. A proposal that her hospital bed should be 'closed', so that the Health Service could fund the equivalent of an extra nurse for her support, was rejected by the local Health Service management, which instead took refuge in the idea of joint funding with social services which never materialised. Meanwhile, the housing department became very interested in the whole exercise and one of its staff just happened to have heard of the community service volunteers One-to-One scheme, which was just being set up for another person in a neighbouring district.

Eventually she did move to her own home with 'CSVs', six years after moving out of the geriatric ward. She had to re-learn to be a manager of her own helpers instead of the plain recipient of help she had been for more than a decade, and initial problems in that respect nearly made it all impossible – but she learned. Because of severe pain she became almost completely bedfast, far less able to pursue an outdoor social life than ten years ago in hospital. But her family visited her regularly, she had friendly relations with the local services (nurses, social services, housing, police – in case there was an emergency) and the Roman Catholic church of which she was a member, and above all, she was in her own place. It was not easy for the volunteers, but with excellent support from nursing and social services they continued to look after her well. To her two small grandchildren she was known as 'granny-in-the-bed'.

After five years in the bungalow her pain did diminish a little, and cautiously she began getting up and about again. She did not fit easily into her wheelchair and a friend added some home-made adaptations to it. Everyone was pleased and impressed with her progress until quite suddenly one day she developed more abdominal distension, severe difficulty with her breathing and a physiological state of shock. There was delay in mobilising the necessary emergency services and within a few hours she had died. A tearful Community Service Volunteer who had been looking after her for several months said that one of her last comments had been that she did not want to become ill again because she had so much to do.

Her memorial service in the local church was attended by family, members of the congregation, community care staff who had come to know her during those five years, and people from the younger disabled unit who had looked after her for the six years before that. I talked to several of them afterwards, her son and daughter-in-law included; they were all convinced it had been right for her to live in her own place and that she had died as she would have wished, in command of her own life and still wholly committed to her family and her various activities. Nearly two years after leaving the younger disabled unit, she had written this about her experience with the volunteers:

> There is so much to be said in order to cover the many aspects of the Independent Living Scheme that it would be impossible adequately to do the subject justice in a brief letter; for now it will be sufficient to say how much I appreciate the care and, at the risk of sounding over-sentimental the compassion – even love – which I have been shown by different CSV couples who have in their turn shared my life. This does not

mean that there are not difficulties at times, for CSVs and clients are simply people who are rather thrown together without prior knowledge of each other in any real sense. Often there is laughter – sometimes the occasional tear. I think that the variety of trials and tribulations shared amongst us all as a small team illustrate both sides of the same 'coin of experience'. This brings me to my second point. All the girls show positive signs of gaining from the experience of hard work, self-discipline and perseverance, a real understanding of their own potential and capabilities for the future. In their turn they have given me a very great deal in terms of re-establishing my identity as an individual within a community, following many years of institutional care where my personal character and preferences had of necessity to remain submerged as part of a cohesive whole.

The presence of CSVs in my life has created a further dimension, a completely new perspective for me where I can emerge once more as an independently responsible, thinking human being with permission to make my own mistakes again and to learn from them. My physical resources have become somewhat more limited as a natural consequence of continuing immobility but my intellect has revived considerably, equally as much from being 'in charge' again at home as it is due to studying and other social activities within my own environment. In conclusion, may I just say 'Thank you'. Long may your organisation prosper and develop for the benefit of your potential Independently Living Clients. We need them, so keep up with the recruiting: it is a valuable service to an increasing minority group within the community.

Appendix 1
The Royal College of Physicians' project

The project's terms of reference have been summarised in Chapter 1. For one person to cover and report on such a wide field in only fifteen months presented obvious problems of judgement. The review would have to be both broad and therefore fairly superficial, the personal contacts would have to be selective, and the subjective nature of many of the observations and their interpretation was inevitable. In the event the chosen course of action was as follows.

1. Review of the literature, including published statistics. The subject is cross-disciplinary and many papers and documents are published neither commercially nor in professional journals, a number of them being issued only for local consumption; retrieval would therefore inevitably be incomplete. Literature from countries other than Britain was not widely consulted unless it was to do with relevant subjects of general importance as, for example, certain clinical and psychological topics and the philosophy of the Independent Living Movement.
2. Informal postal enquiries. A circular letter (not a formal questionnaire) was sent to all the district medical officers and directors of social services in England and Wales, and to directors of social work in Scotland. The issues raised were the provision of residential care for younger disabled people within their own districts, the use their own authorities made of similar resources provided by others, the difficulties that may have been experienced locally in obtaining resources of this nature, and any important developments or future plans which they might wish to report. The proportion of medical officers who replied was over 90 per cent but the proportion of social services directors was only just over 50 per cent; replies from both groups varied enormously in their evident commitment and enthusiasm and their helpfulness. Many were able to supply detailed reports or planning documents; a few social services directors, on the other hand, wrote to say that they felt unable to co-operate. More informal enquiries were sent to the Scottish Home and Health Department and the Northern Ireland Office and to a number of the relevant voluntary organisations; several of these enquiries were followed up by personal visits.
3. A postal questionnaire directed to 245 residential homes and hospital units (Table A1). From the replies to the above enquiries, and from lists supplied by the Department of Health and Social Security (1978), Queen Elizabeth's Foundation for the Disabled (1984), the Leonard Cheshire Foundation and The Spastics Society, as well as certain other voluntary organisations, a total list of 283 was compiled: the lack of replies from half the social service departments meant that the list could not be regarded as complete, but the availability of evidence from other sources suggested that it was very nearly so. Of two versions, the simpler was sent to residential homes: besides asking about data which are set out in Chapter 4 it also included enquiries about the number of beds, documents issued by the home, access to transport, use of special labour schemes, and plans for the future. This version was despatched to the Cheshire Homes at the end of October 1984, the local authority homes in February 1985, and The Spastics Society units in May 1985. Reminders and second copies were not sent. The fuller version was mailed to Health Service units and included all the same questions together with certain others, the responses to which are reported in Chapter 7; it was despatched at the end of October 1984 followed, if necessary, by reminders and second copies in March 1985. These four groups together received 237 of the questionnaires;

Table A.1 *Numbers of homes and units specialising in physically disabled younger adults, with response to questionnaire and number of visits made*

	Number of homes/units	Homes/units replying to questionnaire		Homes/units visited or already known	
		Nos.	(%)	Nos.	(%)
England and Wales					
National Health Service					
(YDUs – purpose built)	(42)	(34)	(81)	(23)	(55)
(YDUs – other)	(33)	(26)	(79)	(9)	(27)
YDUs – total	75	60	(80)	32	(43)
Cheshire Homes	58	30	(52)	11	(18)
Local Authority Homes	58	33	(57)	16	(28)
The Spastics Society residential units	37	21	(57)	2	(4)
Other voluntary and private agencies	At least 45*	8	(62)*	10	(22)
Scotland					
National Health Service	11	6	(55)	1	(9)
Cheshire Homes	3	0	(0)	0	—
Other voluntary and private agencies	At least 6*	0	—	1	(17)
Northern Ireland					
National Health Service	2	2	(100)		
TOTAL	At least 286	160	(64)	73	(29)

* Only 16 were contacted and only 13 were sent the questionnaire: they were all in England.

the other eight were sent to a selection of voluntary or private homes or hospitals, at irregular intervals during the same seven-month period.

4. More than 100 personal visits to individuals, residential homes and Health Service units, and to certain other institutions. The programme extended from August 1984 to July 1985 but was largely concentrated into the five months from December 1984 to April 1985. Visits were deliberately selective, partly on the basis of geographical convenience (the research office was in Birmingham) but also with a bias towards those Health Service units which were purpose-built as a result of the Chronically Sick and Disabled Persons Act.

At the homes and units the routine was unstructured. Usually the first hour or more was spent with the person or persons who had arranged to meet me. In most cases this would be head of home, officer in charge, sister, senior nurse or consultant, but by no means always; in one unit it was a resident's parents. After a fairly quick look round the building, as much time as was available was then spent informally on talking to at least three residents. Visits lasted from two to five hours; besides notes written down during the conversations, a brief account of each one was dictated into a tape recorder immediately afterwards.

Table A1 summarises the number of responses to the questionnaires and the number of visits to the residential units and homes. Tables A2 and A3 give a complete list of the personal contacts which were made during the year. Table A4 displays part of the postal questionnaire which enquired about the severity of physical and mental disability.

Table A.2   *List of units and homes which were visited or already known*

Health Service units – purpose-built

Castle Hill Hospital, Cottingham	Westcliff Hospital, Essex	Gloucester Royal Hospital, Gloucester
Pinderfields Hospital, Wakefield	Linton Hospital, Maidstone	Moseley Hall Hospital, Birmingham
St George's Hospital, Lincoln	St Richard's Hospital, Chichester	
Nottingham City Hospital, Nottingham	Ashurst Hospital, Southampton	Clatterbridge Hospital, Merseyside
Derby City Hospital, Derby	Churchill Hospital, Oxford	
Leicester General Hospital, Leicester	Stoke Mandeville Hospital, Aylesbury	Fazakerley Hospital, Merseyside
Coleman Hospital, Norwich	Manfield Hospital, Northampton	Withington Hospital, Manchester
Hillingdon Hospital, Middlesex	Musgrove Park Hospital, Taunton	Ladywell Hospital, Salford
	Ham Green Hospital, Bristol	Woodend General Hospital, Aberdeen

Other Health Service units

Chapel Allerton Hospital, Leeds	Townlands Hospital, Henley-on-Thames	Dudley Road Hospital, Birmingham
Tickhill Road Hospital, Doncaster	Newcourt Hospital, Exeter	West Park Hospital, Wolverhampton
Frogwell Hospital, Chippenham	Royal Midlands Counties Home, Leamington Spa	Fanny Deakin Hospital, Newcastle under Lyme

Local authority homes

Hull	Leicester	Taunton	Dudley
Doncaster	Norwich	Kenilworth (Warwickshire)	Kidderminster
Nottingham	Camden	Coventry (two)	Walsall
Alfreton (Derbyshire)		Birmingham (two)	Manchester

Cheshire Homes

Holme Lodge	The Grove	Cotswold
Staunton Harold	Mote House	Greenacres
Roecliffe Manor	Le Court	St Anthony's
	St Michael's	Saltways

The Spastics Society

Rutland House Special School	Norwich Hostel	Kyre Park	Meadway Works

Other residential units and homes

York House, Ossett, Yorkshire (Shaftesbury Society)
Combat Care Home, Epping
Royal Hospital and Home for Incurables, Putney
Wellesley House, Wolverhampton
Little Ingestre, Stafford

Stagenhoe Park, Hertfordshire (Sue Ryder Foundation)
Residential and housing units belonging to John Grooms Association in Finsbury Park, Edgware and Southend
Crossways, Birmingham (British Red Cross Society)

Table A.3 *Other visits and personal contacts*

Rehabilitation units at Derby, Cambridge, Southampton, Oxford, Stoke Mandeville, Oswestry, Cardiff and Edinburgh
Chapeltown NHS nursing home, Sheffield
The Grove Road housing project
NHS community units for mental handicap in Kidderminster and Kinver (Staffordshire)
Headway, Nottingham
St Michael's Hospital, Lichfield
In London: The Spastics Society, the Leonard Cheshire Foundation, the King's Fund Centre, the Prince of Wales' Advisory Group, the Spinal Injuries Association, the National Council of Voluntary Organisations, the Association to Combat Huntington's Chorea, the Royal Association for Disability and Rehabilitation, the Royal College of Nursing, the Department of Health and Social Security
The Scottish Home and Health Department
The Welsh Office
Coalitions of Disabled People for Derbyshire and Nottinghamshire; Centres for Independent Living in Norwich, Hampshire and Exeter
The personal advice and help of Dr Elizabeth Badley, Helen Bartlett, Dr Mildred Blaxter, Professor R. S. Bluglass, Professor J. C. Brocklehurst, Professor N. R. Butler, Dr John Cash, Professor V. W. M. Drury, Dr Helen Evers, Vic Finkelstein, Dr Mary Haslum, Tim Marshall, Professor E. A. Marsland, Diana Pomeroy and Professor P. H. N. Wood are also acknowledged with appreciation.

Table A.4 *Extract from the questionnaire*

SECTION E   This section would best be answered by several members of staff in consultation

E1   On 'Census Day' (   ) please identify the numbers of persons according to the following simple scales

	Day attenders		Respite/ holiday		All other residents	
PHYSICAL DISABILITY	*None* ☐	☐	☐	☐	☐	☐
(Needs assistance walking, or wheelchair user who can transfer. Most other functions normal or only mildly affected)	*Mild* ☐	☐	☐	☐	☐	☐
(As above, plus problems of continence/communication/self-care, and/or wheelchair user, unable to transfer without help)	*Moderate* ☐	☐	☐	☐	☐	☐
(All others, including those who need to be fed and/or turned regularly at night)	*Severe* ☐	☐	☐	☐	☐	☐
MENTAL DISABILITY	*None* ☐	☐	☐	☐	☐	☐
(Forgetful/euphoric/lacking initiative/sometimes depressed)	*Mild* ☐	☐	☐	☐	☐	☐
(As above, plus liability to antisocial behaviour/serious difficulty in reasoning/bouts of disorientation)	*Moderate* ☐	☐	☐	☐	☐	☐
(All others, including those who are always badly disorientated/unable to organise the simplest activities/in stupor or coma)	*Severe* ☐	☐	☐	☐	☐	☐

Appendix 2
Outline of a course of teaching in disability medicine

1. *The nature of the principal diseases and injuries which cause severe physical disability*. Much of this component has been set out in Chapter 3; there should be particular attention, not just to the mechanical difficulties that arise from physical disability, but also to the less visible disabilities too. Examples would include:

- the physical sensations (pain, discomfort, fatigue, unaccountable variability) experienced in stroke, head injury, spinal injury, motor neurone disease and other nervous system disorders
- the great varieties of disabilities of performance (perception, concentration, memory, speech, emotion, social awareness) caused by disease or injury of the brain
- the outlook: the chances of improvement or the likelihood of deterioration
- the issues of ageing: the changed perception that ageing brings, and the physiological effects of ageing in the presence of severe physical impairment

2. *The impact of severe disability on the disabled person*

- the inseparability of personality from a disabling condition which dates from birth or early childhood: 'My disability is myself'
- the adjustment to acquired disability: denial, depression, adjustment, rehabilitation and/or resignation, reduced expectation
- greater difficulties with learning power, social acceptability, mobility; a need for greater effort for more limited goals
- discomfort, embarrassment, social inconvenience and frustration
- difficulty with personal (including sexual) relationships
- economic loss
- the crucial importance of a person's aspirations

3. *The impact on families and principal carers*. Many of the effects are like those experienced by the people they care for, but there are others too:

- the practical problems of giving unceasing help with tasks of daily living
- reasonable expectations of the limits of tolerance and responsibility
- altered expectations, loss of freedom, reduced income, isolation and exhaustion
- conflicting emotions which can include affection, resolve and imagination, but also frustration, strain on personal relationships and despair
- the special position of women as carers

4. *The economics and management of service provision*. At least some knowledge of these subjects is desirable so that people not only may understand why things do not appear to happen as they should, but in order to help those who campaign for change:

- evaluation of disability in comparison with other courses of social disadvantage
- the work generated by particular levels of disability, and the need for professional skills
- paid versus unpaid services and help
- the organisation of community services
- the availability and management of wheelchair-adapted housing
- available sources of finance

- ascertainment of those in need; assessment of demands for help
- evaluating effectiveness
- priorities and planning

5. *The hardware of disabled living.* This subject has been discussed in general terms in Chapter 5, but it is necessary to have at least some detailed knowledge of the sort of equipment that can or should be provided. An encyclopaedic set of guides is published by Oxfordshire Health Authority and includes the following titles:

- clothing and dressing
- personal care
- incontinence and stoma care
- communication aids
- walking aids
- wheelchair
- housing and furniture
- hoists and lifts
- home management
- outdoor transport
- equipment for leisure and gardening

as well as special equipment for disabled mothers and disabled children. Other categories include alarms and alarm systems, computer-based equipment, and prostheses (including artificial limbs).

6. *The discipline of residential care.* The importance of this subject is obvious for those who work in any of the residential establishments, but it is also important for those whose work with disabled people lies elsewhere. Only in this way are they likely to be able to give balanced, informed advice to those who, for one reason or another, may be considering entry into a hospital unit or residential home. The aspects to be considered might be as follows:

- do we need residential care?
- admission policies and their consequences
- the ways in which people relate to one another in a large residential community
- the ingredients of a good physical environment
- management issues: residents' rights and opportunities, the bugbear of safety, who should be in charge
- committed care: how far to interfere
- opportunities for (re)assessment and rehabilitation
- programmes of planned short stay and their implications
- accommodating people with unsociable behaviour
- avoiding isolation
- the need for special skills.

7. *An introduction to wider political and ethical aspects of disability.* The potential list is of course very long, but the particular problems of severe physical disability do need to be set in a wider context. Items which might be included are as follows:

- legislation, public administation and social security
- the politics of finance
- the educational challenge; employment; income
- the debate about 'quality of life'
- personal mobility, transport and physical access
- the role, activities and diversity of the voluntary bodies
- disability in less developed countries.

Components such as these should be an integral part of the training of all who work with, and for, severely disabled people, although in courses and curricula other than that of medicine itself there would be differences of emphasis.

References

Abel-Smith, B. (1960). *A History of the Nursing Profession*. London: Heinemann.

Abel-Smith, B. (1964). *The hospitals 1800–1948. A study in social administration in England and Wales*, pp. 352–383. London: Heinemann.

Agerholm, M. (1981). Heenan House: principles and practice in the first two years. In *Handicapped People in our Inner City*, ed. Agerholm, M. London: Heenan House Rehabilitation Centre.

Aitken, C. (1982). Rehabilitation medicine – past or future? *Health Trends* 14, 103–104; *(Scottish) Health Bulletin* 40, 276–78.

Armstrong, A. (1985). *Breath of Life*. London: BBC Publications.

Aronovitch, B. (1974). *Give it Time*. London: André Deutsch.

Baldwin, S., Bradshaw, J., Cooke, K. and Glendinning, C. (1981). The disabled person and cash benefits. In *Disability: Legislation and Practice*, ed. Guthrie, D. London: The Macmillan Press.

Barbellion, W. N. P. (1919, 1920) (republished in 1984). *The Journal of a Disappointed Man, and a Last Diary*. London: Hogarth Press.

Barton, R. (1959). *Institutional Neurosis*. Bristol: John Wright.

Bax, M. and Whitmore, K. (1985). *District Handicap Teams: Structure, Functions and Relationships*. A report to the DHSS. London: Westminster Children's Hospital.

Benson, T. B. and Williams, E. (1979). The younger disabled unit at Fazakerley Hospital, *British Medical Journal*, 2, 369–371.

Berwick, L. (1980). *Undefeated*. London: Epworth Press.

Birrer, C. (1979). *Multiple Sclerosis: a Personal View*. Springfield: Charles C. Thomas.

Blaxter, M. (1976). *The Meaning of Disability. A Sociological Study of Impairment*, pp. 1–17. London: Heinemann.

Bloomfield, R. (1976). *Younger Chronic Sick Units: a Survey and Critique*. Unpublished.

Boucher Report (1957). Survey of services available to the chronic sick and elderly, 1954–55. *Reports on Public Health and Medical Subjects, no. 98*. London: HMSO. Quoted in Means, R. and Smith, R. (1985). *The Development of Welfare Services for Elderly People*, pp. 167–239. London: Croom Helm.

Bowley, A. H. and Gardner, L. (1980). *The Handicapped Child*, 4th ed. London: Churchill Livingstone.

Bowman, G. (1977). Wakerley Lodge: encouragement to living. *Nursing Times* 73, 691–692.

Brattgard, S. O. (1972). Sweden: Fokus: a way of life for living. In *Personal Relationships, the Handicapped and the Community: Some European Thoughts and Solutions*, ed. Lancaster-Gaye, D., pp. 25–40. London: Routledge and Kegan Paul.

Bray, J., Wright, S. (eds.) (1980). *The Use of Technology in the Care of the Elderly and the Disabled: Tools for Living*. London: Frances Pinter, for the Commission of the EEC.

Brearley, P., Hall, F., Gutridge, P., Jones, G. and Roberts, G. (1980). *Admission to Residential Care*. London: Tavistock Publications.

Brechin, A. and Liddiard, P. (1981). *Look at it This Way: New Perspectives in Rehabilitation*. Sevenoaks: Hodder and Stoughton/The Open University Press.

Brechin, A., Liddiard, P. and Swain, J. (eds.) (1981). *Handicap in a Social World*. See especially pp.

5–13 (Safilios-Rothschild, C.), pp. 24–33 (McKnight, J.), pp. 49–57 (Oliver, M.), pp. 58–63 (Finkelstein, V.). Sevenoaks: Hodder and Stoughton/The Open University Press.

Brett, B. (1978). Treat the disabled normally. *Community Care*, 12 April, 16–17.

Brett, B. (1979). A disabled unit from the inside – a consumer's view. In *Living in units for young disabled people*. London: King's Fund Centre.

Briggs, A. and Oliver, J. (1985). *Caring: Experiences of Looking after Disabled Relatives*. London: Routledge and Kegan Paul.

Bristow, A. K. (1981). *Crossroads Care Attendant Schemes: a Study of their Organisation and Working Practice, and of the Families whom they Support*. Rugby: Association of Care Attendant Schemes Ltd.

British Medical Journal (1955). Social problems of the young disabled (report). Vol. 1., p. 163.

British Medical Journal (1960). Chronic disablement from neurological disorders (annotation). Vol. 1, p. 45.

Brooks, N. (ed.) (1984). *Closed Head Injury: Psychological, Social and Family Consequences*. Oxford University Press.

Brown, C. (1970). *Down All the Days*. London: Martin Secker and Warburg (Pan Books, 1971).

Brown, H. J. and Sutcliffe, R. C. G. (1976). Favell House: a young disabled unit. *The Practitioner*, 217, 773–782.

Bryden, J. S. (1985). Paper given at a meeting of the Medical Disability Society, July 1985.

Burnfield, A. (1985). *Multiple Sclerosis: a Personal Exploration*. London: Souvenir Press.

Cantrell, E., Dawson, J. and Glastonbury, G. (1985). *Prisoners of Handicap. A Study of Dependency in Young Physically Disabled People and the Families or Friends upon whom they Rely*. London: Royal Association for Disability and Rehabilitation.

Castree, B. J. and Walker, J. H. (1981). The young adult with spina bifida. *British Medical Journal* 283, 1040–1042.

Challis, L., Day, P. and Klein, R. (1984). Residential care on demand: *New Society*, 5 April, 32.

Checkland, S. G. and Checkland, E. O. A. (eds.) (1974). *The Poor Law Report of 1834*. Harmondsworth: Penguin.

Clough, R. (1982). *Residential Work*. London: The Macmillan Press.

Coe, R. G. (1982). 25 years a tetraplegic. *Lancet* 1, 789–790.

The Consumers' Association (1986). Sounding the alarm. *Which?* pp. 318–321.

Coughlan, T., Ellis, R., Hargraves, E. and Newens, M. (1983). *Survey of Medically Disabled Adults (18–64) Waiting Appropriate Long-term Hospital or Medical Care*. Leeds (unpublished).

Crane, N. and Osborne, P. (1979). *Coincidence . . .? or Meant to Be?* Rugby: The Crossroads Care Attendant Scheme Trust.

Creek, G., Moore, M., Oliver, M., Salisbury, V., Silver, J. and Zarb, G. (1987). *Personal and Social Implications of Spinal Cord Injury: A Retrospective Study*. London: Thames Polytechnic.

Critchley, E. M. R. (1985). Inadequate provision for the young chronic sick. *Practitioner* 229, 91–5.

Cruttenden, D. I. (1975). *The Heritage of Oswestry*. Oswestry: The Robert James and Agnes Hunt Orthopaedic Hospital.

Cunningham, D. J. (1977). *Stigma and Social Isolation: Self-perceived Problems of a Group of Multiple Sclerosis Sufferers*. HSRU Report, No. 27. Canterbury: University of Kent.

Dartington, T., Miller, E. and Gwynne, G. (1981). *A Life Together: the Distribution of Attitudes Around the Disabled*, pp. 49–72. London: Tavistock Publications.

Davis, K. (1981). 28–38 Grove Road: accommodation and care in a community setting. In *Handicap in a Social World*, ed. Brechin, A., Liddiard, P., Swain, J., *op. cit.*

Davis, M. (1976). The institutional tradition. *Nursing Mirror* 13 (142), 65–66.

De Jong, G. (1979). *The Movement for Independent Living: Origins, Ideology, and Implications for Disabled Research*. Michigan: University Centers for International Rehabilitation. (Partly reproduced in *Handicap in a Social World*, eds. Brechin, A., Liddiard, P., and Swain, J., *op. cit.*).

Denly, O. A. (1972). Provision for the younger chronic sick in the South East Metropolitan Region. *Hospital and Health Services Review* 68, 118–121.

Department of Health and Social Security (1971). *Better Services for the Mentally Handicapped*. London: HMSO.

Department of Health and Social Security (1976). *Priorities for Health and Personal Social Services in England: a Consultative Document*. Cmnd 4683. London: HMSO.

Department of Health and Social Security (1977). *Priorities in the Health and Social Services: the Way Forward*. London: HMSO.

Department of Health and Social Security, Statistics and Research Division (1978). *List of Hospital Units and Residential Homes in England for Young Physically Handicapped People*. London: HMSO.

Department of Health and Social Security (1981). *Care in the Community*. A consultative document on moving resources for care in England. London: HMSO.

Derbyshire Centre for Integrated Living (1985). *Strategy 1985–1988*. Ripley, Derbyshire.

Dollar, J. (1986). *Prisoner of Consciousness*. Film shown on Channel 4 television, 14.8.86.

Eames, P. and Wood, R. (1985). Rehabilitation after severe brain injury: a follow-up study of a behaviour modification approach. *Journal of Neurosurgery and Psychiatry*, 48, 613–619.

Elers-Jarleman, H. (1984). *Beyond Sorrow, Beyond Pain*. Film shown on BBC television, 9.2.85.

Ellis, B. (1981). *The Long Road Back*. Great Wakering: Mayhew-McCrimmon.

Equal Opportunities Commission (1980). *The Experience of Caring for Elderly and Handicapped Dependents: a Survey Report*. Manchester.

Fearn, H. (1982). *Time-critical Disability and Planning Hospital Care for the Younger Disabled*. Unpublished.

Field, J. H. (1976). *Epidemiology of Head Injuries in England and Wales, with Particular Application to Rehabilitation*. London: HMSO.

Finch, J. and Groves, D. (1983). *A Labour of Love: Women, Work and Caring*. London: Routledge and Kegan Paul.

Finkelstein, V. (1980). *Attitudes and Disabled People: Issues for Discussion*. New York: World Rehabilitation Fund.

Finkelstein, V. (1981). Disability and the helped/helper relationship: an historical view. In Brechin, A., Liddiard, D., Swain, J., *op. cit.*, pp. 58–63.

Goffman, E. (1961). *Asylums: Essays on the Social Situation of Mental Patients and Other Inmates*, p. 11. Harmondsworth: Penguin.

Goldsmith, S. (1975). *Wheelchair Housing*. London: Department of the Environment.

Goldsmith, S. (1976). *Designing for the Disabled*, 3rd ed. London: RIBA.

Goldsmith, S. (1983). The ideology of designing for the disabled. *Design for Special Needs* 31, 10–15 and 21.

Goldsmith, S. (1984). The independent living paradigm. *Design for Special Needs* 33, 11–14.

Greengross, W. (1976). *Entitled to Love: the Sexual and Emotional Needs of the Handicapped*. London: National Marriage Guidance Council.

Griffith, V. E. (1970). *A Stroke in the Family*. Harmondsworth: Penguin.

Guthrie, D. (1968). *At Home or in Hospital?* National Fund for Research into Crippling Diseases.

Hamilton, Lady (1984). *Am I Living in the Right Place? The Distribution of Health Care*. London: The Royal Association for Disability and Rehabilitation.

Hampshire Centre for Independent Living (1984). *Project 81 – a Housing/Care Programme*. Unpublished.

Hardwick, R. O. F. (1974). Twyford House: a specially designed unit for the care of the younger disabled person. *Royal Society of Health Journal* 94, 30–32.

Harris, A. I. (1971). *Handicapped and Impaired in Great Britain*. London: HMSO.

HCIL Papers (1986). *Source Book towards Independent Living: Care Support Ideas*. Hampshire Centre for Independent Living.

Hearn, D. (1972) *Crash Tackle*. London: Arthur Barker.

Heaton-Ward, W. A. (1977). *Left Behind: a Study of Mental Handicap*. London: Macdonald and Evans.

Hirst, M. (1984). *Moving On: Transfer of Young People with Disabilities to Adult Services*. University of York: Social Policy Research Unit.

Holland, R., Crawford, J. and Peberdy, C. (1985). *Towards a Better Service for People with a Severe Physical Disability in the Basingstoke and North Hampshire Health Authority: a Survey of Needs*. Basingstoke and North Hampshire DHA.

Home Life: a Code of Practice for Residential Care (1984). Report of a working party sponsored by the Department of Health and Social Security and convened by the Centre for Policy on Ageing. London: Centre for Policy on Ageing.

House of Commons (1985). *Second Report from the Social Services Committee, Session 1984–85:*

Community Care, with Special Reference to Adult Mental Ill and Mentally Handicapped People. London: HMSO.

The Housing Corporation (1985). *21st report, 1984/85.* London.

Hunt, J. and Hayes, L. (1980). *Housing the Disabled: Report of a Project to Identify and Meet the Housing Needs of Disabled People Living in the Borough of Torfaen.* Torfaen Borough Council.

Hurley, G. (1983). *Lucky Break?* Horndean, Hampshire: Milestone Publications.

Independent Working Party under the chairmanship of Professor Ian McColl (1986). *Review of Artificial Limb and Appliance Services.* London: DHSS.

Inskip, H. (1981a). *Leonard Cheshire Foundation Handbook of Care (1). Residential Homes for the Physically Handicapped.* London: Bedford Square Press.

Inskip, H. (1981b). *Leonard Cheshire Foundation Handbook of Care (2). Family Support Services for Physically and Mentally Handicapped People in their own Homes.* London: Bedford Square Press.

Jones, D. A. and Vetter, N. J. (1984). A survey of those who care for the elderly at home: their problems and their needs. *Social Science and Medicine* 19, 511–514.

Keeble, U. (1979). *Aids and Adaptations: a Study of the Administrative Process by which Social Services Departments help Clients to Receive Aids and Adaptations to their Homes.* London: The Bedford Square Press.

Keirs, J. (1986). *A Change of Rhythm: the Consequences of a Road Accident.* Nottingham: Headway, and London: The Spastics Society.

Kent County Council and Kent Area Health Authority (1981) *Physical Disability: 'Take a Risk'.*

King, R. D., Raynes, N. V. and Tizard, J. (1971). *Patterns of Residential Care: Sociological Studies in Institutions for Handicapped Children.* London: Routledge and Kegan Paul.

Kitchen, W. H. and 11 colleagues (1982). Collaborative study of very-low-birthweight infants: outcome of two-year-old survivors. *Lancet* 1, 1457–1460.

Klapwijk, A. (1981). Het Dorp, an adapted part of the City of Arnhem (The Netherlands) for severely disabled people. In *An International Seminar on the Long-term Care of Disabled People*, booklet 5/81, pp. 34–35. London: The Development Trust for the Young Disabled.

Knight, R. and Warren, M. D. (1978). *Physically Disabled People Living at Home: a Study of Numbers and Needs.* London: HMSO.

Kurtzke, J. F. (1980). Multiple sclerosis: an overview. In Rose, F. C., *Clinical Neuroepidemiology*, pp. 170–195. London: Pitman Medical.

Lacey, A. (ed.) (1984). *Centres for Independent Living. Proceedings of a Seminar held on 28 November 1983.* London: Centre for Environment for the Handicapped.

La Fane, P. (1981) *It's a Lovely Day, Outside.* London: Gollancz.

Lambeth Social Services (1982) *Strategy for Services for the Physically Handicapped.*

Law, D. and Patterson, B. (1980) *Living after a stroke.* London: Souvenir Press.

Leading article (1969). The young chronic sick. *British Medical Journal* 1, 134–135.

Leading article (1983). Caring for the disabled after head injury. *Lancet* 2, 948–949.

Leading article (1986). Assessment of disability. *Lancet* 1, 591–592.

Lishman, W. A. (1978). *Organic Psychiatry: The Psychological Consequences of Cerebral Disorder.* Oxford: Blackwell Scientific Publications.

Locker, D. (1983). *Disability and Disadvantage: the Consequences of Chronic Illness.* London: Tavistock Publications.

Lorber, J. and Ward A. M. (1985). Spina bifida – a vanishing nightmare? *Archives of Disease in Childhood* 60, 1086–1091.

Lovelock, R. (1981). *Friends In Deed: Three Care Attendant Schemes for the Younger Physically Disabled in Hampshire.* Portsmouth: Social Services Research Division and Intelligence Unit.

Lowe, C. R. and McKeown, T. (1950). The care of the chronic sick II: Social and demographic data. *British Journal of Social Medicine* 4, 61–74

McAndrew, L. (1984). *The Survey of the Younger Chronic Sick in Hospital in the Lothian Health Board Area.* Rehabilitation Studies Unit, University of Edinburgh.

McCoy, L. (1978). *Policy Issues in Residential Care: a Discussion Document.* London: Personal Social Services Council.

McEwan, P. and Laverty, G. G. (1949). *An Investigation and Analysis of 701 Chronic Sick and Elderly Patients in Bradford hospitals, including a Scheme for a Geriatric Service.* Bradford (B) Hospital Management Committee.

Martin, G., Pfingst, A. and Goldring, J. (1987). *Constructing Services for People with Severe Physical Disabilities in Bloomsbury District Health Authority*. London: Bloomsbury DHA.

Martin, J. P. (1984). *Hospitals in Trouble*. Oxford: Blackwell Scientific Publications.

Martin, N. (1982). *In a Changing World*. London: John Grooms Association for the Disabled.

Mattingly, S. (ed.) (1981). *Rehabilitation Today in Great Britain*. London: Update Books.

Miller, E. J. and Gwynne, G. V. (1972). *A Life Apart: a Pilot Study of Residential Institutions for the Physically Handicapped and the Young Chronic Sick*. London: Tavistock Publications.

Morris, B. (1981). Residential units. In *Handbook of Psychiatric Rehabilitation Practice*, eds. Wing, J. K. and Morris, R. Oxford: Oxford University Press.

Mutch, W. J., Dingwall-Fordyce, I., Downie, A. W., Paterson, J. G. and Roy, S. K. (1986). Parkinson's disease in a Scottish city. *British Medical Journal* 292, 534–536.

National Association of Health Authorities (1985). *Registration and Inspection of Nursing Homes: a Handbook for Health Authorities*. Birmingham.

Newson-Smith, J. (1983). Who cares for the adult brain damaged? *Bulletin of the Royal College of Psychiatry* 7, 181–3.

Oliver, M. (1983). *Social Work with Disabled People*. London and Basingstoke: The Macmillan Press.

Olsen, M. R. (ed.), (1979). *The Care of the Mentally Disordered: an Examination of Some Alternatives to Hospital Care*. Birmingham: British Association of Social Workers.

Oswin, M. (1984). *They Keep Going Away. A Critical Study of Short-term Residential Care Services for Children who are Mentally Handicapped*. London: King Edward's Hospital Fund.

Owen-Smith, B. D. (1982). Experience of a later younger disabled unit. Donald Wilson House, Chichester. In *Younger Disabled Units: report of the Conference held in Leeds in October 1982*, pp. 11–18. University of Leeds.

Peaker, C. (1986). *The Crisis in Residential Care*. London: National Council for Voluntary Organisations.

Pellatt, D. J. R. (1976). Caring for the younger disabled. *Nursing Mirror*, 142 (23), 57–9.

Pharoah, P. O. D. (1985). The epidemiology of chronic disability in childhood. *International Rehabilitation Medicine*. 7, 11–17.

Pillar, G. (ed.) (1984). *Unmet Needs of Handicapped Young Adults*. Liverpool: The Children's Research Fund.

Pinder, N. R. (1984). Coping with the young chronic disabled. *Update 29*, pp. 755–762.

Prince of Wales' Advisory Group on Disability (1985). *Living Options*. London.

Prinsley, D. M. (1973). The younger disabled in hospital. *Health and Social Services Journal* 83, *Supplement on Aids for the Disabled*, pp. 8–9.

Queen Elizabeth's Foundation for the Disabled (1984). *List of Opportunities for School Leavers*. Leatherhead.

Report of the Committee on Child Health Services (1976) Fit for the Future. Cmnd. 6684. London: HMSO.

Report of the Committee of Enquiry into Mental Handicap Nursing and Care (1979). Cmnd. 7468. London: HMSO.

Report of the Ministry of Health for the year ended 31st March 1948, p. 191. Cmnd. 7734. London: HMSO.

Report of the Ministry of Health for the year ended 31st March 1949, p. 244. Cmnd. 7910. London: HMSO.

Ritchie, D. (1960). *Stroke: a diary of recovery*. London: Faber and Faber.

Rogers, M. A. (1986). *Living with Paraplegia*. London: Faber and Faber.

Roth, J. A. (1963). *Timetables: Structuring the Passage of Time in Hospital Treatment and Other Careers*. Indianopolis, Bobbs-Merrill.

Royal College of Nursing (1975). *Improving Geriatric Care in Hospital: a Handbook of Guidelines*. London.

Royal College of Physicians (1986a). Physical Disability in 1986 and Beyond. *Journal of the Royal College of Physicians* 20, 160–194.

Royal College of Physicians (1986b). *The Young Disabled Adult: the Use of Residential Homes and Hospital Units for the Age Group 16–64*. London.

Ryan, J. and Thomas, F. (1980). *The Politics of Mental Handicap*. London: Penguin.

Safilios-Rothschild, C. (1970). *The Sociology and Social Psychology of Disability and Rehabilitation.* pp. 53–92. New York: Random House.

Sandford, J. R. A. (1975). Tolerance of debility in elderly dependents by supporters at home: its significance for hospital practice. *British Medical Journal* 3, 471–3.

Scott, C. J. (1984). Hospitals for the disabled. *International Rehabilitation Medicine* 6, 166–69.

Scott, C. J. (1985). The first year of a new young disabled unit. *Health Bulletin* 43, 102–108.

Scull, A. T. (1979). *Museums of Madness: the Social Organisation of Insanity in Nineteenth-century England*, pp. 254–66. London: Allen Lane.

Scull, A. T. (1984). *Decarceration: Community Treatment and The Deviant: a Radical View.* 2nd edition: Cambridge: Polity.

Shearer, A. (1974). Housing to fit the handicapped. In *The Handicapped Person in the Community.* eds. Boswell, D. M. and Wingrove, J. M., pp. 61–73. London: Tavistock Publications.

Shearer, A. (1982). *Living Independently.* London: Centre on Environment for the Handicapped and King Edward's Hospital Fund for London.

Sheffield Regional Hospital Board (1973). *Younger Chronic Sick: Report of the Working Party.*

Shone (1968). The young chronic sick. *Nursing Mirror* 126 (23), 21–25.

South West Thames Regional Health Authority (1985). *Towards Independent Living: Services for Younger Severely Physically Disabled People.*

Social Work Service Development Group Project (1984). *Fifty Styles of Caring*, London: DHSS.

Spath, F. (1977). *How the Cheshire Homes Started.* London: Leonard Cheshire Foundation.

Stewart, W. F. R. (1979). *The Sexual Side of Handicap: a Guide for the Caring Professions.* Cambridge: Woodhead-Faulkner.

Stokes-Roberts, A. E. (1972). *A Short History of the Royal Hospital and Home for Incurables.* London: RHHI.

Stone, D. A. (1984). *The Disabled State*, pp. 29–89. Basingstoke: Macmillan.

Swingler, R. J. and Compston, D. A. S. (1986). The distribution of multiple sclerosis in the United Kingdom. *Journal of Neurology, Neurosurgery and Psychiatry* 49, 1115–1124.

Swithinbank, J. M., Beswick, N. and Mayberry, J. F. (1984). The forgotten people: survey of the chronic younger sick in Welsh hospitals. *Journal of the Royal Society of Medicine* 77, 375–377.

Symons, J. (1974). *Residential Accommodation for Disabled People.* London: Centre on Environment for the Handicapped.

Thomas, A., Box, M., Coombes, K., Goldson, E., Smyth, D. and Whitmore, K. (1985). The health and social needs of physically handicapped young adults: are they being met by the statutory services? *Developmental Medicine and Neurology* 27, Suppl. 50: Spastics International Medical Publications.

Thompson, J. D., Goldin, G. (1975). *The Hospital: a Social and Architectural History.* Yale: Yale University Press.

Topliss, E. (1975). *Provision for the Disabled.* Oxford: Basil Blackwell and Martin Robertson.

Topliss, E. and Gould, B. (1981). *A Charter for the Disabled.* Oxford: Basil Blackwell and Martin Robertson.

Torrens, M. and Cummins, B. (undated). *What is Head Injury?* Nottingham: Headway.

Townsend, P. (1979) *Poverty in the United Kingdom*, pp. 717–722. Harmondsworth: Penguin.

Trieschmann, R. B. (1980). *Spinal Cord Injuries.* New York: Pergamon Press.

Wade, B., Sawyer, L. and Bell, J. (1983). *Dependency with Dignity: Different Care Provision for the Elderly.* London: Bedford Square Press.

Wade, D. T., Hewer, R. L., Skilbeck, C. E. and David, R. M. (1985). *Stroke: a Critical Approach to Diagnosis, Treatment and Management.* London: Chapman and Hall.

Walker, A. (1981). Disability and income. In *Disability in Britain*, ed. Walker, A. and Townsend, P., pp. 52–72. Oxford: Martin Robertson.

Waller, J. (1984). *Love was my Fortune.* Kendal: Westmorland Gazette.

Warren, M. W. (1946). Care of the chronic aged sick. *Lancet* 1, 841–2.

Weddell, J. M. (1980). Applications of a stroke register in planning. In Rose, F. C., *Clinical Neuroepidemiology.* London: Pitman Medical.

Wedgwood, J. (1982). *Long-term Hospital Care in the United Kingdom: the RHHI model* (booklet 1/82). London: The Development Trust for the Young Disabled.

Wedgwood, J. (1984). Residential care in the United Kingdom. In *The dynamic approach to the residential care of disabled people in an integrating society* (booklet 2/84). London: The Development Trust for the Young Disabled.

Weir, S. (1981). Our image of the disabled, and how ready we are to help. *New Society* 55, pp. 7–10.

Wells, T. J. (1980). *Problems in geriatric nursing care*. London: Churchill Livingstone.

West Midlands Regional Health Authority Operational Research unit (1984). *Results of survey of inappropriate occupancy of beds*. Birmingham.

Williams, E. S. and McKeran, R. O. (1986). Prevalence of multiple sclerosis in a south London borough. *British Medical Journal* 193, 237–239.

Wilson, D. S. (1978). The planning and running of a young chronic sick unit. *Journal of the Royal Society of Medicine* 71, 448–451.

Wint, G. (1965). *The Third Killer: Meditations on a Stroke*. London: Chatto and Windus.

World Health Organisation (1980). *International Classification of Impairments, Disabilities and Handicaps*. Geneva.

Wynn-Parry, C. B. (1986). Rehabilitation long-term issues. Appendix II to the *Review of Artificial Limb and Appliance Services (Report of an Independent Working Party)*. London: DHSS.

Subject index

Name index